De Musica Verbali Libri Duo

Gaspar Stoquerus's treatise, *De musica verbali* (ca. 1570), is the only Renaissance treatise as yet discovered that is devoted entirely to the problem of text placement in vocal polyphony. Salient portions of Stoquerus's treatise were first discussed in 1961 by Edward E. Lowinsky, and a more detailed synthesis of Stoquerus's treatise is contained in one chapter of Don Harrán's *Word-Tone Relations in Musical Thought from Antiquity to the Seventeenth Century* (1986). The present volume of *Greek and Latin Music Theory* offers the first critical edition of Stoquerus's entire treatise, preceded by an extensive introduction and accompanied by a translation and annotations facing the Latin text. Indexes of terms, names, and subjects are also included.

The critical edition of the text provides a precise reading and comprehension of its contents, while the translation enables readers to examine more closely the contents of the entire treatise, especially Stoquerus's contextual arguments justifying his subject in general and his fifteen rules for text placement in particular. The introduction and annotations reveal Stoquerus's immersion in his historical milieu as a scholar, humanist, and pedagogue. As a pedagogue in particular, Stoquerus is deeply immersed in the scholastic method of argumentation and advances his thought with precision and logic, culminating in his closely reasoned set of fifteen rules for text placement and a simplification of the Guidonian method of solmization already in progress in Renaissance choir-instruction books.

Albert C. Rotola, S.J., is an assistant professor of music history and literature at St. Louis University.

Greek and Latin Music Theory

Thomas J. Mathiesen,
General Editor
Indiana University

Jon Solomon,
Associate Editor
University of Arizona

Previously published in this series

Prosdocimo de' Beldomandi, *Contrapunctus*
edited and translated by Jan Herlinger

The Berkeley Manuscript, University of California
Music Library, MS. 744 (*olim* Phillipps 4450)
edited and translated by Oliver B. Ellsworth

Sextus Empiricus, ΠΡΟΣ ΜΟΥΣΙΚΟΥΣ,
Against the Musicians (Adversus musicos)
edited and translated by Denise Davidson Greaves

Prosdocimo de' Beldomandi, *Brevis summula
proportionum quantum ad musicam pertinet*
and *Parvus tractatulus de modo
monacordum dividendi*
edited and translated by Jan Herlinger

Gaspar Stoquerus

DE MUSICA VERBALI
LIBRI DUO

Two Books On Verbal Music

A new critical text and
translation on facing pages,
with an introduction, annotations,
and *indices verborum*
and *nominum et rerum* by

Albert C. Rotola, S.J.

University of Nebraska Press
Lincoln and London

Copyright © 1988 by the University of Nebraska Press
All rights reserved
Manufactured in the United States of America

The paper in this book meets the minimum requirements of
American National Standard for Information Sciences—
Permanence of Paper for Printed Library Materials,
ANSI Z39.48–1984.

Library of Congress Cataloging-in-Publication Data
Stoquerus, Gaspar.
  [De musica verbali. English & Latin]
  De musica verbali libri duo = Two books on verbal music / Gaspar
Stoquerus; a new critical text and translation on facing pages, with an
introduction, annotations, and indices verborum and nominum et rerum by Albert C. Rotola.
      p.   cm.—(Greek and Latin music theory)
  Includes indexes.
  ISBN 0-8032-4163-1 (alk. paper)
  1. Music and language—Early works to 1800. 2. Musical accentuation—Early works to 1800. 3. Music—Theory—16th century—
Early works to 1800. 4. Counterpoint—Early works to 1800.
I. Rotola, Albert C. II. Title. III. Title: Two books on verbal music.
IV. Series.
MT5.5.S7613   1988   88-25045
781.0′6—dc19   CIP
MN

To my parents

CONTENTS

SERIES EDITOR'S PREFACE ix

PREFACE xi

INTRODUCTION 1

  Gaspar Stoquerus and the Madrid Codex 6486 1
  Discovery and Dating of Codex 6486 5
  Stoquerus's Life and Character 6
  Stoquerus's Treatises in General 7
    His Topics and Their Establishment 7
    His Sources 9
    His Humanist and Scholastic Milieu 9
  De musica verbali 13
    The Form and Contents of the Treatise 13
    Chapters 1–31 16
  The Manuscript 95
    Description and Contents of the Manuscript 96
  The Edition 97

CONSPECTUS CODICIS ET NOTARUM 99

GASPARIS STOQUERI GERMANI
DE MUSICA VERBALI LIBRI DUO 100

  Caput I 100
  Caput II 104
  Caput III 108
  Caput IIII 116
  Caput V 118
  Caput VI 120
  Caput VII 128
  Caput VIII 138
  Caput IX 142
  Caput X 144
  Caput XI 156
  Caput XII 160
  Caput XIII 166
  Caput XIIII 170
  Caput XV 174
  Caput XVI 180
  Caput XVII 182

Caput XVIII	186
Caput XIX	192
Caput XX	202
Caput XXI	208
Caput XXII	212
Caput XXIII	216
Caput XXIIII	220
Caput XXV	226
Caput XXVI	232
Caput XXVII	240
Caput XXVIII	242
Caput XXIX	246
Caput XXX	252
Caput XXXI	254
PLATES	256
INDEX VERBORUM	259
INDEX NOMINUM ET RERUM	293

SERIES EDITOR'S PREFACE

We are pleased to present in this volume Gaspar Stoquerus's *De musica verbali libri duo*, the only Renaissance treatise yet discovered that is devoted entirely to the problem of text placement in vocal polyphony. Albert C. Rotola, S.J., has prepared the first critical edition and translation of the treatise and has introduced it with a masterful illumination of Stoquerus's life, sources, and humanist and scholastic milieu. With the publication of this volume, the fifth in the series Greek and Latin Music Theory, we also pause to review our work since 1984, when the inaugural volume was published, and to offer our readers a projection for the next five years.

When the series was first conceived in 1982 and we began the process of finding scholars interested in the very special problems of preparing critical texts and parallel translations, with extensive introductions and annotations to assist our readers in their study of the treatises, we were confident that there would be sufficient interest—both on the part of prospective editors and on the part of readers—to maintain a series. We were also determined to offer a high level of quality in production with a reasonable sale price for the volumes so that they might be within the reach of students and private individuals as well as large research libraries. We have been very gratified with the reception of Greek and Latin Music Theory on all fronts, and we are pleased to report that, even as this fifth volume is in hand, we are in the editorial and production stages of the next four volumes. We hope to continue to offer one or two volumes a year for the foreseeable future.

Readers who have followed our development from the first will note that we have progressed from a camera-ready format produced with IBM typewriters (volumes 1–3) to one produced with advanced computer technology that allows us to achieve a much higher level of typography. Volumes are now prepared by their editors in any of a number of word processing programs, and beginning with this volume, the camera-ready pages are assembled in Letraset®'s program Ready, Set, Go™, version 4.0a. Allotype Typographics' Kadmos font is used to produce the Greek type (a small sample of which appears on p. 102 of the present volume) and various graphics programs, including Crickct Draw™ (vcrsion 1.1) are used to create the figures and illustrations. We hope our readers will enjoy the new appearance of the volumes in Greek and Latin Music Theory.

While we have modified our method of production, the editorial principles of the series remain steadfast, and it may be worthwhile to repeat them here.

The series aims to establish truly critical texts for the many works of ancient, medieval, and (occasionally) renaissance music theory in Greek and Latin that do not presently exist in critical editions and to provide translations on facing pages with annotations illuminating the content of the treatise. Each volume will include a major introductory essay discussing, as appropriate, the significance of the treatise to its theoretical tradition; the life of its author (or, for anonymous works, the probable authors); the design, sources, and theoretical premises of the treatise; the manuscripts used to establish the text and the actual establishment of the text itself; *loci paralleli* and quotations; and special considerations involved in the translation. The texts will be based on a full collation of every relevant manuscript—insofar as possible—and the collation will be reported in a critical apparatus at the bottom of each text page. The text critical work will largely follow Martin L. West's *Textual Criticism and Editorial Technique Applicable to Greek and Latin Texts* (Stuttgart: B. G. Teubner, 1973). The translations are intended to be readable, but at the same time, they will attempt to preserve in large measure the consistency, variety, and subtlety of the original. Special care will be given to the treatment of technical vocabulary, syntactic subtleties, and consistency of terminology. Finally, each volume will also include *indices verborum, nominum et rerum*. Each volume is prepared in camera-ready format by the various volume editors and the series editors, and each volume follows the series' *Style Guide* to insure consistency from volume to volume. Copies of the *Style Guide* are available from the editorial office for the series.

It is a pleasure to acknowledge the encouragement and helpful advice we have received in the past five years from readers and reviewers. We also express our appreciation for past support from the College of Fine Arts and Communications at Brigham Young University. With this volume, we announce the new location of the editorial home of Greek and Latin Music Theory at the School of Music at Indiana University, and we express our appreciation for the generous support already extended the series by the School of Music and the Division of Research in Advanced Studies at Indiana University.

Thomas J. Mathiesen
General Editor,
Greek and Latin Music Theory

School of Music
Indiana University
Bloomington, Indiana 47405

PREFACE

The discovery in 1959 of Gaspar Stoquerus's treatise, *De musica verbali libri duo*, in the Biblioteca Nacional in Madrid brought a new chapter to the history of text-music relations, particularly in the middle-to-late sixteenth century, and inaugurated a new and more confident era of modern editorial procedure for Renaissance vocal polyphony. Stoquerus's treatise, the only Renaissance treatise as yet discovered that is devoted entirely to the problem of text placement in vocal polyphony, has found its leading exponents in Edward E. Lowinsky and Don Harrán, whose writings have provided excellent syntheses of Stoquerus's thought and whose editions of music effectively incorporate his rules for text placement.

The time is now ripe for a critical edition, translation, and commentary on Stoquerus's entire treatise. The present critical edition of the text and its translation on facing pages provide a precise reading of the text and comprehension of its contents. An extensive introduction and annotations to the translation discuss the manuscript itself and Stoquerus's immersion in his historical milieu as a scholar, humanist, and pedagogue. As a pedagogue in particular, Stoquerus is deeply immersed in the scholastic method of argumentation and advances his thought with precision and logic, culminating in his closely reasoned set of fifteen rules for text placement and a simplification of the Guidonian method of solmization already in progress in Renaissance choir-instruction books.

Whatever is of value in this edition can only have come about through the collaboration of various institutions and individuals whom I now happily acknowledge. For anything that is controversial or faulty I hold myself alone responsible. The College of Fine Arts and Communications of Brigham Young University and its dean, James A. Mason, provided generous grants in support of the series Greek and Latin Music Theory; the NEH-Andrew W. Mellon Faculty Development Fund of the College of Arts and Sciences of St. Louis University provided generous financial assistance in the final stages of this project; my colleagues in the Department of Fine and Performing Arts at St. Louis University exhibited constant patience and enthusiasm for its successful completion; and the editorial staff of *Review for Religious* generously and cheerfully provided computer assistance.

I am most indebted to Thomas J. Mathiesen, whose expertise, knowledge, and taste combined in as perfect an editor as anyone could have the good fortune to work with.

Among all the members of my Jesuit community at St. Louis University who accompanied me on my journey, I would like to single out Daniel T. Costello, truly a Renaissance man whose broad knowledge of Latin and philosophy helped to explicate much of Stoquerus's style and thought. My debt of gratitude to him is immeasurable. I am grateful also to Francis J. Guentner for his constant interest and support of my work and to John F. Kavanaugh for some philosophical clarifications, but most of all for his unfailing encouragement.

I wish to express a debt of gratitude to Don Harrán and the late Edward E. Lowinsky, each of whose expertise clarified some issues and whose enthusiasm for this project provided invaluable motivation throughout.

I am happy to dedicate this book, a grandchild as it were, to my parents, Albert and Mary, whose wisdom has been a constant inspiration to me in my work.

INTRODUCTION

Gaspar Stoquerus and the Madrid Codex 6486

The writings of the sixteenth-century German theorist Gaspar Stoquerus survive in a single codex[1] in the Biblioteca Nacional in Madrid, shelved there as Codex 6486 and titled *Gasparis Stoqueri Germani de musica verbali libri duo*. This title, presented alone and in large letters on the page preceding the numbered folios, gives only a partial indication of the contents of the entire codex, for upon closer inspection, it proves to be the title only of Stoquerus's first work, a treatise of major proportions occupying the first forty of the forty-nine folios of the codex, the thrust of which concerns his now well-established fifteen rules for text placement. The second treatise, occupying the next five folios (ff. 41r–45v), is titled *Gasparis Stoqueri Germani de vera solfizationis quam vocant docendae ratione ad Magistrum Franciscum Salinam Dominum suum* (hereafter *De vera solfizationis docendae ratione*). As the title indicates, this is addressed to Salinas and concerns Stoquerus's method of teaching solmization, part of which is treated in four chapters of the first treatise. The third treatise, separated from the second by a blank page (f. 46r) and comprising the remainder of the codex (ff. 46v–49r), is titled *De modo, tempore, et prolatione* and concerns Stoquerus's own approach to an understanding of the topics indicated by the title—modus, tempus, and prolatio.

Of these treatises of Stoquerus, *De musica verbali libri duo* (hereafter *De musica verbali*) has proved to be the most influential. The treatise was first discussed by Edward E. Lowinsky in 1961 in his study, "A Treatise on Text Underlay by a German Disciple of Francisco de Salinas."[2] The publication of

---

[1]With the exception of a tetrastich comprising two elegiac distichs published at the beginning of Francisco de Salinas's *De musica libri septem* (Salamanca: Mathias Gastius, 1577), f. 2v. See the facsimile edition by Macario Santiago Kastner in Documenta musicologica, I/13 (Kassel: Bärenreiter, 1958).

[2]In *Festschrift Heinrich Besseler*, ed. Ernst H. Meyer (Leipzig: VEB Deutscher Verlag für Musik, 1961), pp. 231–51. Stoquerus's treatise is also

1

this study was an important and far-reaching event for musicology: important because Stoquerus's treatise is unique for its exclusive and detailed attention to the proper text declamation of Renaissance polyphony; far-reaching because Lowinsky's discussion of the treatise and his translation and commentary on its salient portions now form a well-established *vade mecum* for editions and studies of Renaissance polyphony[3] and have moreover provided a stimulus for further research into the historical progress of text-music rela-

---

discussed at length in one chapter of Don Harrán's *Word-Tone Relations in Musical Thought from Antiquity to the Seventeenth Century*, Musicological Studies and Documents, no. 40 (Neuhausen-Stuttgart: American Institute of Musicology and Hänssler-Verlag, 1986), pp. 218–58. Because his study was published after the conclusion of my own research (1985) and during this edition's final stages of preparation, I was unable to incorporate all of his work into the body of this edition. Professor Harrán, however, kindly showed me the galley proofs (not yet supplied with musical examples) of his chapter on Stoquerus. This was his gracious way of clarifying some questions I had concerning my own findings. I gratefully acknowledge his assistance here and at various other places in this edition.

[3]Professor Lowinsky was the first to employ his own findings in his edition, *The Medici Codex of 1518*, Monuments of Renaissance Music, vols. 3–5 (Chicago: University of Chicago Press, 1968). See in particular his discussion of Stoquerus's principles as governing the editing of the codex's text underlay in "The Problem of Text Underlay" in vol. 3, pp. 90–107. For other references to Stoquerus after Lowinsky, see, for example, the following editions in Corpus mensurabilis musicae, Armen Carapetyan, gen. ed.: *The Anthologies of Black Note Madrigals*, ed. Don Harrán, 5 vols., Corpus mensurabilis musicae, no. 73 ([Rome]: American Institute of Musicology, 1978–1981), especially vol. 1, no. 1, "Text Underlay," pp. xvi–xvii; *Bertrandi Vaqueras Opera omnia*, ed. Richard Sheer, Corpus mensurabilis musicae, no. 78 ([Rome]: American Institute of Musicology, 1978), especially "Principles of the Edition," p. xi; *Johannis Lupi Omnia opera*, ed. Bonnie J. Blackburn, 2 vols., Corpus mensurabilis musicae, no. 84 ([Rome]: American Institute of Musicology, 1980–86), especially vol. 1, "Text Underlay," pp. xi–xiv; and *Huberti Naich Opera omnia*, ed. Don Harrán, Corpus mensurabilis musicae, no. 94 ([Rome]: American Institute of Musicology, 1983), p. ix. See also *The Mellon Chansonnier*, 2 vols., ed. Leeman L. Perkins and Howard Garey (New Haven: Yale University Press, 1979), 2:137–48.

tions.[4] Indeed, Lowinsky's exposition of Stoquerus's treatise has so clarified the procedure of text placement for modern editorial practice as to establish a clear line of division between the often arbitrary choices of editors and com-

---

[4]Don Harrán has significantly advanced the understanding of text-music relations in the Renaissance by tracing lines of historical development from the early fifteenth century to and beyond Stoquerus. See his (in chronological order of publication) "New Light on the Question of Text Underlay Prior to Zarlino," *Acta musicologica* 45 (1973): 24–56; "Vicentino and His Rules of Text Underlay," *The Musical Quarterly* 59 (1973): 620–32; "The Theorist Giovanni del Lago: A New View of the Man and His Writings," *Musica disciplina* 27 (1973): 107–51; "Burney and Ambros as Editors of Josquin's Music," in *Josquin des Prez: Proceedings of the International Josquin Festival-Conference*, ed. Edward E. Lowinsky in collaboration with Bonnie J. Blackburn (London: Oxford University Press, 1976), pp. 148–77; "In Pursuit of Origins: The Earliest Writing on Text Underlay (c. 1440)," *Acta musicologica* 50 (1978): 217–40; and *Word-Tone Relations*. See also Leeman L. Perkins, "Toward a Rational Approach to Text Placement in the Secular Music of Dufay's Time," in *Papers Read at the Dufay Quincentenary Conference, Brooklyn College, December 6–7, 1974*, ed. Allan W. Atlas (Brooklyn, N.Y.: Brooklyn College, 1976), pp. 102–14; Jay Rahn, "Text Underlay in French Monophonic Song circa 1500," *Current Musicology* 24 (1977): 63–79; Frank Tirro, "La Stesura del testo nei manoscritti di Giovanni Spataro," *Revista italiana di musicologia* 15 (1980): 31–70; Ross W. Duffin with Belinda Slobin, "Rules for Text Underlay ca. 1440–ca. 1590," *The International Society of Early Music Singers: Newsletter* 1, no. 1 (Sept. 1983): 5–7; and Allan Atlas, "Paolo Luchini's *Della musica*: A Little-Known Source for Text Underlay from the Late Sixteenth Century," *Journal of Musicology* 2 (1983): 62–80.

mentators before 1961 and the more sophisticated and rational choices of those since then.[5]

Stoquerus's two other treatises have as yet received little or no attention.[6] This is most likely because of the overshadowing historical import of *De musica verbali* and its relevance to modern editorial procedure, in contrast to the emphasis of the other two treatises' relevance to past procedures alone.

---

[5]Harrán ("New Light," p. 25 and n. 8) also points to the scarcity of bibliography on text underlay "*ante* Lowinsky" and claims "Lowinsky is the only scholar, to my knowledge, to have systematically addressed himself to the problems of achieving a rational coordination of text and music in transcriptions of Renaissance polyphony. The results of his efforts have been twofold: the study of text underlay, only incidentally considered in earlier writings, has been placed on a disciplinary footing; the determination of the correct alignment of text and music, often treated as secondary to the determination of the correct pitches and rhythms, has been pushed into the foreground of the modern editor's attention." One can also point to the contrast in *Die Musik in Geschichte und Gegenwart* (hereafter MGG) between the more systematic treatment of the problem of text underlay by Gustave Reese and George M. Jones ("Textunterlegung," *MGG* 16 [1979]: 1843–52 and musical examples on the unnumbered sides opposite the entry) and the more general, tentative approach by Hans Albrecht ("Editionstechnik, sec. IV," *MGG* 3 [1953]: 1117–28, especially 1124–28). Reese and Jones rely heavily on Stoquerus's treatise and Lowinsky's study. The discussions of text underlay in *The New Grove Dictionary of Music and Musicians* are on a general level, but this is due to the contributors' preference rather than lack of available sources. See, for example, Howard Mayer Brown, "Editing, sec. 3," *New Grove Dictionary of Music and Musicians* 5 (1980): 844–45; and Don Harrán, "Stoquerus," *New Grove Dictionary of Music and Musicians* 18 (1980): 179. For a helpful summary of writings on text underlay before 1961, see Tirro, "La Stesura del testo," pp. 33–35 and notes 4–18; and Harrán, "New Light," p. 25 and nn. 7–8.

[6]*De vera solfizationis docendae ratione* is usually cited as the only other writing of Stoquerus comprising the remainder of the Madrid codex, with *De modo, tempore, et prolatione* presumably implied as a part of this second treatise. See Lowinsky, "Treatise on Text Underlay," p. 232, and Harrán, "Stoquerus," *New Grove Dictionary of Music and Musicians* 18 (1980): 179. That *De modo, tempore, et prolatione*, however, stands alone as a writing distinct from *De vera solfizationis docendae ratione* is shown by (1) its separation from the preceding treatise by a blank page (f. 46r), (2) the title's flush position at the left margin as opposed to the centered subheadings of the preceding treatise, and (3) its subject matter, which stands apart from the organization of the preceding treatise. The absence of Stoquerus's name from the title may indicate that the writing is a part of a longer work in progress, the title of which has not yet been fully formulated.

Yet they do have historical value not only as other works authored by Stoquerus but also as revealing other concerns of his as a pedagogue and theorist. *De vera solfizationis docendae ratione*, too, stands alone as a treatise devoted exclusively, passionately almost, to Stoquerus's concern for a simplification of the method of solmization so integral to the elementary instruction of choirboys. *De modo, tempore, et prolatione*, brief as it is, sheds further light on Stoquerus as a theorist in his attempt to put further order into these selected mensural topics.

Discovery and Dating of Codex 6486

The manuscript containing Stoquerus's treatises was discovered by Paul Oskar Kristeller in 1959 in the Biblioteca Nacional in Madrid, where he found it listed not among the music treatises given in the *Catálogo músical de la Biblioteca Nacional de Madrid* compiled by Higinio Anglés and José Subirá[7] but as *De musica verbali libri duo Gasparis Stoqueli 6486* under *M* in volume three of a handwritten index (*Indice*) of four volumes. Kristeller further confirmed the Stoquerus manuscript in a card file titled "Inventario Topographico Nuevo," where it is listed as "6486. Gasparis Stoqueri Germani de musica verbali libri duo. s. XVII."[8]

Lowinsky has shown that although the Madrid codex is assigned on its index card (from the "Inventario Topographico Nuevo") to the seventeenth century, internal evidence suggests an earlier date for its composition. Lowinsky's reasoning is careful and cogent. Basing his conclusion on theorists and composers either named or quoted in the treatises, he establishes 1559 and 1587 as constituting the codex's widest *termini ante* and *post quem* respectively: 1559 as the year of publication of Willaert's *Musica nova*[9] and 1587 as the year of Salinas's retirement from the University of Salamanca. Since Stoquerus mentions in *De musica verbali* that Salinas urged him to compose his rules for text placement for use in the University's curriculum, the treatise was most certainly written after Salinas began his career there in 1567. Furthermore, while Stoquerus cites or quotes from the works of other

---

[7] 3 vols. (Barcelona: Consejo superior de investigaciones cientificas, Instituto Español de musicologia, 1946–51).

[8] Lowinsky, "Treatise on Text Underlay," pp. 231 and 249, n. 1.

[9] Lowinsky also cites 1559 as the date of publication of Zarlino's *Istitutioni harmoniche*, from which Stoquerus quotes from Part 4, chapter 33. Because of some ambiguities, the date and quotation from this work will be discussed in their appropriate place in the annotations rather than here, since they only strengthen Lowinsky's findings.

theorists (Zarlino, Gaffurius, Vicentino, and Glareanus), he does not quote from Salinas, his avowed master and supreme authority. This is plausibly explained by the fact that Salinas's *De musica libri septem* was published in 1577 and was therefore not yet available in print at the time Stoquerus wrote his treatises. From this evidence, Lowinsky narrows the composition of Stoquerus's treatises to the interval 1567–1577, most likely sometime around 1570.[10] Lowinsky further confirms this dating from external evidence: Stoquerus's tetrastich included at the beginning of Salinas's work, an inclusion that could not have taken place unless a close professional relationship had developed between them during Salinas's career at the University, and quite possibly at the time Salinas's work was being written.[11]

Stoquerus's Life and Character

If it were only for his tetrastich, Stoquerus would have been known only as a poet—and a not especially imaginative one. His treatises, so far as is known, were never published, nor were his ideas in them disseminated to the point where he was quoted or even acknowledged by his contemporaries as an authority on text placement or on solmization. Any information about his life, professional bent, and character must therefore be gleaned from his treatises themselves. This evidence is amply presented and discussed by Lowinsky[12] and may be summarized in the paragraphs that follow.

As indicated by the full titles of his first two treatises, Stoquerus was of German descent.[13] His vernacular name was probably Kaspar Stocker. At the time of the writing of his treatises, he was residing in Spain and engaged in a professional relationship with Salinas at the University of Salamanca, both as a student who had attended his lectures there and as his teaching assistant.[14] There is no indication in the treatises that Stoquerus himself was steadily employed in an established professional career; rather, the writing of at least the first treatise and his other occupations at the same time seem to be

---

[10]Lowinsky, "Treatise on Text Underlay," pp. 231–32.

[11]Lowinsky further suggests here that Stoquerus possibly assisted the blind Salinas in preparing his work. See his essay, "Gasparus Stoquerus and Francisco de Salinas," *Journal of the American Musicological Society* 16 (1963): 241–43.

[12]"Treatise on Text Underlay," pp. 232–33.

[13]The title of the third treatise, of course, does not bear his name. Cf. n. 6 *supra*.

[14]In the opening paragraph of *De vera solfizationis docendae ratione*, Stoquerus relates that Salinas had assigned him a pupil for instruction in solmization.

related to some compelling circumstance ("fortuna ita cogente")[15] that remains unidentified: perhaps a hope, at his mature age, for a position with Salinas at the University, for which his treatise may afford an example of his abilities. Before his association with Salinas at Salamanca, Stoquerus resided in Italy, possibly in Venice, where he would doubtless have become acquainted with the works of Willaert and Zarlino, who figure so prominently in his first treatise.

As a professional, Stoquerus emerges from his pages more as a theorist strongly intent on applying his ideas to practice in both performance and composition rather than as a performer or composer.[16] His treatises show not only a familiarity with the works of other theorists in addition to Zarlino—notably Gaffurius, Vicentino, and Glareanus—but also a maturity of expression that can only have come from wise perceptions of daily life and a broad education in the humanities and in the scholastic method of argumentation. In all, Stoquerus writes with color and advances his thought carefully, thoroughly, and systematically, betraying a temperament altogether congenial to bringing order to the troublesome state of the topics he addresses.[17]

Stoquerus's Treatises in General

A brief discussion of all three of Stoquerus's treatises will serve to provide a wider perspective from which to view the more detailed commentary on *De musica verbali* that will follow.

His Topics and Their Establishment

Stoquerus's three treatises are characterized by a total absorption with single topics that in other writings of his era constitute smaller divisions of subjects more ambitious and comprehensive in scope. Within his own sphere of thought and capabilities, however, Stoquerus brings to his subject matter an ambition and comprehension that is equal, in intent at least, to the larger theoretical and practical concerns of the major writers of his era. The happy result is that Stoquerus's topics are themselves expanded to treatise or near-treatise proportions, thus giving these topics a breadth of treatment absent

---

[15]*De musica verbali*, chap. 1.

[16]His interest in methods of teaching also emerges in the discussions of solmization in his first two treatises.

[17]He also writes with a passionate conviction of the correctness of his ideas, and his remarks concerning those who do not proceed in the direction of his method often border on contempt, as in such terms as "insani," "stulti," "caeci caecos sequentes," "indigni ... hominis vocabulo."

from other writings of which they are only a part. Thus, *De musica verbali* is devoted exclusively to the topic of text placement—the application of words to music, or of music to words—and is treated within a framework of two books comprising thirty-one chapters. *De vera solfizationis docendae ratione* is a recasting of his chapters from *De musica verbali* on this same topic, but now within a larger plan of learning solmization by means of a method that is easy and certain. And his brief *De modo, tempore, et prolatione* is a promising treatment of these topics within the context of definition, notes, signatures, and mensuration.

In order to establish his subject matter, Stoquerus points to the theoretical and practical tradition of his era and notes the insufficiency or lack of clarity with which the topics of his concern have been expressed. Thus, in chapter 2 of *De musica verbali*, Stoquerus observes that of the three branches of vocal music, the third—music with words—has not been treated with the same completeness as the first branch—solmization. He remarks further that to merely list his own rules for text placement, as others have done in their writings—and particularly Zarlino, would be to establish them on the basis of authority rather than reason and would therefore eliminate the need for establishing this third branch as an art with its own definition, divisions, and rules of procedure.

Stoquerus's second treatise is grounded on his premise that the methods of determining the progression of the syllables along the gamut for use in solmization had heretofore been various and in each instance laborious and confusing for the beginner. This premise had already been addressed and a solution offered in chapters 6 through 9 of *De musica verbali*; now, in this second treatise, he not only recasts his method of determining the syllables for use in solmization but also demonstrates how his procedure works in the actual solmization of a given melody. This treatise, addressed as it is to Salinas, originates from the occasion of Salinas assigning Stoquerus a pupil for tutoring in solmization. The ensuing report to Salinas consists in contrasting his own easier and surer method with those that continue to use the Guidonian gamut with its interlocking hexachords from which one syllable from a group of two or three must be chosen, a procedure that Stoquerus claims is difficult and confusing to the beginner.

Stoquerus's third treatise, it must be admitted, is not as original or fully developed as the other two. It consists, nevertheless, of his own synthesis of the approaches of Zarlino, Gaffurius, and Glareanus on the subjects of modus, tempus, and prolatio.

His Sources

Stoquerus makes use of the writings, both theoretical and practical, of his era, but only to the extent that he locates the topics from these writings that he then expands into a more detailed discussion. As to his sources for *De musica verbali*, Stoquerus culls from Gaffurius's list of the three types of vocal music (solmization of a melody, vocalization of a melody, and the application of words to a melody) in his *Practica musicae* and selects the third as the focus of his treatise. Stoquerus grants a nod to Vicentino (*L'antica musica ridotta alla moderna prattica*), but only to support his assessment of the difficulty of the second type of vocal music (vocalizing without syllables). Stoquerus quotes from the passage in *Istitutioni harmoniche*, Part 4, chapter 33, where Zarlino states he will give some rules that should be of help to the singer and composer. The heart of Stoquerus's treatise seems to be based on Zarlino's rules (though he never quotes them as such) as the two greatest composers of his era—Josquin and Willaert—and their followers have observed them. For chapter 6 of this treatise, Stoquerus draws from a wide array of pedagogical books (without naming them or their authors) for his own survey of methods for determining the progression of syllables along the gamut in solmization, only to reject them later in favor of his own system, which he doggedly formulates in chapter 7 by means of a series of interrelated hypotheses.

For the separate treatise on his method of teaching solmization (*De vera solfizationis docendae ratione*), Stoquerus relies chiefly on his own resources, although his terminology is based on that found in Renaissance choir-instruction books.

His brief third treatise, *De modo, tempore, et prolatione*, is basically a recasting of the approaches of Zarlino, Gaffurius, and Glareanus on the subjects of modus, tempus, and prolatio.

His Humanist and Scholastic Milieu

Stoquerus's treatises lie comfortably in both the humanist and scholastic traditions of the Renaissance—the humanist tradition in their manner of stylistic expression and tendencies, the scholastic tradition in their manner of thought progression and development.[18] As to the humanist tradition in his

---

[18] For an account of the influence of the humanist tradition on music at the University of Salamanca during the Renaissance, see Nan Cooke Carpenter, *Music in the Medieval and Renaissance Universities* (Norman: University of Oklahoma Press, 1958; reprint ed., New York: Da Capo, 1972), pp. 210–22,

three treatises in general, Stoquerus casts his thought in Neo-Latin style (including some Graecisms), with Seneca seemingly as his basic model, and substantiates it with references from Classical Greek and Latin literature (Isocrates, Plutarch, Zeno, Terence, Cicero, Vergil), Roman law (Justinian), philosophy (Aristotle), and Sacred Scripture (Deuteronomy, Paul's Letter to the Romans).[19] In particular, *De musica verbali* grows out of the central humanist concern, in music, for the proper subjection of melody to text, a concern that had its beginnings with Aristotle and Plato and was voiced most urgently, for Stoquerus at least, by Zarlino in his *Istitutioni harmoniche*—the immediate background, it seems, for Stoquerus's own rules in this treatise on the proper placement of text to the melody.[20] In relation to this central humanist concern for the proper placement of text to melody, Stoquerus's second and third treatises can be regarded as remote preparations, discussing as they do matters related to the purely musical aspect of *musica verbalis*: the easiest and surest way to sing the tones themselves in a melody by means of solmization—*De vera solfizationis docendae ratione*; and a convenient way to

---

316–17; and for an account of the scholastic tradition (to which Stoquerus may have been exposed during his attendance at lectures other than those on music at the University), see Frederick Copleston, S.J., *History of Philosophy*, vol. 3: *Ockham to Suarez* (London: Burns and Oates, Ltd., 1968), pp. 335–36.

[19]These references will be identified more fully in the annotations to the translation.

[20]A comprehensive treatment of this humanist concern for the proper subjection of music to the text, beginning with Plato and Aristotle and including Zarlino, is given by D. P. Walker in his essay "Musical Humanism in the 16th and Early 17th Centuries," *The Music Review* 2 (1941): 1–13, 111–21, 220–27, 288–308; and 3 (1942): 55–71. A favorable review of this essay reissued in its original German form (*Der musikalische Humanismus im 16. und im frühen 17. Jahrhundert* [Kassel: Bärenreiter, 1949]) is given by Edward E. Lowinsky in *The Musical Quarterly* 37 (1951): 285–89. See also idem, "Music in the Culture of the Renaissance," *Journal of the History of Ideas* 15 (1954): 509–53 (note in particular his seventh "thesis," p. 552). The influence of humanism on Renaissance music is also discussed by Paul Oskar Kristeller, "Music and Learning in the Early Italian Renaissance," *Journal of Renaissance and Baroque Music* 1 [1947]: 255–74; reprinted in *Renaissance Thought and the Arts: Collected Essays* (Princeton, New Jersey: Princeton University Press, 1980), pp. 142–62 (see p. 153). For a detailed study of Italian musical humanism, see Claude V. Palisca, *Humanism in Italian Renaissance Musical Thought* (New Haven: Yale University Press, 1985).

understand the mensural aspects of the tones—*De modo, tempore, et prolatione.*

Within this humanistic framework, Stoquerus advances and develops his thought almost exclusively by means of the scholastic method of argumentation.[21] In the light of Stoquerus's intent in his treatises—not merely to present a new approach to his chosen areas of music practice but also to teach these areas to others to learn and eventually use—his decision to advance and develop his thought by means of the scholastic method is pertinent.[22] The scholastic method itself is a method of both teaching and learning whereby a subject or problem is investigated in order to reach a solution or conclusion consistent with authorities, facts, and human reason.[23]

---

[21]For the coexistence of humanism and scholasticism in the Renaissance, see Paul Oskar Kristeller, "Humanism and Scholasticism in the Italian Renaissance," in *Renaissance Thought and Its Sources*, ed. Michael Mooney (New York: Columbia University Press, 1979), pp. 85–105. It is quite possible that Stoquerus himself experienced this humanist-scholastic coexistence during his years in Italy. For the interaction of humanism and scholasticism in the Renaissance, see Walter J. Ong, S.J., *Ramus, Method, and the Decay of Dialogue* (Cambridge: Harvard University Press, 1958), pp. 57–59 and 92–96. For the revival of scholasticism itself in Spain during the sixteenth century, see the reference to Frederick Copleston, S.J. in n. 18 *supra*; Maurice de Wulf, *Scholasticism Old and New: An Introduction to Scholastic Philosophy, Medieval and Modern*, trans. P. Coffey (Dublin: M. H. Gill and Son, Ltd., 1907), pp. 145–46; and Maurice de Wulf, *History of Medieval Philosophy*, trans. Ernest C. Messenger, vol. 2: *From St. Thomas Aquinas to the End of the Sixteenth Century* (New York: Longmans, Green and Co., 1926), pp. 300–306 (see especially p. 301, where Salamanca and Alcalá are mentioned as the starting points of this revival).

[22]The scholastic method as employed by Stoquerus warrants a separate and longer exposition than the brief note presented here, especially in regard to the employment of this method in Renaissance writings on music. For further reading, an excellent source with which to begin would certainly be Martin Grabmann, *Die Geschichte der scholastischen Methode*, 2 vols. (Berlin: Akademie-Verlag, 1956); see 2:44–47 and 122–23. The intent here, however, is to report, as already established, those elements of scholastic methodology employed by Stoquerus in his argumentation. To this effect, the sources employed for documentation in this section are general ones but sufficient for a basic understanding of Stoquerus's approach in his treatises and as a starting point for further exploration by the interested reader.

[23]This description is adapted from James A. Weisheipl, "Scholastic Method," in *New Catholic Encyclopedia*, 17 vols., ed. William J. McDonald et al. (New York: McGraw-Hill Book Company, 1967–79), 12:1145–46; see beginning of the article.

The chief means employed for teaching and learning in the scholastic method are division, definition, and reasoning.[24] "Division" is the process of dividing and further subdividing a subject or topic into its component parts. The preferred scholastic division is division by two, or "dichotomization."[25] Stoquerus employs division or dichotomization both to establish or eliminate topics he wishes or does not wish to discuss and to advance his thought in an orderly and logical fashion. In regard to the latter, Stoquerus will indicate his general divisions by such terms as "ratio," "differentia," "limitatio," etc.

A "definition" is a statement or proposition explaining exactly what a term means. In scholastic terminology, a definition may be "operational" if it describes a process or how something acts, "essential" if it explains the composition of a term or thing.[26] Stoquerus uses definition both to establish the identity of something as apart from something else and to provide a means of further argumentation.

"Reason" or "reasoning," from a scholastic viewpoint, admits of various usages: discursive thinking, or the act of drawing a conclusion from other judgments; the basis or evidence behind a conclusion or judgment; and the explanation offered for something.[27] Stoquerus uses all these modes of reason or reasoning throughout his treatises.

In the advancement and progression of the reasoning process, scholastic methodology employed an entire network of means to establish a convincing argument. Apropos of Stoquerus's use of the scholastic method in his treatises, some of these means are (1) the axiomatic method, i.e., argumentation from self-evident propositions (axioms) as the basis of a deductive system;[28]

---

[24]Ibid., p. 1145.

[25]Dichotomization may occasionally employ a three-fold division. See John J. Glanville, "Division (Logic)," *New Catholic Encyclopedia* 4 (1967): 926–28. See also Bernard Wuellner, S.J., *A Dictionary of Scholastic Philosophy*, 2d ed. (Milwaukee: Bruce Publishing Company, 1966), s.v. "division," *senses* 3 and 5. For the origin of dichotomization in class logic, see Ong, *Ramus, Method, and the Decay of Dialogue*, pp. 199–202.

[26]See Wuellner, *Dictionary of Scholastic Philosophy*, s.v. "definition," *sense* 1 and its divisions. See also de Wulf, *Scholasticism Old and New*, pp. 10–11.

[27]Selected and summarized from Wuellner, *Dictionary of Scholastic Philosophy*, s.vv. "reason" and "reasoning." See also Jean Ladriere, "Reasoning" (subsection "Scholastic Analysis"), *New Catholic Encyclopedia* 12 (1967): 120.

[28]Adapted from Wuellner, *Dictionary of Scholastic Philosophy*, s.vv. "axiom"; and "axiomatic method" under "method." For an account of the use of axioms in scholastic methodology, see M.-D. Chenu, O.P., *Toward*

(2) commonly held opinions ("sententiae communes"), hypotheses, theorems, and propositions, i.e., argumentation from principles that are not immediately self-evident but are provable from evident premises and serve as foundations for other proofs, explanations, and applications;[29] (3) images or examples drawn from experience, i.e., argumentation by analogy or comparison;[30] and (4) the *quaestio*, i.e., argumentation by calling into question a position ("Utrum ...") and its settlement by means of (a) the presentation of objections opposing the position ("Videtur quod non"), (b) the presentation of the author's denial of the opposing position by a statement to the contrary ("Sed contra") followed in turn by the statement of his own position ("Respondeo"), and (c) the presentation of the author's replies to the objections ("Ad primum," etc.). This formal structure of a *quaestio* is commonly termed an "articulus" or article;[31] moreover, within the framework of an article, most of the means of argumentation may be employed.

De Musica Verbali

The Form and Contents of the Treatise

His use of the scholastic method, especially that of division and subdivision, enables Stoquerus to guide readers smoothly through the intricacies of his treatise. Before discussing the form and contents of *De musica verbali* in

---

Understanding Saint Thomas, translated with authorized corrections and bibliographical additions by A.-M. Landry, O.P., and D. Hughes, O.P. (Chicago: Henry Regnery Company, 1964), pp. 186–88.

[29] These terms are grouped together here because, as used by Stoquerus, they originate from a specifically musical context and are further applied to it (unlike axioms, which originate within a specifically philosophical context). "Sententiae communes" are not as immediately self-evident as axioms but are commonly regarded as true. Stoquerus uses hypotheses and theorems interchangeably, in the sense of suppositions or assumed principles. See Wuellner, *Dictionary of Scholastic Philosophy*, s.v. "supposition," *sense* 6, and compare "hypothesis," *sense* 2. On the other hand, Stoquerus uses proposition in the sense of a theorem or thesis to be proved by deduction from accepted premises (ibid., s.v. "theorem,") such as, for example, "sententiae communes" and definitions.

[30] See Chenu, *Toward Understanding Saint Thomas*, pp. 169–72.

[31] This structure is found in its pristine form as used by St. Thomas Aquinas. For an excellent discussion of the construction of an article, see ibid., pp. 93–96. Stoquerus's use of the article, as will be seen, follows this structure closely enough to be clearly traceable to its pristine source.

particular, however, a few questions should be addressed. The first two of these concern the full title of the treatise, *De musica verbali libri duo*. The numbering of the chapters from the beginning to the end clearly suggests a single undivided work. What, then, are the two "books" this title suggests, and where is their point of division? The third question concerns the plan of the entire treatise as Stoquerus conceived it, for the treatise as it stands is incomplete, with the final chapter (31) broken off abruptly at the very beginning in mid-sentence and followed by the scribal notation "Caetera desiderantur" ("the rest is missing").[32] What is missing? Obviously, the remainder of the final chapter. Is there more, however? Perhaps just as internal evidence was used to suggest details of Stoquerus's life and character, it may also be used here to suggest a division into two books and to indicate what is missing from the treatise as Stoquerus conceived it. In this respect, a schema of the treatise may be helpful not only to illuminate the internal evidence that bears on these questions but also to furnish an orientation for the detailed discussion of the treatise that will follow these general observations. The schema may be presented as follows. The sections set in brackets indicate what is suggested from internal evidence; the chapter numbers of the treatise as it stands are enclosed in parentheses.

> [Book I: Establishment of *musica verbalis* as an art]
>   Introduction (1)
>   Division of music in general (2)
>   Theory
>   Practice
>   Instrumental
>   Vocal
>   With solmization syllables
>   With vocalise or random syllables
>   With words
>   An art distinct from solmization (3)
>   Name and definition (4)
>   Division of *musica verbalis* (5)
>   Words
>   Tones (6-9)

---

[32]That the manuscript is a copy will be discussed in more detail below in its proper section.

[Book II: Rules of *musica verbalis* as an art]
    Origin of the rules (10)
    Division of the rules (11)
        Necessary rules
            The rules themselves (12-16)
            Their use (17)
        Discretionary rules
            In general (18)
            In particular (19)
                Rules of the older generation
                    The rules themselves
                        The rules listed as a group
                        The rules individually (20-24)
                    How the rules are used (25)
                Rules of the newer generation
                    The rules themselves
                        In general (26)
                        In particular (27-31)
                    [How the rules are used]
[Conclusion]
[Appendix: Music examples]

As can be seen from this schema, Stoquerus's thought seems to be anchored in two broad divisions that suggest the "books" of his title. The first book, then, would concern the establishment of *musica verbalis* as an art (chapters 1–9); the second would be a discussion of the rules of *musica verbalis* in particular (chapters 10–31). In the first book, Stoquerus introduces the topic of his treatise (chapter 1), locates it in relative neglect as the third species of vocal music (chapter 2), asserts that this third species can be treated as an art in its own right (chapter 3), names this art *musica verbalis* and provides a definition (chapter 4), divides it into two parts, words and tones (chapter 5), and presents his own manner of solmizing the tones corresponding to the letter names of the Guidonian gamut (chapters 6–9). In the second book, Stoquerus discusses the rules proper to *musica verbalis* as an art. In this book, Stoquerus establishes the origin of his rules (chapter 10), divides them into necessary and discretionary ones (chapter 11), discusses the necessary rules individually (chapters 12–16) and suggests how they are used (chapter 17), discusses the need for discretionary rules in addition to the necessary rules (chapter 18), divides the discretionary rules into those of the older generation of composers headed by Josquin and those of the newer generation headed by Willaert (chapter 19), and discusses the rules of each generation in particular—those of the older generation (chapters 20–24) and how they are used (chapter 25) and those of the newer generation in general (chapter 26) and in particular (chapters 27–31), at which point the treatise ends abruptly.

With this, it is now possible to suggest what is missing. It would seem that a chapter following the last as the treatise stands would be devoted to the application of the rules of the newer generation. This chapter would correspond to Stoquerus's model in regard to the necessary rules (chapter 17) and the discretionary rules of the older generation (chapter 25). Following this chapter might be a final one in the form of a conclusion to the treatise as a whole. And finally, as Stoquerus promises in chapter 18, there would have followed a set of musical examples illustrating the application of his discretionary rules. This might be in the form of an appendix, as indicated in the schema.

Chapter 1: The Method of Applying the Words to the Notes Is Shamefully Ignored by Musicians and Cannot Be Easily Learned without Precepts.

This chapter functions as Stoquerus's introduction to his treatise. Accordingly, he opens his treatise in a straightforward manner, indicating the circumstances surrounding the writing of his treatise and his subject matter and readership. He admits to being compelled by circumstance ("fortuna ita cogente") to take on a number of seemingly humble tasks, one of which is the writing of this treatise.[33] He does not specify these other tasks or the particular circumstance prompting the treatise itself. Stoquerus, however, seems to have reconciled himself to drawing the most out of his situation (any wise man would, he implies) and has channeled his enthusiasm to the work at hand.

Stoquerus indicates that the focus of his treatise will be the correct application of words to music, which he perceives as the ultimate goal of musicianship and music instruction. Solmization, the method of singing a melody by means of the solmization syllables, is an intermediate goal, ordered to singing the melody correctly so that a text can eventually be substituted in

---

[33]The germination of the treatise can quite possibly be traced to Stoquerus's discipleship with Salinas, who, as Stoquerus himself will relate in chapter 3, encouraged him to draw up a set of rules for text placement for possible use in the University curriculum at Salamanca. At this time, then, Stoquerus was most likely enrolled at the University, was working closely with Salinas, and in conjunction with his tasks (one of which may have been assisting Salinas in the preparation of his *De musica libri septem*), had to set aside his own independent projects. See Lowinsky, "Treatise on Text Underlay," p. 232; and idem, "Gasparus Stoquerus and Francisco de Salinas," pp. 241–43.

place of the solmization syllables. Stoquerus does not conceal his disgust with the traditional educational emphasis on solmization at the expense of neglecting the method of applying words to the melody, a technique for advanced students but one to which beginners should at least aspire. He thus perceives his treatise to be important in that it leads to this goal: the correct application of the words to the music by means of rules.

It does not matter to Stoquerus that some musicians (singers especially, but composers as well) already possess this technique naturally, without the aid of rules. The treatise will help them to develop this technique more surely and with less effort if they are guided by its rules. For the less talented, however, Stoquerus maintains that his rules are indispensable because they will supplement any natural deficiencies these musicians might have. Stoquerus therefore envisages a wide readership, since all can profit from his treatise.[34]

Chapter 2: The Division of Music

In this chapter, Stoquerus discusses the division of music in order to bring into clearer relief the third branch of vocal music, music with text, as the ultimate end or goal of vocal music. In so doing, Stoquerus establishes, justifies, and delineates the subject of his treatise, thus locating it more clearly for his reader within the context of previous musical studies.

Stoquerus accordingly points out that the theoretical branch of music has already been treated adequately by his teacher Salinas.[35] On the other hand, Stoquerus points out that although both branches of practice (instrumental and vocal music) have also been treated by others, vocal music has not been ade-

---

[34]The tripartite division of this chapter (circumstances of the treatise, its subject matter, and readership) relates directly to that of the *exordium* or *proemium*, a rhetorical means employed at the beginning of a speech to render the audience well disposed ("benevolum"), attentive ("attentum"), and receptive ("docilem"). See Cicero *De inventione* 1.15.20–16.23; and Quintilian *Institutio oratoria* 4.1.1–79. Thus, Stoquerus's willingness to draw good from his circumstances puts his reader in a favorable disposition toward him; his promise to offer something new ("rei novitatem") for consideration attracts his reader's attention; and his contention that all can profit from his treatise makes the reader receptive to what will follow.

[35]Surely referring to Salinas's lectures at the University of Salamanca and to his *De musica libri septem*, with which Stoquerus was assisting Salinas in its preparation for publication, perhaps at the time he was writing his own treatise. See n. 11 *supra*.

quately treated, especially in regard to its ultimate purpose or goal, the most important aspect of any activity.[36]

Stoquerus employs for his purposes the three branches of vocal music as given by Gaffurius: solmization, intended for beginners; vocalization of a melody without syllables or words, intended for advanced students; and singing a melody with words, the goal of vocal music and intended for clerics.[37]

---

[36]Stoquerus is here referring to the scholastic (ultimately Aristotelian) principle of final causality, the direction, that is, of any activity to its ultimate goal or end. The final result of any activity, of course, is preceded by intermediate goals, but they are secondary, or subordinate to the final goal. Stoquerus's statement is perhaps best understood in the context of the scholastic dictum, "Finis est nobilior iis, quae sunt ad finem." See St. Thomas Aquinas, *Summa theologiae*, I–IIae, q. 111, art. 5, *ad contra*: "Semper autem finis potior est his quae sunt ad finem." The dictum itself is explained by Nuntio Signoriello, *Lexicon peripateticum philosophico-theologicum*, 5th ed. (Rome: Fredericus Pustet, 1931), p. 153, no. 4.

[37]Gaffurius's division of vocal music is as follows: "Tones which notes indicate are usually expressed in three ways. The first is through solfege [*solfizando*], that is, singing the syllable names of the tones, *ut, re, mi, fa, sol, la*, as illustrated here [example]. This manner of singing is the preferable method of instructing children. The second way is by producing only sounds and tones, and omitting entirely letters, syllables, and words. A skilled singer does this easily, as shown here [example]. The third way is by singing the words subjoined to the notes of a song, as in antiphons and responsories. This manner of singing, an example of which follows, is the desired goal of the best ecclesiastical singers [example] (Franchinus Gaffurius, *Practica musicae*, translated and transcribed by Clement A. Miller, Musicological Studies and Documents, no. 20 [(Rome): American Institute of Musicology, 1968], pp. 30–31) (Tribus insuper modis voces quas notulae declarant pronuntiari solent. Primo modo solfizando idest syllabas ac nomina vocum exprimendo scilicet ut re mi fa sol la [exemplum]. Quem quidem pronunciationis modum tanquam legem initiandis pueris praeponendam tradunt. Secundo modo: sonos ac voces tantum emittendo omissis penitus litteris ac syllabis et dictionibus: quod exercitatus cantor facile prosequitur hoc modo [exemplum]. Tertio modo: quascumque dictiones ut antiphonas et responsoria: et ipsarum verba cantilenarum notulis ipsis subscripta pronuntiando: Ad quem tanquam ad finem ellecti modulaminis clerici deducuntur [exemplum] [*Practica musicae* (Milan, 1496; reprint ed., Farnborough: Gregg Press, 1967), Bk. I, chap. 3, ff. A4v–5r])." Cf. *The Practica musicae of Franchinus Gafurius*, translated and edited with musical transcriptions by Irwin Young (Madison: University of Wisconsin Press, 1969), pp. 21–22.

With this division laid as groundwork, Stoquerus proceeds to supplement Gaffurius's division of the three branches of vocal music in several ways and moves closer to establishing and justifying the subject of his treatise.

First, in regard to the vocal utterances proper to each branch of vocal music, Stoquerus includes in the second branch not only the random sounds made by the voice in, say, humming a melody, analogous to birds chirping a melody and functioning much like a musical instrument's production of sound alone, but also nonsense syllables such as "fa la la" or onomatopoetic utterances in imitation of horns and birds, such as "ta ran ta ra" or "ti ri li." These syllables are different from solmization syllables in that they are not used in reference to any specific pitches and at the same time are not words, properly speaking, but are much like modern utterances used to sing a melody, as for example "tum de dum." Stoquerus probably includes such utterances in this second branch so as to exclude them from the third branch, which is concerned only with words conveying a complete meaning. Moreover, while Gaffurius seems to include in the third branch primarily plainchant, Stoquerus includes any meaningful text that induces an emotional response.

Second, Stoquerus understands the three branches as having an interrelatedness that is more unified than Gaffurius indicates. While Gaffurius associates each branch with a certain age group (solmization for beginners, wordless melody for the advanced, and texted melody for clerics), Stoquerus associates the three branches according to a hierarchy of goals, a hierarchy that places first in the order of intention the ultimate goal of vocal music, that of declaiming a text to a melody.[38] For Stoquerus, solmization is ordered to singing a melody correctly, which in turn is ordered to singing a melody independent of the syllables, which then is ordered to texting a melody. The third branch of vocal music, then, has a primacy of goal because the other two branches are but intermediate steps to that goal.

---

[38]Stoquerus here utilizes another aspect of final causality: that the end of an activity is first in the order of intention but last in the order of execution. See St. Thomas Aquinas, *Summa theologiae*, I, q. 5, art. 5, *ad contra*: "Videmus enim quod id quod est primum in causando, ultimum est in causato." The corresponding scholastic dictum "finis est primum in intentione et ultimum in executione" is explained by Mariano Fernández García, *Lexicon scholasticum philosophico-theologicum* (Quaracchi. St. Bonaventura, 1910; reprint ed., Hildesheim: Georg Olms, 1974), p. 861. Thus, while singing a melody to a text is the ultimate goal of the beginner, the beginner must be able simply to sing a melody first with and then without the solmization syllables. Only after this is the beginner equipped to sing a melody to a text.

Third, Stoquerus relates the three branches of vocal music in terms of their historical evolution. Of the three, solmization is the most recent and has been explained by numerous theorists. The second and third branches were already in use in antiquity, long before solmization, and utilized letters to indicate the pitches of a melody, to which words might or might not be sung.[39] As "proof" of the prior existence of these two branches, Stoquerus refers to a line from Vergil, "Numeros memini; si verba tenerem."[40] Of the second and third branches, however, the third is even older and, according to Stoquerus, is as innate to man as song is to birds, beginning as it did from the very moment of creation. Thus, the third branch of music has primacy over the other two by reason of its age.

With these considerations of the three branches of vocal music in general and the primacy of the third branch in particular, Stoquerus establishes and justifies the subject of his treatise. It is the proper way of singing melody with text, the ultimate goal of vocal music and the oldest branch, which renders the completely formed musician.[41]

Chapter 3: Whether This Third Species of Vocal Music Can Be Handled by Means of Art.

Having identified for his reader the third branch of vocal music, music with text, as the subject of his treatise, Stoquerus now proceeds to establish this branch as an art (*ars*) distinct from the other two branches, and therefore one having its own set of rules.[42]

---

[39] For a convenient example of an ancient melody with letters to indicate pitch, see the Epitaph of Seikilos in Egert Pöhlmann, *Denkmäler altgriechischer Musik*, Erlanger Beiträge zur Sprach- und Kunstwissenschaft, vol. 31 (Nürnberg: Hans Carl, 1970), pp. 54–55.

[40] *Eclogae* 9.45.

[41] Concerning the union of words and music and at the same time the Renaissance ideal of the perfect musician, cf. Lowinsky, "Treatise on Text Underlay," p. 235: "With these words [the last sentence of chapter 2], Stocker expresses the classical attitude of the Renaissance musician, and determines the point of view that governs his whole treatise. If music was invented to express words, what more urgent task can there be than to teach how properly to coordinate words with tones?"

[42] Here and elsewhere in his treatise, Stoquerus uses *ars* to indicate an activity accomplished by following established rules. He uses *usus*, on the other hand, to indicate an activity accomplished by judgments responding to the individual requirements of a given situation, whether or not they conform to established rules. For his employment of these terms in these senses, Stoquerus seems to be influenced by Hermann Finck's definition of *musica arti-*

Stoquerus's method in establishing this third branch as an art accords closely with that of the scholastic *quaestio*.[43] The elements of the *quaestio* as a method of argumentation in this chapter can be observed in (1) the chapter's title (introduced by the particle *an* with the verb in the subjunctive mood), (2) the four arguments forming the negative response to the question, (3) Stoquerus's own position to the contrary, and (4) his response to the four arguments, thus settling the question in his favor.

The four arguments raised in objection to this third branch of vocal music represent the central issues that Stoquerus must address in order to establish this branch as a distinct art with its own set of rules: solmization as a sufficient preparation for singing a melody with text (argument 1), the ability of musicians with a thorough grounding in solmization to text a melody from practice alone (*usus*[44]) (argument 2), the freedom of the composer to set the text as he sees fit (argument 3), and the natural ability to put words to melody, an ability that the other two branches, in their respective spheres, can attain only through art (argument 4).

Stoquerus's own position argues from authority, scholastic reasoning, and a common-sense understanding of the requirements of this third branch of vocal music. Arguing first from authority, Stoquerus claims he can merely list his rules for this third branch because other theorists, notably Zarlino (in his *Istitutioni harmoniche*, Part 4, chapter 33), have done exactly this before him and because Salinas encouraged him to draw up a set of rules for instruction at Salamanca. In view of the wide influence of these two theorists, their rules and advice would undoubtedly weigh heavily in the balance toward Stoquerus's position.

Aware, however, that an argument from authority alone is not sufficient,[45] Stoquerus advances two philosophical arguments supporting the

---

ficialis as "quando praeter usum etiam praecepta addunt" and of *musica usualis* as "quae magis usu quam praeceptis comparatur." See Hermann Finck, *Practica musica* (Wittenberg: Georg Rhaw, 1556; reprint ed., Bologna: Forni, 1969), f. 5v.

[43] See p. 13 *supra*. Moreover, the *quaestio* as a scholastic method of argumentation was generally reserved for fields of learning other than the arts, as for example, jurisprudence, theology, and philosophy. See Kristeller, "Humanism and Scholasticism," in *Renaissance Thought*, p. 99. In this respect, it is noteworthy that Stoquerus uses this method in his treatise, for in so doing, he supplies a treatise on practice with a solid rational underpinning.

[44] Cf. n. 42 *supra*.

[45] An argument from authority might well be true but was used mainly as an adjunct to a more reasoned and valid approach to the truth. Cf. its defini-

rational basis underlying his position. His position, put succinctly, is: If solmization has rules, then should not this third branch of vocal music also have rules? For his first argument, Stoquerus invokes the scholastic axiom "propter quod unumquodque tale est, magis est tale (that on account of which something is what it is, is that and more)" in order to emphasize that singing a melody with text is the very reason or formal cause ("propter quod") for solmization.[46] Thus, solmization is ordered to the third branch of vocal music not only according to its ultimate end (final, or extrinsic cause), as chapter 2 emphasized, but also as dependent on it for its very being (formal, or intrinsic cause). Or in the negative, if there were no need to learn how to sing a melody, either with or without words, there would be no reason for learning solmization. Stoquerus thus concludes: If solmization has its rules, then this third branch of music, as the formal cause of solmization, has even more reason to have rules.

For his second argument, Stoquerus contrasts the content of solmization and texted melody by means (apparently) of the axiom "non potest esse minus in abstracto quam in concreto (there cannot be less in the abstract than in the concrete)."[47] In regard to Stoquerus's application of this principle, the "concrete" refers to a solmized melody, the "abstract" to a melody in which the solmization syllables are taken away, or abstracted, and a text is inserted in their place. Stoquerus points out that in the process of this abstraction, "more," not "less" is involved, because in texting a melody, one not only has to be able to sing a melody correctly, thus accomplishing the function of solmization, but also must take into consideration factors that solmization does not involve: word accent, syllabic quantity, note values, and ligatures.

---

tion as a "proof based on the testimony of others or on authentic citations from intellectual authorities but not based on intrinsic evidence or on one's own immediate knowledge of the truth," in Wuellner, *Dictionary of Scholastic Philosophy*, s.v. "argument from authority" under "authority." For a thorough treatment of the argument from authority, see Chenu, *Understanding St. Thomas*, pp. 126–55.

[46]This axiom, from Aristotle (*Metaphysica* 993b24 and *Analytica posteriora* 72a25), is more commonly translated "propter quod unumquodque tale, et illud magis." For the axiom and a detailed explanation, see Signoriello, *Lexicon peripateticum*, pp. 324–25. For its application to formal causes, see Wuellner, *Dictionary of Scholastic Philosophy*, s.v. "Propter quod ... magis."

[47]This axiom is not contained in the sources consulted, but *abstractum* and *concretum* suggest philosophical usage. Moreover, in the context of Stoquerus's argumentation, the statement functions as the major premise of a syllogism.

Thus, according to Stoquerus, more (that is, additional) rules are needed to address these instances.

Having presented his own position, Stoquerus proceeds to respond to each of the four arguments opposing his position. The first argument, Stoquerus recapitulates, is that solmization is as sufficient for singing the text as a rush plant is for learning how to swim. For his response, Stoquerus asserts that the philosophical axiom supporting this argument, "subrogatum naturam sapit eius in cuius locum subrogatur (a substitute resembles the nature of that in whose place it is substituted),"[48] does not apply in this instance, because solmizing a melody and texting a melody involve different factors. One cannot, therefore, merely substitute the text for the solmization syllables, because the procedures for note-to-syllable correspondence are not identical. Hence, the two branches of vocal music are not similar in nature. Likewise, neither does a rush plant, as a flotation aid for learning how to swim, fully substitute for swimming independently, for eventually a beginner will have to "let go" and follow rules specifically designed for swimming.

The second argument is that most musicians with a thorough grounding in solmization have acquired the ability to text a melody from experience in doing it. Stoquerus replies, probably from his own observation, that not everyone has this ability to learn from experience, and even those who have done so could have learned more quickly with rules to guide them.

The third argument concerns the freedom of composers to set their texts as they see fit, a freedom that is unhampered by rules and that performers should respect by not applying other rules. In his reply to this objection, Stoquerus presents for the first time in his treatise his distinction between rules that are necessary and those that are discretionary. Stoquerus indicates that even presupposing the freedom of composers to set their text as they see fit, all of them observe the necessary rules, while the better ones observe the discretionary rules as well, which account for their better acceptance by the public.

The fourth argument utilizes Stoquerus's own assertion in chapter 2 that the expression of words to music began at the creation of the human race and asserts that this third branch of vocal music is therefore natural and not dependent on any skill acquired by following rules. By contrast, the first and second branches are "artificial," or accomplished by art, with their ease of

---

[48]For this axiom and its application, see St. Thomas Aquinas, *Commentum in quatuor libros sententiarum P. Lombardi*, d. 42, q. 2, art. 1, *solutio* and *ad* 6. St. Thomas is discussing here an adopted child as a substitute for a real offspring, the adopted child resembling the nature (as a son or daughter) of a real offspring of the adoptive parent.

procedure accomplished by following rules, thus imitating the "natural" procedure of the third branch. Stoquerus's reply to this objection cleverly develops his own assertion to his advantage. In comparing *all* the branches of vocal music to the faculty of speech considered as natural but developed by art, Stoquerus indicates that all the branches of vocal music are alike in that they are natural ("naturales") and uncultivated ("rudiores") but developed by art ("artificiales") and refined ("politae"). Indeed, since the urge to express syllables and sounds is innate to man, Stoquerus would have the reader believe that the first and second branches, too, are natural, with solmization being the more recent development into an art in its own sphere. Moreover, the tendency to put words to music is also innate to man, and the manner of doing so was at first awkward but gradually developed into a more perfect art with the passage of time and the evolution of rules. For Stoquerus, then, the natural and the artificial are not mutually exclusive; rather, the artificial is the natural in the state of perfection.

Stoquerus's concluding statements confirm his argumentation from the viewpoint of the art involved in each of the three branches and the degree of difficulty involved in attaining their art, with the third branch, as the goal of the other two, involving the greatest difficulty. Thus the unique difficulty of the third branch of vocal music and its character as the end of the other two branches justifies Stoquerus's establishment of it as an art with its own set of rules.

Chapter 4: On the Definition of Verbal Music.

Having indicated this third branch of vocal music as the topic of his treatise (chapter 2) and justified it as an art in its own right (chapter 3), Stoquerus now assigns it a name and definition.

In deciding upon a name for this third branch of vocal music, Stoquerus refers to its proper activity, the singing of words or a text ("verba canere"). He accordingly names this branch *musica verbalis* ("music with words" or "verbal music"), hence the title of his treatise. The name is apt, since this branch so named is thereby distinguished from the other two branches of vocal music, which are concerned with the singing of syllables, either the solmization syllables ("voces musicales") of the first branch or the random syllables ("syllabae") or even none at all of the second branch. For an additional rationale behind his title, Stoquerus refers to the grammarians, who, as he claims, list *verbum* (word) as a species under the genus *vox* (vocable or utterance).⁴⁹ Hence, by analogy, *musica verbalis* is a species under the genus *musica vocalis*.

Stoquerus's care to locate precisely and name *musica verbalis* as a special branch of vocal music manifests, of course, his scholastic methodology. This is no less true in his care to define *musica verbalis*, since definition of terminology and subject matter is one of the "topics" proper to the scholastic method and ordered to effective discourse and reasoning. Stoquerus's definition is operational, defining *musica verbalis* from the aspect of its method or what it does.⁵⁰ The two most important aspects of *musica verbalis* are, first, that the setting of words or syllables of words to the notes be correct, since unlike solmization not all notes can receive syllables, and second, that in this setting no "barbarism" occur to offend the ear, that is, a wrong pronunciation of a word,⁵¹ perhaps here due to a discrepancy between a note value and a syllabic quantity. In mentioning these instances, Stoquerus is merely explaining his definition and indicating its thrust.

Chapter 5: The Division of Verbal Music.

So as to delineate further the subject of his treatise, now named and defined, Stoquerus divides *musica verbalis* into words and tones. The motivation for this further division of his subject matter is at bottom pedagogical,

---

⁴⁹Stoquerus's reference to the grammatical distinction between *verbum* and *vox* is probably meant to be understood as a general rather than technical statement. In grammatical usage, *vox* indicated any articulated vocal sound and *verbum* an action word or verb; *dictio* indicated a word in general, and one that bears a complete meaning, as opposed to *syllaba*, which did not. For a discussion of these terminological ambiguities, see Quintilian *Institutio oratoria* 1.5.2.

⁵⁰The root meaning of topics is "places," hence the Latin *loci*, "areas" or "places" from which argumentation is drawn, with definition included among these. See Cicero *Topica* 1.7–8. Ultimately traceable to Aristotle's *Topica* in the *Organon*, these *loci* were considered authoritative starting points for argumentation and discourse. In the Renaissance, they formed an essential part of the scholastic method, observed not only in the definition of terms, but in the many axioms and maxims that proliferated and were cited in syllogistic and other reasoning. For a detailed account of *loci* in Renaissance dialectic, see Ong, *Ramus, Method, and Decay of Dialogue*, pp. 63–65. For the operational definition, see Wuellner, *Dictionary of Scholastic Philosophy*, s.v. "operational definition" under "definition."

⁵¹Quintilian *Institutio oratoria* 1.5.5–33.

as manifested by his concern to treat his subject adequately and in its entirety.⁵²

By "tones" Stoquerus means, of course, anything that pertains to the purely musical aspect of *musica verbalis*. In the ordinary course of instruction, this should have all been learned at the elementary level along with solmization of chant (clefs, modes, transposition) and mensural music (notes, ligatures; time signatures, modus, tempus, prolatio; the various kinds of puncti; coloration, augmentation, diminution, proportions).⁵³ Stoquerus can therefore legitimately excuse himself from a reiteration of these matters, since anyone ready for this third stage of instruction must already have learned it, or at least know where to go for freshening.⁵⁴

In regard to solmization method, however, Stoquerus expresses a concern about the effectiveness of the methods of teaching the easiest progression or alignment of the solmization syllables along the gamut for their eventual selection for the solmization of the tones of a melody. Stoquerus will discuss these methods as well as systematically present his own new and easier method in the following four chapters. This portion of his treatise seems as good a forum as any to discuss these methods and his own, especially since solmization was directly ordered to the correct singing of melody and preceded whatever instruction there was, if any, in textual declamation. Accordingly, in chapters 6–9, Stoquerus presents the various methods of teaching the progression of the syllables, his own method, his criticism of the other methods, and a different division of the syllables as used in mutation.

Chapter 6: On the Progression of the Six Musical Syllables.

Stoquerus's presentation of the various ways in which the six solmization syllables progress along the gamut of pitches available for vocal melody is not detailed in full, nor are the methods themselves necessarily exclusive of one another. Rather, he organizes his presentation according to efficient and sure ways in which the progression of syllables is learned for their eventual use in

---

⁵²For a fuller account of this tendency to divide and in most instances dichotomize subject matter, particularly for pedagogical purposes, see Ong, *Ramus, Method, and the Decay of Dialogue*, pp. 199–202.

⁵³Any elementary instruction book for choirboys includes most—if not all or others besides—of the topics given here. See, for example, *passim*, Finck, *Practica musica*; and Gallus Dressler, *Musicae practicae elementa* (Magdeburg: Wolfgang Kirchner, 1571).

⁵⁴Stoquerus's third treatise, *De modo, tempore, et prolatione*, however, does discuss the topics indicated by its title.

the solmization of a given melody. His criticisms of these methods in chapter 8 will be aimed directly at the practical difficulties and ambiguities these methods involve when they are applied to a given melody. Stoquerus's ultimate purpose in presenting these methods is to contrast them with his own method of ordering the syllables along the gamut, a method that he submits is new and far easier in practice.[55]

The first and classic method of learning and using the syllables is that of the so-called "Guidonian hand,"[56] possibly the most celebrated and applied visual aid in the history of music. Its features are well known. Each of the twenty letters (*claves*) of the pitch spectrum comprising the full vocal range was arranged in a spiral pattern along the joints and digits of the left hand, with the topmost letter, ee, located beyond the hand above the middle finger. The six solmization syllables (*voces musicales*) were assigned to these letters and "progressed" (hence the title of this chapter) along the gamut by means of a series of overlapping hexachords beginning with ut and applied on the letters G, C, and F. In their instruction, the teacher would drill his charges by pointing to or tracing the locations of the syllables with his right hand. To solmize a melody with the mnemonic aid of the hand was no mean feat. One had to know from memory which syllables were available for any given letter, which hexachord could be correctly used to narrow the selection to one syllable, and which of the many possible mutations could be employed in order to ascend or descend from one hexachord to another.[57]

---

[55]Moreover, in *De solfizationis docendae ratione*, Stoquerus demonstrates that his method is not only easy (arguing *a facili*) but also certain (arguing *a certitudine*).

[56]For a concise explanation of Guido of Arezzo's association with the hand as a teaching device, see Oliver B. Ellsworth, *The Berkeley Manuscript*, Greek and Latin Music Theory, vol. 2 (Lincoln: University of Nebraska Press, 1984), pp. 33–35, n. 1.

[57]The Guidonian hand was used in numerous elementary instruction books during the Renaissance, even as late as Stoquerus's time. Among these was Bonaventura da Brescia's widely circulated *Regula musice plane*, first published in Venice in 1497 and followed by other editions in Venice, Milan, and London from 1505–1550. An edition in Italian was published in Venice in 1570. The 1497 edition shows an illustration of the hand and its explanation (chap. 1), the mutations on the entire gamut (chap. 8), and a description of Guido's method of singing (chap. 42). See Bonaventura da Brescia, *Rules of Plain Music (Brevilogium Musicale)*, trans. Albert Seay, Colorado College Music Press Translations, no. 11 (Colorado Springs: Colorado College Press, 1979). See also Johannes Aventinus, *Musicae rudimenta* (Augsburg, 1516), trans. and ed. T. Herman Keahy (New York: Institute of Medieval Music, 1971), pp. 7–9; the anonymous *Compendium*

The second method utilizes just the seven letters from the middle range (*claves acutae*) of the gamut, extending, that is, from A-la-mi-re to G-sol-re-ut.[58] Since the *claves acutae* contain all the syllables from all three hexachords needed for melodic ascent and descent, not just for the middle range but by octave transposition for the upper and lower ranges as well, this method simplifies learning all the syllables along the gamut.

The third method that Stoquerus describes reduces further the effort required to associate from memory the correspondence of letters and syllables along the gamut by suggesting that only ut be memorized as beginning on C of the natural hexachord (*cantus naturalis*), F of the soft hexachord (*cantus mollis*), and G of the hard hexachord (*cantus durus*). Only three letters are therefore required as orientation points for ut. The remaining syllables can easily be located on the gamut by inference, based on the order of the hexachord syllables progressing from ut. This method of determining the progression of the syllables along the gamut is found in many instruction-books under their discussions of *cantus*, that is, the arrangement of the hexachord syllables beginning with ut and spanning C-A, F-D, and G-E.[59]

The fourth and fifth methods represent two stages in the mid-sixteenth century toward a simplification of the process of associating the syllables with the letters along the gamut. The emphasis or point of orientation in both concerns the pivotal syllables of mutation, re and la respectively in ascent and descent. The fourth method associates the syllables re and la with their corresponding letters in the context of the three *cantus* or hexachordal spans beginning on C, F, and G, and uses only these syllables for mutation, thus considerably simplifying the procedure of mutation and thereby lessening the

---

musices confectum ad faciliorem instructionem cantum choralem discentium (Venice, 1513), f. 4r; Guillaume Gerson, *Utilissimae musicales regulae necessariae plane cantus* (Paris: François Regnault, 1518), ff. Aiv–Bi; and Michael Koswick, *Compendiaria musicae artis editio* (Leipzig: Wolfgang Stökel, 1517), ff. Aiii–iv.

[58]Johannes Tinctoris defines *acutae claves* as "... those comprised in the [Guidonian] hand from the lower to the higher a *la mi re* [a to a'] including the former but not the latter (*Johannes Tinctoris: Dictionary of Musical Terms [Terminorum Musicae Diffinitorium]*, translated with Latin text on facing pages by Carl Parrish [New York: The Free Press of Glencoe, 1963], p. 7) (... illae quae in manu ab alamire inferiori inclusive et usque ad alamire superius exclusive continentur [ibid., p. 6])." Cf. ibid., where Tinctoris defines *graves claves*, pp. 34–35, and *superacuta loca*, pp. 60–61.

[59]For examples, see Lampadius, *Compendium musices* (Bern: Samuel Apiarius, 1554), pp. Bvi–vii; and Heinrich Faber, *Compendiolum musicae pro incipientibus* (Nürnberg: Johann vom Berg, 1548), chap. 3, pp. A4v–5r.

demands placed on the memory. The fifth method, on the other hand, associates re and la along the gamuts of two scales, which are in effect combinations of the natural hexachord with either the soft or hard hexachord. The two *cantus*—*mollis* and *durus*—(now meaning "scales") are differentiated respectively by the presence or absence of B^b in the signature heading the staff. In both methods, however, the syllables for mutation, as well as their corresponding letters are identical.[60] The only difference is that the former method presupposes only one gamut with three interlocking hexachords, while the latter presupposes two gamuts or scales, the *cantus mollis* and the *cantus durus*.

The sixth method of learning the progression of syllables consists in the memorization of the syllables corresponding to the letters of the pitches located within a given vocal range. The range, in turn, is indicated by its characteristic clef sign both with and without B^b in the signature. This process is done systematically for each range, using both scales (the *cantus durus* and the *cantus mollis*) with the clef sign variously placed within each range.[61]

---

[60]Heinrich Faber, for example, clearly understands the three *cantus* as characteristic hexachordal spans (*Compendiolum*, chap. 3, p. A5r) and within this context gives his rules for mutation employing re and la (chap. 4, pp. A5r–5v). Martin Agricola, however, employs only two *cantus*—*mollis* and *durus*—considered as scales comprising the entire gamut and distinguished by the function of B as fa (*cantus mollis*) or mi (*cantus durus*), according to the presence or absence of B^b in the signature. Within this context, he then presents his rules (in dactyllic hexameters) for mutation on re and la according to their corresponding letters in each *cantus* (see Martin Agricola, *Rudimenta musices* [Wittenberg: Georg Rhaw, 1539], ff. B3v–5r). This change in meaning of *cantus* from hexachord to scale is noted by Martin Ruhnke ("Hexachord," *MGG* 6 [1957]: 355): "Seit der Mitte des 16. Jh. lehrte man die Mutationsregeln mehr und mehr schematisch, ohne sich des Hexachordwechsels bewusst zu werden. Die Namen *cantus mollis* und *durus* bezeichnen jetzt bei den meisten Theoretikern nicht mehr die Hexachorde auf *f* und *g*, sondern die ganzen Skalen mit und ohne generelle b-Vorzeichnung." See also Carl Parrish, "A Renaissance Music Manual for Choirboys," in *Aspects of Medieval and Renaissance Music: A Birthday Offering to Gustave Resse*, ed. Jan LaRue (New York: W. W. Norton and Co., 1966), pp. 657–58.

[61]Sebald Heyden proposes this method of learning the syllables. In his *De arte canendi* (Nürnberg: Johannes Petreius, 1540; reprint ed., Monuments of Music and Music Literature in Facsimile, II/139, New York: Broude Brothers, 1969), Heyden illustrates the location of the syllables of the three hexachords in relation to the clef signs (*characteristicae claves*) pertaining to the high, middle, and low ranges (p. 25) and then presents musical examples for practice in each range, with and without B^b in the signature (pp. 26–39).

The example given in the illustration in this section is presumably for the more adventurous pupils who might want to learn all the ranges: discant, alto, tenor, and bass.

The seventh method of learning the syllables, lightly sketched here by Stoquerus, is that of a Spanish theorist who locates fa on F of the natural hexachord, B^b of the soft hexachord, and C of the hard hexachord, presumably as the points of departure for determining the remaining syllables in relation to their respective letters and hexachords.[62] The basis of this method is possibly the location of the important mi-fa interval along the gamut, with all the remaining intervals easily recognized as whole tones.

The eighth method is Stoquerus's own, one that he devised during his stay in Italy and before becoming acquainted with the method of the Spanish theorist noted above. Stoquerus's method is similar to the Spanish method in that he also uses fa as a point of departure, but only as an orientation syllable for determining the location of re and la as these syllables are distributed along the lines and spaces of the staff comprising the gamut. Where fa is on a space or line, re and la of the hexachord are also in the spaces or lines immediately adjacent. This method would seem to be a convenient means for locating re and la in systems that employ these syllables as the easiest and most practical for use in mutation.

In presenting these systems, Stoquerus shows himself to be knowledgeable and well read in solmization theory; he also reveals his pedagogical interests. And if, as will be seen, he reveals himself as something of an iconoclast, this image will be tempered by the fact that he knows his field and argues from evidence and reason rather than from emotion or prejudice.

Chapter 7: Theorems Showing the True Way of Tracing the Syllables.

In this chapter, Stoquerus presents a series of eighteen hypotheses that are intended to furnish the rationale governing his method and the criteria by which the weaknesses of the methods different from his will be revealed in chapter 8. Stoquerus intends the hypotheses themselves to be evident upon

---

[62]It has not been possible to identify this theorist; however, the German theorist Dietrich Tzwyvel (or Tzwiefel), in his *Introductorium musicae practicae* (Münster: Georg Richolff, 1508; rev. ed., Cologne: Heinrich Quentel, 1513), seems to anticipate this approach. With fa as the syllable of orientation on C of the hard hexachord, F of the natural hexachord, and B^b of the soft hexachord, he distributes the remaining syllables and their full hexachords over the Guidonian gamut (see Wilfried Kaiser, *Dietrich Tzwyvel und sein Musiktraktat* [Marburg: Bärenreiter, 1968], pp. 92–93 and 217–18).

inspection and, by their arrangement, to lead the reader to an understanding of his own method, which is succinctly stated in the corollary following his hypotheses.

Stoquerus first establishes the syllables that are available for each of the seven letters in the hexachords along which these syllables lie (hypotheses 1–8). He then makes some observations about the intervallic relationships of the hexachords, one to another, and those of the corresponding syllables one to another on each letter (hypotheses 9–12). Proceeding from these general observations, Stoquerus next establishes (1) how, from all these letters and syllables, an ascending and descending progression of seven syllables corresponding to seven letters is derived and (2) where the mutations should take place to bring about these progressions (hypotheses 13–15). Stoquerus then shows how these progressions can be repeated at every octave (hypothesis 17). Finally, he gives the guideline for determining the focal syllable (B as fa or mi) governing the choice of a particular ascending or descending progression in a given instance (hypothesis 18). Thus, with B as fa or mi, the remaining six syllables can be determined, and the ascending and descending progressions corresponding to seven letter names can continue to ascend and descend indefinitely (corollary).

Stoquerus's first hypothesis presents the raw materials of solmization theory and practice: the six syllables that are used in reference to seven letters. This hypothesis also points to the fundamental problem of solmization theory and practice: how to supply a syllable for each letter. The second hypothesis indicates the repetition of letter names and syllables at their octaves, with the resulting series progressing in ascending and descending order. This hypothesis also serves to establish the octave as the focal area for the solution to the problem of supplying a syllable for each letter. The third hypothesis narrows the observations of the first and second hypotheses to the octave span C–C, with a syllable from the natural hexachord available for each letter except B, which it does not reach:

C	D	E	F	G	A	B	C	D	E	F	G	A
ut	re	mi	fa	sol	la		ut	re	mi	fa	sol	la

The problem now becomes how to determine a syllable for the letter B. In order to determine this logically, Stoquerus begins by advancing his fourth hypothesis, which states that the span of the octave requires the (conjunct) addition of a semiditone to the (major) sixth. Then, in the fifth hypothesis, reasoning on the basis of the two kinds of the semiditone (distinguished by the location of the semitone above or below the whole-tone interval), Stoquerus establishes fa and mi as the only two possible syllables for this seventh degree. According to the sixth hypothesis, the seventh letter, B, can bear the two syllables mi and fa, because of its dual character, that is, ♮ (hard) and b (soft). In practice, however, it can bear only one of the two syllables. Thus, if B is mi, the syllable is taken from the hard hexachord; if fa, from the soft hexachord, since the natural hexachord does not reach B.

Next, with the letter B given only one possible syllable for either of its pitches, Stoquerus posits his seventh hypothesis. This situates mi and fa in relation to their respective hexachords, since the solmization of the semiditone should ascend or descend in relation to the hexachordal series in which mi and fa are located. These series, like that of the natural hexachord, begin of course on ut. All three hexachords can be located in relation to each other, with their first syllable, ut, located on their corresponding letters: C of the natural hexachord, F of the soft hexachord, and G of the hard hexachord. Stoquerus indicates that these letters are also used as clef signs, presumably to indicate the basic ranges for the syllables, since all three hexachords are used in every range. In turn, the eighth hypothesis establishes the location of the syllables of each hexachord on their respective letters, with each letter showing three or two syllables, one from each hexachord, depending on whether the letters lie in or outside the gamut of each hexachord. At this stage of Stoquerus's argumentation, the three hexachords are related as follows, with B-fa-B-mi occupying the central locus of orientation:

```
C    D    E    F    G    A   |B|  C    D    E    F    G    A
ut   re   mi   fa   sol  la  | |  ut   re   mi   fa   sol  la
               ut   re   mi  |fa|  sol  la
                         ut  re  |mi|  fa   sol  la
```

Having established where the hexachords lie along their gamuts in relation to B-fa and B-mi, and what and how many syllables are available for each letter name, Stoquerus now considers the various intervallic relations of the hexachords one to another and of the syllables one to another on each letter. Accordingly, his ninth hypothesis establishes that in descent from the soft and hard hexachords, the natural hexachord lies respectively a fourth and fifth lower, but in ascent, a fifth and fourth higher. In turn, the hard hexachord is one interval higher than the soft hexachord. This can be observed in the figure above, which can also serve as a convenient reference for many of the remaining hypotheses. In the tenth hypothesis, the intervallic relations of the syllables one to another on each letter are established as bearing the same intervallic relations as those of the corresponding hexachords. The hexachords, however, are distant in pitch, while the syllables are "distant" at the unison, except B-fa-B-mi, which is not a unison, but two pitches.

With the next two hypotheses, Stoquerus further specifies the intervallic relations of the syllables to each other on each letter. The eleventh hypothesis establishes the comparative distance of one syllable from another on each letter as the converse of the comparative distance of their respective hexachords. For example, on G-sol-re-ut, sol is four degrees higher than re because the natural hexachord is four degrees lower than the soft hexachord; re is one degree higher than ut because the soft hexachord is one degree lower than the hard hexachord. In Stoquerus's example, on B-fa-B-mi, mi is one degree lower than fa, because the hard hexachord is one degree higher than the soft. The twelfth hypothesis further systematizes the relations of the hard and soft hexachord syllables (the "accidental" syllables) in relation to the syllable of the natural hexachord on each letter. Thus, on letters of three syllables, the "hard" and "soft" syllables bear the relation of a fourth or fifth to the "natural" syllable. The letters of two syllables, however, lack a third syllable because the letter is not reached by one of the three hexachords. Thus on F-fa-ut, there is no syllable possible that is one degree lower than ut (of the hard hexachord), as ut (of the soft hexachord) in turn is three degrees lower than fa; in E-la-mi, there is no syllable possible that is one degree higher than la (of the soft hexachord), as la (of the hard hexachord) in turn is three degrees higher than mi; on B-fa-B-mi, with fa being higher than mi, there are no corresponding possible syllables available from the natural hexachord that would be three degrees higher than fa, or four degrees higher than mi.

At this point in Stoquerus's argumentation, these last four hypotheses (9–12) are simple observations; however, it is safe to say that their significance lies in their providing for Stoquerus and his readers the rationale underlying the process of mutation from the hard or soft hexachord to the natural (or vice versa), in which the mutations, required because of the need for additional syllables from another hexachord, can be shown to be consistent because of these various intervallic relationships.

Thus far, Stoquerus's hypotheses have established the positions of the hexachords along a portion of the gamut and all the possible syllables available for each of the seven letters. Now, in his thirteenth hypothesis, he observes that each letter reveals a plurality of available syllables, but the order of syllables in any given hexachordal span reveals only one possible syllable for each letter. In solmization, then, it is easier and more certain to refer to the hexachordal order of syllables rather than to each letter. This implies that if one syllable is associated with one letter, the remaining five syllables will automatically and correctly correspond to their five letters. Since, however, the fundamental problem of solmization is one of supplying a syllable for each of the seven letters, it is obvious that two hexachords must be used, thus involving mutation. In the fourteenth hypothesis, Stoquerus therefore proposes that the way to give one syllable to each of the seven letters is to use the lower syllables of two hexachords for ascent and the higher syllables for descent. More specifically, on the basis of the division of the span of the seventh into two groups of three and four units, it is necessary to use three syllables from one hexachord and four from another (or vice versa). Thus for example, the span C–B^b can be solmized as ut-re-mi-ut-re-mi-fa, with the mutation to the soft hexachord taking place on the lowest syllable, ut, of the four-syllable series. Or, the span C–B can be solmized as ut-re-mi-fa-ut-re-mi, with the mutation to the hard hexachord taking place on its lowest syllable, ut.

In the fifteenth hypothesis, Stoquerus establishes that mutation to the second hexachord is easier if it occurs at the interval of the whole tone between the two hexachords. This principle he shows to be especially applicable in ascent. Instead of ut-re-mi-ut-re-mi-fa, in which the half tone occurs between mi and ut, the series re-mi-fa-re-mi-fa-sol is preferred, in which a whole tone occurs between fa and re. Presumably this is easier to sing in ascent. It should be noted, however, that Stoquerus establishes this principle on the basis of the descending series la-sol-fa-la-sol-fa-mi and la-sol-fa-mi-la-sol-fa. Yet, since the series la-sol-fa-la-sol-fa-mi shows a half tone between fa and la, there is no way this principle can be applied in this instance. If Stoquerus is using this as a general principle, perhaps the series la-sol-fa-la-sol-fa-mi would be the only series involving a half tone, since the other three series all involve a whole tone. Indeed, in the ascending series beginning with re, the whole-tone intervals are connected by a curved line in the manuscript. In any event, the series beginning on re will also correspond to seven letters, and the principle established in the fourteenth hypothesis is still valid.

Stoquerus's sixteenth hypothesis systematizes hypotheses 13 through 15 using B as the focal letter for mutation to the natural hexachord. Since B is reached only by the soft or hard hexachord, mutation to the natural hexachord takes place above B in ascent and below B in descent. According to Stoquerus's system, since the first syllable of each descending series is la and of each ascending series re, these syllables are the syllables where the mutation occurs, that is, where the next hexachord series of three of four syllables begins. Below B then, the natural hexachord is entered directly, that is, on its first descending syllable, la. Above B, the natural hexachord is entered indirectly, that is, on its second syllable, re, with fa or sol of the hard or soft hexachord intervening for ut, which is not a suitable syllable for mutation. The descent to the natural hexachord from B-fa is fa-la; from B-mi is mi-la. Ascent to the natural hexachord from B-fa is fa-sol-re; from B-mi is mi-fa-re.

At this point in his argumentation, Stoquerus has established a set of ascending and descending syllables corresponding to seven letters, with B as the focal letter of reference and either one of its two syllables, fa or mi, as the focal syllable for ascending or descending to the natural hexachord. Now, in the seventeenth hypothesis, he shows how the order of seven syllables progresses to the octave and beyond. To show this, Stoquerus distributes the series of seven syllables twice along the span of a double octave comprising two equal conjunct octave-spans, with the octaves themselves comprising a conjunct but unequal tetrachord and pentachord. With the seven-syllable series distributed over these spans, the two octave-spans will have the same series of seven syllables, because the mutations at the octave are identical. Within the octave, however, the interior mutations are different, and the tetrachord will therefore have three different syllables, the pentachord four. For example, using B-mi, the following mutations might occur:

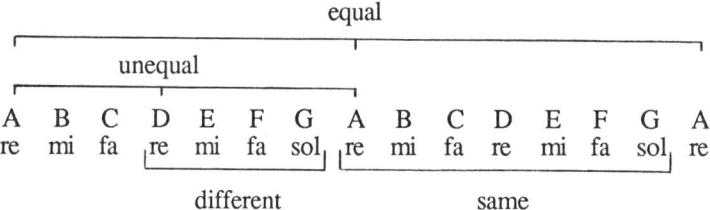

To continue to and beyond the octave, alternating the series of three and four syllables is all that is required, with each syllable of the series thus corresponding to its letter at the octave.

Stoquerus's eighteenth and final hypothesis posits the way to determine whether B is mi or fa in a given instance, that is, whether or not B is indicated as B♭ in the signature.

Stoquerus's corollary stands at the end of this chapter as the conclusion of his logically progressing hypotheses. The corollary is therefore his method of determining the ascending or descending progressions of seven syllables corresponding to seven letters, progressions that can be repeated indefinitely. Using B-fa (B♭ in the signature), the ascending order, for example, of seven syllables can be derived as follows. Since B-fa is from the soft hexachord, the ascent by mutation to the natural hexachord is fa-sol-re. This reveals fa-sol as the top two syllables of the soft hexachord and re as the bottom syllable of the natural hexachord. Fa-sol and re-mi are therefore a four-syllable series. Hence re as the bottom syllable of the natural hexachord series must be followed by mi-fa to make a three-syllable series. The order of seven syllables is therefore re-mi-fa-sol-re-mi-fa, corresponding to G-A-B♭-C-D-E-F. This same reasoning can of course be used with B-fa in descent and with B-mi in ascent and descent. And once each series of syllables is determined in any instance, it may then be repeated indefinitely at every octave. The figure illustrating this corollary is absent from the manuscript, but it is not necessary to an understanding of Stoquerus's method.

Chapter 8: The Rejection of the Various Ways Handed Down by Different Authors Concerning the Progression of the Syllables, and the Indication of the Errors They Contain.

From the perspective of the simplicity and rational basis of his method, Stoquerus points out in this chapter the weaknesses of the methods different from his. He points to three problems inherent in the pedagogy of the first method, which employs the full Guidonian gamut. First, the method was difficult, involving as it did a number of mental gymnastics: (1) the correlation of each written note with its corresponding letter on the twenty-note gamut, (2) the selection of one of the two or three syllables available for that letter, and (3) the singing of the syllable corresponding to the letter. Second, the time required to produce the correct syllable proved to be a particular obstacle in passages of shorter note values. Third, a soft hexachord was often required below the first hard hexachord (beginning on Gamma-ut) in order to accommodate the solmization of the B^b in the bass range, thus adding re and mi to the heretofore monosyllabic Gamma-ut and A-re.

Stoquerus points out that the same problem of a complex of letters and syllables also appears in the second method, which advocates the use of only seven letters. Furthermore, Stoquerus makes an important distinction between using the letters as a basis for selecting the syllables in solmization and as a way of understanding why they are so selected and used. According to Stoquerus, the latter function of the letters is the more important one.[63] But in respect to the actual selection of syllables in a given passage, it is easier to refer to the order of syllables from the passage's present hexachord, with the other syllables falling into place until a mutation is necessitated. If this is done correctly, each syllable will necessarily correspond to its correct letter name without any direct reference to each letter name.

---

[63]The chief characteristic of the hexachord series of syllables is the intervallic relationship of the syllables to one another (TTSTT) as derived by Guido from the hymn *Ut queant laxis*. It is this order of syllables and their intervallic relationships that determines the placement of the syllables along the spans C–A, G–E, and F–D. See J. Smits van Waesberghe, *De musico-pedagogico et theoretico Guidone Aretino eiusque vita et moribus* (Florence: Leo S. Olschki, 1953), pp. 89–90; and Andrew Hughes, "Solmization, I," *New Grove Dictionary of Music and Musicians* 17 (1980): 458–59.

The basic insight of the third method is common to Stoquerus's own method—the hexachordal order of the syllables rather than the letters as the point of reference. Nevertheless, to use ut as the syllable of orientation for determining the remaining syllables involves the difficulty of locating this syllable on three letters, C, F, and G. The same result of this method is achieved more easily with Stoquerus's method by the use of only B, with the order of the remaining syllables determined from either of its two syllables, fa or mi, in a given instance. Stoquerus also points to the use of ut as the syllable heading the mutation to the next hexachord—a use that is wrong according to his own method.[64]

The next two methods (5 and 6) bear an outward resemblance to Stoquerus's own in that they also use re and la as the respective ascending and descending syllables heading the mutation into the next hexachord. The only difference, however, is that both methods associate re and la with their corresponding letters as an aid to memory. Moreover, both methods involve two syllables and six letters (the first method in relation to three hexachords, the second to two scales), presumably as orientations for the remaining letters and syllables. Stoquerus's method, on the other hand, arrives at the same results, but by means of the letter B and either of its two syllables, fa or mi, with no direct reference to the letters on which re and la fall in the mutation.

The difficulty pointed out by Stoquerus concerning the sixth method, which associates the syllables in relation to the clef signs, is this: since the clefs are movable on the staff, the memory is taxed to an even greater degree and more practice is required before facility is attained. Furthermore, such a reliance on local memory is purely mnemonic with no real theoretical foundation of the kind Stoquerus laid with his hypotheses.

The seventh method, Stoquerus maintains, falls into the same trap as methods 3, 4, and 5, in which one syllable (in this method, fa) is multiplied by its association with one letter for each hexachord. Stoquerus's method, on the other hand, uses only one letter name, B, with only one unambiguous syllable, with the remaining syllables falling easily and quickly into line on

---

[64]Loys Bourgeois, in his *Le droict chemin de Musique* (Geneva: Jean Gerard, 1550), strongly opts for the use of ut in ascent to the next hexachord (see *The Direct Road to Music,* translated on facing pages with Bourgeois's text in facsimile and introduced by Bernarr Rainbow [Co. Kilkenny: Boethius Press, 1982], pp. 48–57). See also Hughes, "Solmization," *New Grove Dictionary of Music and Musicians* 17 (1980): 462 and *table* 5; and Eberhard Preussner, "Solmizationsmethoden in Schulunterricht des 16. und 17. Jahrhunderts," in *Festschrift Fritz Stein*, ed. Hans Hoffmann and Franz Kuehlmann (Braunschweig: Henry Litolff, 1939), pp. 117–18.

their respective letter names. Indeed, Stoquerus is so convinced of the simplicity and certainty of his method that he dissociates himself from the method he devised during his stay in Italy.

Chapter 9: The Division of the Syllables Faulted.

Having established his own method as the surest one and having demolished the methods different from his, Stoquerus discusses in this chapter the syllables themselves and proposes a new division that is necessitated by the demands of his own method, a division differing in approach from that found in most of the writings of his era.

In many practical treatises and choir instruction-books, the six solmization syllables are divided into two groups, according to their function as mutation syllables. The lower syllables, ut, re, and mi are "ascending" syllables, because each of them continues, after mutation, the melodic motion upward into another hexachord to accommodate the range of a given melody; the higher syllables, fa, sol, and la, are "descending" syllables, because each continues the melodic motion downward into its own hexachord.[65]

---

[65]Sebald Heyden explains this division: "We divide them into upper and lower vocables. We call the lower ones *ut, re, mi*; if, on keys of two or three vocables, they cannot continue upward through *fa, sol, la,* as far as necessary, then they usually substitute for the missing vocables. We call the upper ones *fa, sol, la*; in the same way they substitute for lower vocables whenever in keys of two or three vocables they cannot be lowered through *mi, re, ut,* as far as the lower melody requires (Sebald Heyden, *De arte canendi*, translated and transcribed by Clement A. Miller, Musicological Studies and Documents, no. 26 [(Rome): American Institute of Musicology, 1972], p. 33) (Nobis [syllabae] in inferiores et superiores dividuntur. Inferiores vocamus Ut, Re, et Mi. Nam si in clavibus bisyllabis aut trisyllabis, per Fa, Sol, La, quantum oportet, scandi non potest, hae pro illis deficientibus succenturiare solent. Superiores vocamus Fa, Sol, La. Quod itidem et hae succenturiant inferioribus, quoties in clavibus bisyllabis aut trisyllabis, per Mi, Re, Ut, tantum descendi non possit, quantum vocis remissio flagitat [*De arte canendi*, p. 13])." Stephano Vanneo also explains this division of the syllables and offers an elegiac distich as a mnemonic device (see Stephano Vanneo, *Recanetum de musica aurea* [Rome: Valerius Doricus, 1533; facsimile reprint, ed. Suzanne Clercx, Documenta musicologica, I/28, Kassel: Bärenreiter, 1969], p. 16r). Tinctoris, in his *Expositio manus*, gives all the possible mutations from these syllables in a set of elegiac distichs, one for ascent and one for descent (see *Johannis Tinctoris Opera theoretica*, 2 vols., ed. Albert Seay, Corpus scriptorum de musica, no. 22 [(Rome): American Institute of Musicology, 1975], 1:48). In most choir instruction-books, however, this division is

Within Stoquerus's method, this division of syllables is applicable only to re and la as ascending and descending syllables of mutation. The division as a whole, however, is senseless and misleading, at least in terms of his method, which never uses ut in ascending mutations and which uses mi, fa, and sol in ascent and in descent, not as mutation syllables but as syllables continuing the progressions from re or la. Since the customary division of syllables into ascending and descending ones was made for purposes of mutation on any one of the syllables, the division is useless in respect to Stoquerus's method. A more accurate division of syllables conforming to Stoquerus's own method would be one that describes the function of each syllable in relation to his ascending and descending progressions spanning seven letters and comprising the higher and lower syllables of two hexachords. Stoquerus therefore proposes a six-fold division of the syllables, with each syllable categorized according to its ascending or descending function within the three- and four-syllable progressions he has determined in the hypotheses of chapter 7.

The following table showing all the ascending and descending progressions of Stoquerus's method illustrates the function of each syllable in terms of ascent and descent:

			la	la
		sol	sol	sol
↑	fa	fa	fa	fa
	mi	mi	↓ mi	
	re	re		

According to Stoquerus, ut is used neither in ascent nor in descent (thus it is not included in the table); re in ascent only; mi in ascent and "sometimes" in descent; fa in both ascent and descent; sol in descent and "sometimes" in ascent; la in descent only. Stoquerus emphasizes, however, that such a division of syllables is necessary only when mutation is required. If there is no need for mutation, all six syllables can be used in ascent and descent.

Taken together, these four chapters on solmization are of interest for several reasons. Stoquerus appears to be the first theorist to provide a survey of the various methods that were current and pedagogically useful in his time, although with varying degrees of efficiency. Stoquerus's own method rests on a solid rational foundation, as shown by the systematic arrangement of his eighteen hypotheses. This approach to his subject matter and purpose fur-

---

merely mentioned with no elaboration. See, for example, Johann Spangenberg, *Quaestiones musicae* (Nürnberg: Johannes Petreius, 1536), p. B8v.

nishes an opportunity to view a Renaissance pedagogue at work in his effort to arrive at a method that is founded on clarity and accomplished with ease. While Stoquerus's method does use the same mutation syllables—re for ascent and la for descent—that are proposed in many instruction manuals, his own method provides a simpler way of arriving at these syllables, that is, from the context of B as fa or mi rather than from their direct association with corresponding letters. Finally, with B-fa-B-mi as the only letter and syllables needed for learning the remaining syllables, Stoquerus's method might well be the simplest one possible before all the methods yielded to the octave system without the use of two interlocking hexachords.

Chapter 10: On the Second Part of Verbal Music and Whether or Not the Words Should Be Delivered According to the Intention of the Sinfonista.

With *musica verbalis* established as a separate branch of vocal music and as an art with its own definition and division into words and tones, Stoquerus is now ready to present his rules for setting words to music. These rules and Stoquerus's explanation of them constitute the remaining chapters of his treatise.[66] Chapter 10 serves as an introduction to his rules and—more specifically—establishes their origin and their relationship to composition and performance. Stoquerus casts this chapter in the form of a *quaestio*:[67] (1) the statement of the question about the origin of his rules and their relationship to the composer and performer, (2) three possible answers to the question, with supporting arguments, (3) Stoquerus's own position and supporting arguments, and (4) his replies to the three opposing answers.

Stoquerus poses the question: Do his rules precede the intention of the composer, do they arise during the composition (as decisions the composer makes while composing), or are they simply a collation of what has been found to be the common practice of previous composers? The question is an important one, for it challenges not only the authority of his rules but also their validity and that of his enterprise in general. If Stoquerus's rules are the absolute determining factors for proper text setting, composers and performers must observe them. If they are not, the composer's intention is the regulatory factor and the performer must follow whatever the composer intended in a given composition. In this case, Stoquerus would be forced to admit that rules for proper text setting either could not be formulated or, if they could,

---

[66]For these chapters as constituting the second "book" of the treatise, see p. 15 *supra*.

[67]Cf. the full form of the *quaestio*, see p. 13 *supra*.

would represent a kind of synthesis of practice. The authority of his rules would then be founded merely on previous composers' preferences.

Stoquerus provides three answers for the question, representing the adversary position (the *videtur quod non*).[68] He presents strong empirical, legal, and philosophical arguments supporting the claim that his rules do not antedate compositions but rather must yield to the authority of the composer as the sole proprietor of the composition. In support of the first answer—that his rules do not antedate compositions—is the lack of any empirical evidence of the prior existence of his rules. They simply have not been seen anywhere.

The second answer—that rules arise from the choices each composer makes during the course of his work—is the most threatening to the validity and authority of his rules. The first consideration in support of this answer is the legal right of any artist in general to create as he wills; the second consideration is the close relationship between the composer, performer, and the composition. In regard to the second consideration, Stoquerus offers two philosophical axioms to establish this relationship. The first axiom, "correlativorum eadem est ratio (the basis of correlatives is the same),"[69] points to the correlative relationship between the composition and the performer, whose basis of unity ("ratio") is the nature ("natura") of the composition, that is, the version given by the composer. The performer therefore has no other choice but to perform the composition as the composer intended. The second axiom, "qui conveniunt uni tertio inter se conveniunt (those who relate to a third thing relate also to each other),"[70] points to the mutual relationship of the performer and the composer to the composition. In this instance, the composer writes the composition and the performer reproduces it. Here too, the performer must simply do what the composer intended. In either of these two instances, the authority of the composer is

---

[68]Stoquerus presents most of his opposing arguments as articulated by unspecified others. It is quite possible that he discussed and debated his treatise with others; yet his arguments are more likely rhetorical formulations of the problems he had to solve in order to establish his rules.

[69]This axiom is more usually worded "relata sunt simul natura." For the explanation of this axiom, see Signoriello, *Lexicon peripateticum*, pp. 361–62 and 364. The axiom has its source in Aristotle *Categoriae* 6a36–8b25.

[70]This axiom is more usually worded "eadem uni tertio sunt eadem inter se." See Signoriello, *Lexicon peripateticum*, pp. 125–27. Closer to Stoquerus's wording is "quae conveniunt in uni tertio, ea conveniunt inter se." See Stephanus Chauvin, *Lexicon philosophicum* (Leeuwarden: Franciscus Halma, 1713; reprint ed., Düsseldorf: Stern-Verlag Janssen and Co., 1967), s.v. "convenientia."

supreme, and any rules extrinsic to the composer's intent would be superfluous and carry no authority. Rather, there are as many rules for performance as there are compositions, and the rule governing all these rules is that which each composer intends in each individual composition.

The third answer is willing to grant that rules do exist, but qualifies them as being a synthesis of the practice of past composers in the same way that rules of grammar are a synthesis of linguistic tradition. But while rules of grammar may also regulate present and future usage, Stoquerus's rules may not do so, because composers writing after his rules would be unable to compose as freely as their predecessors. Nor can Stoquerus's rules be used to emend a faulty passage in a composition previous to his rules, especially when the emendation would affect a chain of performers extending from the chorus to the instrumentalists and even the dancers. Furthermore, a performer who emends a text to fit the music is usurping the authority of the composer and in addition is perhaps applying a slick and quick change to something on which the composer may have deliberated for a long time. Even in this third answer, the composer—past, present, or future—has the final say, and the performer must simply go along with the composer's intent. In this position, it results that Stoquerus's rules, interesting as they might be as a kind of synthesis of common practice, would nevertheless have no regulatory authority for the performer over that of the composer.

In regard to his rules, Stoquerus takes the position (the *respondeo* to the answers) that they antedate any composer or composition. As such, his rules are endowed with far more authority than rules of grammar, even to the extent that performers may emend any composition that violates his rules.

Stoquerus supports his position by two arguments. First, there are rules in general for *musica verbalis* because it is an art in itself and is a part of music, which taken as a whole is an art governed by rules. To support this assertion, Stoquerus invokes the axiom "eadem ratio est de parte quae de toto (the basis is the same concerning the part as that concerning the whole)."[71] Second, his rules preexisted any composer or composition, since they are the expressions of innate principles of behavior—in this instance, of proper musical procedure—common to all men ("sententiae communes natura mentibus omnium insculptae") and stemming from the very nature of man as a reasoning being. The composer, therefore, who observes these "natural"

---

[71]Most certainly in reference to the axiom "eadem est ratio totius et partis (the basis of the whole is the same also of the part)," for which see George Reeb, S.J., *Thesaurus philosophorum seu distinctiones et axiomata philosophiae* (Brixen: Weger, 1871), p. 255.

rules will be recognized as a far better composer than one who does not and forces instead his own will on his work, thus departing from the common judgment of the ear.

This origin of Stoquerus's rules in man's very nature as a reasoning being is the basis for the greater part of his replies to the arguments favoring the authority of the composer rather than that of the rules. In response to the first argument—that his rules have not appeared before—Stoquerus argues that they did in fact exist, though in an unformulated state. He likens their prior existence, first, to that of the natural (moral)[72] law directing and sanctioning man's moral actions even before its formulation in the Decalogue and, second, to that of unwritten law or custom, which in legal terminology is as binding as written, formulated law. His rules, then, are the formulations of what should always have been done according to custom and the natural inclinations of reason in regard to the relationship between words and music.

In response to the second argument—that no rules existed but those of the composer as the supreme authority that the performer must honor—Stoquerus qualifies the authority of the artist as being derived from his following these rules as expressive of "right reason" ("recta ratio").[73] Hence, these rules have existed and form the basis for the composer's authority in his compositions. Likewise, the relationships obtaining between the composer, performer, and the composition can be improved by following these rules as expressive of right reason. For by means of Stoquerus's rules, the performer, as a correlative of the composition, can discern clearly whether or not the "nature" of a composition, that is, the composer's version, is good and to be performed as

---

[72]The following definitions of the natural law are helpful: "(1) 'the sharing in the eternal law by the rational creature' (Saint Thomas, *Summa theologiae*, I–II, q. 91, a2). (2) the dictates of right reason concerning the necessary order of human nature. (3) the universal practical obligatory judgments of right reason concerning the duties and rights of human beings inasmuch as they are human and knowable by the use of right reason" (Wuellner, *Dictionary of Scholastic Philosophy*, s.v. "natural law" under "law"). For a thorough discussion of the natural law, including its sanctions, see Austin Fagothey, S.J., *Right and Reason: Ethics in Theory and Practice*, 4th ed. (St. Louis: C. V. Mosby Co., 1967), pp. 115–30, 139–53.

[73]"Right reason" as used by Stoquerus seems to be any practical, objective judgment in regard to musical matters that is based on reason unhampered by subjective preferences to the contrary. Cf. the following definitions of right reason in Wuellner, *Dictionary of Scholastic Philosophy*, s.v. "reason": "(1) reason that is objectively controlled by and functions according to the objective measure of truth or of human conduct. (2) hence, reason conformed to objective evidence."

is, or bad and to be emended. Furthermore, Stoquerus's rules as expressive of right reason are at bottom the third element to which both the performer and composer relate in a finished composition. For this reason, the performer may emend a composition if the composer has not followed these dictates of right reason in his composition. Indeed, such an adjustment by the performer sets this relationship on its proper basis, for, as Stoquerus points out, every composer wants to compose well but might fall short of his goal through ignorance of proper procedure.

In response to the third argument—that his rules are new and represent, as do rules of grammar, a summary of past practices—Stoquerus distinguishes musical rules from rules of grammar by likening musical rules to mathematical principles, which are founded on universal laws and are unlike rules of grammar, which are founded on particular usages of various geographical locales and synthesized from them. Thus, Stoquerus says that although there can be no common grammar for language in general because of its local and national diversity, his rules can apply to any composition. Furthermore, since his rules are based on right reason, they are not new but merely the formulated expressions of what any good composer should think in the deep recesses of his right reason. And if the composer does not think accordingly, then the performer, if he does so think, may function as the composer and emend a composition before performing it. In this respect, it does not matter that the performer does this "on the spot," for even though the composer may have sweated much longer over his work, he may have nevertheless been ignorant of at least some of the rules because he never really reflected upon them or allowed them to influence his composition.

In regard to knowing some rules and not knowing others, Stoquerus ends the argument by dividing his rules into necessary rules (those that are most known) and discretionary ones (those that are less known). This division will be explained more fully in the next chapter.

Chapter 11: On the Division of the Rules into Necessary and Discretionary Rules.

Stoquerus addresses his division of the rules in terms of the scholastic philosophy of human nature. In so doing, he locates his rules more firmly in human nature and clarifies further why some rules are better known than others.

Stoquerus explains the division of his rules by developing a simple analogy: just as man as man (*homo in quantum homo*) does some things necessarily and others freely, so also does man as musician (*homo in quantum musicus*) act out of necessity and out of free choice. The distinction Stoquerus makes between the necessary and voluntary actions of man *qua* man is based on the distinction, drawn in the scholastic philosophy of human nature, between those acts of a man over which he has no voluntary control (or that are instinctually made) and those that he can freely choose to do or not do. Such acts as man's sensory acts (seeing, hearing, to use Stoquerus's examples), muscular acts at rest or in motion (sleeping, uttering sounds), and vegetative processes (nourishment, digestion) are necessary acts because they are performed not freely but spontaneously in the presence of a need or stimulus. Other acts, however, proceed from rational deliberation and free will and can change according to circumstance and choice. Such acts as eating one thing rather than another, walking, saying this or that, and singing are voluntary acts and proceed from man's ability to rationally choose or not choose to do an action for a particular purpose or end.[74]

By means of analogy, Stoquerus applies this distinction to those necessary and voluntary acts of man *qua* musician. At this level, singing or composing is no longer a free act of man simply *qua* man (such as extemporaneous singing in the bathtub at the top of his voice with no concern for exactness of pitch or rhythm) but an art he has deliberately chosen and must now pursue according to proper procedures, some of which are absolutely necessary (the necessary rules, analogous to the necessary actions of man *qua* man) and others of which have some leeway (the discretionary rules, analogous to the free acts of man *qua* man).

By identifying the necessary and discretionary rules with the necessary and free actions of man *qua* musician, Stoquerus clarifies further the division of the rules made in the previous chapter. Accordingly, the necessary rules are better known than others because they proceed from a musician's instinctual knowledge concerning what should be done in a given situation. The

---

[74]Stoquerus's examples of necessary actions are called in scholastic terminology *actus hominis* ("acts of man"). They are performed by man but not in a specifically human manner, that is, not by any deliberate act of the will. They are non-voluntary or instinctual. Stoquerus's examples of voluntary acts are called *actus humani* ("human acts"). These are performed freely by the will acting toward a deliberately chosen end and, in this sense, are voluntary acts. This distinction is important chiefly in ethics, for only human acts have moral significance. See St. Thomas Aquinas *Summa theologiae*, I–II, q. 1, a. 1, *resp*. For an explanation of this distinction, see Fagothey, *Right and Reason*, pp. 10–11; and Vernon Bourke, *Ethics* (New York: Macmillan, 1951), pp. 6, 18–19. To locate precisely Stoquerus's distinction, see the chart "Divisions of Acts of Man and of Human Acts" in Wuellner, *Dictionary of Scholastic Philosophy*, p. 127; see also ibid., s.vv. "human act"; and "act of man" under "man."

discretionary rules, however, are lesser known because they proceed from choices that some musicians may fail to make correctly.

Stoquerus closes this chapter with his set of five necessary rules, each of which will be separately explained in detail in the next five chapters.

Chapter 12: The Explanation of the First Rule.

Stoquerus's first necessary rule cautions against assigning a larger number of syllables to a smaller number of notes.[75] It is clear from his discussion that Stoquerus is referring not to an unequal proportion between the number of notes and syllables as such, but rather to one between the number of notes that can legitimately take syllables and the number of syllables intended for these notes. Stoquerus identifies those notes that cannot legitimately take syllables: the *punctus augmentationis* (hereafter, punctus) after a note, the note or notes of a ligature after its first note, and most semiminimae and notes of smaller value. Since Stoquerus indicates that he will later give a fuller explanation of these, he most likely intends this rule to be a general but necessary directive to assure that syllables be given only to notes that may properly receive them.[76]

The two musical examples showing how this rule is violated in a composition or in its performance are not given on the staves provided in the manuscript. One can, however, easily imagine a section of a composition as defective owing to a lack of suitable notes for the intended syllables. And Stoquerus himself points to a situation in which singers assign only a few syllables at the beginning of a section and then must end it by omitting some syllables or dividing the remaining notes or giving syllables to notes that cannot carry them. Stoquerus asserts that such errors in composition or perfor-

---

[75] For additional remarks on this rule, see Reese and Jones, "Textunterlegung," *MGG* 16 (1979): 1844–45; and Lowinsky, "Treatise on Text Underlay," pp. 236–37. Reese and Jones discuss this rule in the light of its exceptions (which Stoquerus does not present at this stage in his argumentation); Lowinsky, however, discusses this rule within the context of the present chapter.

[76] This rule is not contained in Zarlino's canon of rules (*Istitutioni harmoniche* [1558], pp. 340–41), but Harrán understands it as a formulation of one of Zarlino's implications in the preface to his rules lamenting the carelessness of text setting in his time: "Now he [the singer] sees many notes comprising two syllables, now many syllables comprising two notes" (Harrán's translation; see "New Light," p. 50). This may account for Stoquerus's discussion in this chapter of the situation where there are more notes for fewer syllables.

mance render a composition damaged (*mutila*) and thereby establishes the absolute necessity of this first rule.

The opposite situation—in which more notes are given to fewer syllables—is more flexible for both the composer and the performer. In bringing up this situation as the opposite of the first rule (*de eius contrario [praecepto]*), Stoquerus introduces an implied rule that a few syllables may be assigned to a larger number of notes. This rule is not stated as such in his list of fifteen rules, but like the first necessary rule, it can well be regarded at this point in his argumentation as a general directive that is developed later into specific rules. Unlike the first rule, however, this one is discretionary in observance, as shown by the preference of Willaert and his generation for a more syllabic setting of the text and by the preference of the older generation for a more melismatic setting.

A situation allowing for more notes than syllables arises either from musical necessity (*necessitas cantionis*) or aesthetic preference (*dulcior harmonia*). For either of these reasons, the composer or the performer may extend the number of notes beyond that of the syllables. For reasons of musical necessity, the composer might be forced to add more notes so as to align all the parts for fuller counterpoint or imitation, or to complete a tempus (*temporis implendi gratia*) with, for example, part of a standard cadential formula. A performer, too, might find it necessary to divide a note (or even to tie several together) in one part in order to provide a more exact imitation of the text setting of the other part or parts. But even for aesthetic reasons, a composer may want to emphasize the meaning of a word or repeat some text, thus occasioning a more extended melody; or, apart from any textual considerations, he may simply prefer a more melismatic type of melody. For aesthetic reasons, the performer, too, may want to ornament a melody by diminution, according to his improvisational skill or established formulae.

Stoquerus's acknowledgment of both a syllabic and melismatic style reveals his respect for all the music of his era, even though he betrays a fondness for that of the modern generation, with its humanist preference for a more syllabic style.[77] His discretionary rules for the older generation of composers confirm this respect, and performers and editors (both functioning as composers with Stoquerus's blessing) can give these works new life by applying these rules conscientiously if the composer (or scribe) did not.

---

[77]Cf. Lowinsky, "Treatise on Text Underlay," pp. 236 and 244.

Chapter 13: On Ligatures.

Stoquerus now discusses the necessary rule prescribing that a ligature receive only one syllable, which is given to its first note and extended along its remaining notes.[78] Stoquerus discusses this rule under four aspects he considers pertinent: (1) the reason why this rule is necessary, (2) its first exception—more than one syllable to a ligature, (3) its second exception—no syllable at all to a ligature, and (4) the various kinds of ligatures. Stoquerus's discussion of this rule under these aspects broadens the common understanding of the rule and clarifies its applicability in given situations.[79]

Stoquerus reasons to the necessity of this rule from two directions. The first is by way of an analogy with notes of the same pitch that are notated and sung as one note and given one syllable, as in Stoquerus's second rule concerning the punctus after a note.[80] In like manner, notes of different pitch but combined in ligature should receive only one syllable. The second is by way of the intention of composers to spread a few syllables over many notes, for the various textual or aesthetic reasons enumerated in chapter 12. To make their intention clear, composers use ligatures to indicate how many notes they intend to carry only one syllable. From either point of view—the notation

---

[78] The most frequent reference to this rule is Zarlino's formulation as rule 2 of his canon of rules in his *Istitutioni harmoniche* (1558), pp. 340–41; however, Harrán has uncovered Zarlino's dependence on Lanfranco's formulation in his *Scintille di musica* (1553) (see "New Light," pp. 38–39). Harrán has also discovered a formulation dating from the mid-fifteenth century (see his "In Pursuit of Origins," pp. 220 and 228).

[79] Stoquerus indicated a similar division at the beginning of chapter 12 and will continue to do so for most of the remaining chapters of his treatise. This division of a section of a work into smaller sub-sections is scholastic in intent and assures discussion of a subject from all of its relevant aspects. For an example of this scholastic procedure in the outlining of a discussion, see in St. Thomas Aquinas, *Summa theologiae*, I–II, the introduction to *quaestio* 7 ("De circumstantiis humanorum actuum") immediately before *articulus* 1.

[80] The rule concerning the punctus is listed in chapter 11 as Stoquerus's second necessary rule, which he will discuss in chapter 14. (That he considers the punctus to be a note is clear from his statement in chapter 12: "Notae syllabis non omnes aptae videntur, sicut ligaturae ⟨et⟩ puncta.") Perhaps Stoquerus discusses his ligature rule before the rule concerning the punctus because the discussion follows logically from the end of his discussion (in the previous chapter) concerning the assignment of few syllables to many notes. The rule concerning the punctus, however, bears a relation to the fourth rule in that both are concerned with notes of the same pitch, though they are handled differently.

itself or the composer's intention—only one syllable should be assigned to a ligature. To do otherwise is to violate the very meaning or essence of a ligature and to treat the ligature not as a ligature at all but simply as a group of separate notes.

The first exception to this rule concerns a situation in which the performer is forced to divide a ligature in order to accommodate more than one syllable. Stoquerus points out, however, that the performer does not necessarily violate the rule by making this adjustment. Rather, the composer (or scribe) himself was at fault for using a ligature instead of separate notes. While the rule itself is binding and valid, it does not apply in this situation, for the ligature is a notational error and must be separated.[81]

The second exception to this rule concerns a situation in which no syllable at all is given to the first note of a ligature. The musical example intended to illustrate this exception is not given in the manuscript. Stoquerus's discussion regarding the various kinds of ligatures, however, clarifies how this exception is recognized and handled.

In his discussion, Stoquerus shows that of the nine possible two-note combinations of semibrevis (S), brevis (B), and longa (L), only five are customarily notated as ligatures: SS, BB, BL, LB, and LL. The remaining four combinations are not notated as ligatures but can nevertheless be considered to be implied ligatures: SB, SL, BS, and LS. This is behind Stoquerus's statement that there are more ligatures in reality than are indicated by customary ligature notation.

It would seem that Stoquerus, in making this distinction, had in mind a musical example that would include a notated ligature intended to extend a syllable set to a note immediately preceding the ligature, such as (x=syllable):

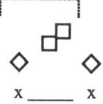

In this instance, the syllable set to the note preceding the ligature would extend along the ligature as well. The first note of the ligature would thus not receive a syllable, because the ligature is only an interior portion of an implied

---

[81]Cf. Lowinsky, "Treatise on Text Underlay," pp. 237 and 244. For a discussion and examples of this exception, see idem, "The Problem of Text Underlay," in *The Medici Codex*, 3:106. See also the discussion and musical example in Reese-Jones, "Textunterlegung," *MGG* 16 (1979): 1845 and example 3 on the unnumbered pages following the entry.

ligature, the first note of which cannot be combined with the first note of the ligature to form one continuous notated ligature.[82] It is in this sense that Stoquerus's conclusion concerning the absent musical example should be understood ("prima ligaturae figura exprimi non potuit"). That is to say, the first note (*prima*) of the notated ligature (*ligaturae*) could not be bound with the first note carrying the syllable so as to be expressed (*exprimi*) by a figure (*figura*) of a ligature.

The distinction Stoquerus makes concerning implied and notated ligatures is directed toward a better understanding of the custom of the earlier generation of composers to assign one syllable to any number of notes and note values. Many of them, however, did not bother to use even the notated ligatures available.

Stoquerus also includes among the various kinds of implied ligatures groups of two notes smaller in value than semibreves but equal in value with each other, such as:

He does not discuss these in this chapter because nothing can be said about these implied ligatures that is necessary to follow. They will be discussed instead among the discretionary rules.

Chapter 14: On Puncti.

In this chapter, Stoquerus discusses his second necessary rule prescribing that the punctus receive the same syllable as the note to which it is attached.[83] For his discussion, Stoquerus (1) distinguishes between the punctum in chant notation and the punctus in mensural notation, (2) indicates that only the *punctus augmentationis* is the concern of this rule, (3) gives the reason for the

---

[82]For an illustration of this, see in Lowinsky's transcription and text setting of Josquin des Prez's "Nimphes des bois" the alto declamation of *cou(v)re* (*The Medici Codex*, 4:343, mm. 96–100). Here the syllable *cou-* is set in part to a S followed by a BB ligature. In this instance, *cou-* is extended along the ligature, but there is no way to make this absolutely clear in the notation because the S cannot be combined in ligature with the first note of the BB ligature. The combination SBB, however, is an implied ligature and therefore the notated ligature does not carry a new syllable.

[83]I.e., his second necessary rule in the order given at the end of chapter 11 (see n. 80 *supra*). This rule appears as rule 3 in Zarlino's canon, which in turn is derived from Lanfranco's "rule 4" as listed by Harrán in "New Light," p. 39.

necessity of the rule, and (4) points out how a possible exception to the rule might be determined and handled in performance.

Stoquerus's reference to the use of the punctum in plainchant is meant to be understood as a general term designating the symbol ■ (or any combination and variant thereof) for every tone. Thus, a punctum would always carry at least one syllable, either alone or in combination with other puncta.[84] Since the rule under discussion, however, concerns a situation in which a punctum is not given a separate syllable, the rule has application only to mensural music, in which the punctus, expressed in notation as a dot · has its own specific function.

Stoquerus indicates that this rule concerns only the *punctus augmentationis* because, of all the various puncti used in mensural music, it alone has the force of a note ("vim notae obtinet"), that is, it is sung. Although a kind of note in its own right, the punctus, however, is integrally related to the note to which it is attached. Identical in pitch with its related note, and half its durational value, the punctus is essentially an extended part of its companion note and not a separate note of the same pitch, as is the case in the fourth necessary rule.[85] As a part of the note, the punctus must receive the same syllable as the note. This association of the punctus with its note is therefore the reason behind the obligation of this rule.

Stoquerus does allow for an exception to the rule. The musical example intended to illustrate this exception is left blank in the manuscript, but it is presumably meant to show an ostensible error on the part of the composer (or scribe) who used a punctus after a note when two separate notes would have been preferable in order to accommodate all the syllables of the given text. Yet, Stoquerus advises caution in hastily concluding to this exception, for the composer might have used the punctus precisely to soften a dissonance in the counterpoint that might be unduly emphasized if the punctus were expressed as a separate note with its own syllable. If this is in fact the case, Stoquerus does not permit the exception, even if it would seem more convenient (*commodius*)[86] for textual reasons to separate the punctus from its note. Sto-

---

[84]Zarlino incorporates this chant rule in rule 1 of his canon. Commenting on this part of the rule and its derivation from part of Lanfranco's "rule 2," Harrán observes that the "square notes" in chant indicate puncta and virgae (see "New Light," p. 36).

[85]Lanfranco also understood the punctus as an extension of a note. See Harrán's juxtaposition of Zarlino's rule 3 and Lanfranco's "rule 4" in ibid., p. 39.

[86]The implication, then, is that if a dissonance is present in the counterpoint, the syllabic setting will have to be handled in a less convenient manner.

querus's position, then, is to follow the rule except in a situation where two syllables must clearly and with no doubt be given to a note and its punctus with no dissonance lurking under the punctus. In this respect, the rule favors the intention of the composer who, in a given situation, might decide that textual necessity must yield to musical necessity. Any exception to the rule must keep the composer's intention intact, even in the doubtful case of a seeming error of text underlay.[87]

Chapter 15: On Several Notes in the Same Place.

In this chapter, Stoquerus discusses his fourth necessary rule, prescribing that a separate syllable be set to successive notes of the same pitch. For his discussion, Stoquerus (1) compares and (2) contrasts this rule with the previous rules, (3) shows why the rule is necessary, (4) raises the question whether separate syllables should be given to notes of different pitch, and (5) presents some exceptions to the rule.

As far as is known, Stoquerus is the first writer to give this rule separate and detailed treatment.[88] He justifies the existence of this rule scholastically by showing its similarity (*convenientia*) to his previous rules and contrast (*differentia*) with them, in particular (so it seems, since he is discussing notes of the same pitch) with the first rule and the third rule (in the order of discus-

---

[87]Lowinsky sees this exception as an "extraordinary concession" and considers it one of the "significant additions to Zarlino's ideas" (see "Treatise on Text Underlay," pp. 237, 245 [on p. 245, "Commentary on rule 4 (chapter XIII)" should read: "Commentary on rule 2 (chapter XIV)"]). Further comments on this exception and a musical example showing it at work in a situation where there is no doubt about its application are given by Reese-Jones, "Textunterlegung," *MGG* 16 (1979): 1845 and example no. 2 on the unnumbered pages following the entry. The caution against setting a syllable to a dissonant note is given by Vicentino (see Harrán, "Vicentino and His Rules," pp. 628–29).

[88]Lowinsky, "Treatise on Text Underlay," p. 244, suggests that this rule is not found in Zarlino's canon because Zarlino probably regarded it as self-evident. Nor does this rule appear in any of Harrán's findings as given in "New Light," "Vicentino and His Rules of Text Underlay," and "In Pursuit of Origins." Jeppesen, however, summarizing Vicentino's and Zarlino's rules for text placement as well as the common practice of Palestrina's contemporaries, does list this rule as no. 9: "Repetition of tones requires new syllables of the text, with the exception of tonal entries that have ornamental character (as with the anticipation)" (see Knud Jeppesen, *Counterpoint: The Polyphonic Vocal Style of the Sixteenth Century*, trans. Glen Haydon [New York: Prentice-Hall, Inc., 1939], pp. 159–60).

sion) concerning the punctus. If one note receives only one syllable, as in rules 1 and 3, then by extension two or more notes of the same pitch would receive separate syllables; however, just as rules 1 and 3 prohibit the division of one note to accommodate additional syllables, this rule prohibits the contraction of two or more notes of the same pitch into one in order to accommodate only one syllable. Indeed, as Stoquerus further observes, the allotment of more than one syllable to one note, or one syllable to more than one note, equally affects the individuality of the notes in question: in the former instance, one note is divided into two or more notes, and in the latter instance, two or more notes are treated as one note. Rules 1 and 3 guard against the former instance; this rule guards against the latter.

Stoquerus establishes the necessity of this rule by reasoning that each successive note of the same pitch is an integral unit, that is, a whole (*totum*). To assign only one syllable to successive notes of the same pitch is to treat them as parts (*partes*), with the effect, in performance, that they are heard as blurred together (*confusae*) rather than as distinct notes (*distinctae*). Therefore, each note should receive its own syllable.

Stoquerus raises the question whether a series of notes of different pitch should also receive separate syllables. By means of his part-whole argument, Stoquerus concludes that it should. He argues that just as successive notes of the same pitch cannot become parts of a whole by being assigned only one syllable, so neither can notes of different pitch become parts of a whole (except presumably notes intended as parts of a notated ligature[89]) by being assigned only one syllable. Thus Stoquerus concludes that a series of notes of different pitch should in principle receive separate syllables. But Stoquerus is enough of a realist to concede that this should not be done necessarily, for sometimes one syllable is intended for a series of notes of different pitch that cannot be grouped in an available notated ligature.

The only exception Stoquerus allows in regard to this fourth rule occurs in the instance of two notes of the same pitch, the first of which is valued at a semiminima or less. In this instance, a syllable may be given only to the second of the two notes, or preferably to neither of them:

---

[89]See pp. 48–49 *supra*, where Stoquerus establishes the obligation of the ligature rule.

Presumably the first two of the three staves provided in this section, with the headings "Exemplum prioris" and "Exemplum posterioris," were intended to show these two choices.

For this exception to occur, however, Stoquerus presents various conditions that must precede the two notes of the same pitch. Of these conditions, only one was intended to be exemplified by Stoquerus, but it is not given on the third staff provided in the manuscript. A discussion of these conditions followed by examples at the end may serve to illustrate all the conditions that Stoquerus had in mind.

1. The semiminima (or shorter note) must be preceded by a note of equal value, so that as a result both semiminimae (or shorter notes) would be bound in an implied ligature. Thus, the second semiminima—the first of the two notes of the same pitch—would go without a syllable, i.e., it would carry the same syllable given to the first semiminima. The second note of the same pitch, however, may receive a syllable (see example a below).

2. The second of the two notes of the same pitch may go without a syllable, because it follows a semiminima, as Stoquerus will discuss later in his tenth rule (i.e., his fifth discretionary rule for the older generation of composers)[90] (see example b).

3. A punctus equal in value to a semiminima in place of a semiminima itself may precede the first semiminima (see example c, either or both of which may have formed the central context of the examples Stoquerus had in mind for the third staff provided in this section).[91]

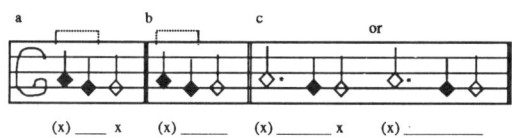

---

[90]In the third section of his discussion of this rule, Stoquerus cautions against assigning a syllable to the first longer note following a series of semiminimae. Lowinsky discusses this situation and offers an example of what Stoquerus may have had in mind (see "Treatise on Text Underlay," p. 237).

[91]For a discussion of this situation and a musical example, see Reese-Jones, "Textunterlegung," *MGG* 16 (1979): 1845 and example no. 4 on the unnumbered pages following the entry. Further examples, particularly in cadential formulae, can be noted abundantly in Lowinsky, *The Medici Codex*, 5: *passim* (for just one example, see in Boyleau, "In principio erat verbum," the cantus setting of *verbum*, f. 4v, score 5, and Lowinsky's transcription, ibid., 4:6, mm. 28–30).

These conditions are negated, however, when the first of the two notes of the same pitch is preceded by (1) a note of different value or (2) perhaps no note at all (that is, when the first note—a semiminima or less—is the first note set to a textual unit) or (3) a note with a punctus not equal in value to the semiminima. In all three of these instances, the semiminima is necessarily given a syllable, and by reason of this rule, the second note is given a syllable as well.[92] For example:

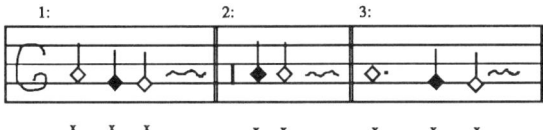

Chapter 16: On Combining the Order of the Syllables with the Order of the Notes.

Stoquerus now discusses his fifth and last necessary rule, which prescribes that the first and last syllables of a unit of text be assigned to the first and last notes of their corresponding melodic unit.[93]

Stoquerus begins his discussion of this rule by presenting a division of syllables and notes into first, middle, and last ones. Among the middle syllables are included the antepenultimate and penultimate syllables of the last word of a textual unit.[94] The purpose of this division is to establish the terminology for the remainder of his discussion, which includes all three kinds of syllables and notes.

---

[92]I am deeply indebted to Don Harrán for sending me a copy of the preliminary galley proofs (not yet containing his musical examples) of the Stoquerus section of his *Word-Tone Relations*. Although my interpretation of this chapter is somewhat different from Harrán's, his clarification of the issues presented here were extremely helpful to me.

[93]"Unit" here is a rendition (not a translation) for Stoquerus's term *sententia*, which he uses, in reference to the text, as any meaningful group of words that grammatically speaking could be a phrase, a clause, or even an entire sentence, and in reference to the melody, as a group of notes set off from another group by a rest or cadence. Stoquerus will discuss his usage of *sententia* in more detail in the second section of chapter 20.

[94]The mention of these syllables is perhaps an anticipation of his first discretionary rule of the older generation of composers, which expressly concerns the setting of the penultimate and antepenultimate syllables.

In the second section of his discussion, Stoquerus justifies the necessity of this rule in two ways. First, his first necessary rule requires that each syllable be given at least one suitable note. This rule would seem to have special import here in regard to an erroneous division of single notes (wholes into parts), particularly at the end of a phrase. Hence, only the first syllable should be given to the first note, only the middle syllables to the middle notes, and only the last syllable to the last note. Second, since the melody is written to express the text, the order of the notes of the melody must be congruent with the order of syllables of the text (hence the title of this chapter). In this respect also, the first note must carry the first syllable of text, the middle notes the middle syllables, and the last note the last syllable.

In regard to both these considerations, Stoquerus might appear to be belaboring the obvious: begin at the beginning, continue on through the middle, and end at the end. This is not entirely the case. Rather, he is supplying a rational explanation for what appears obvious and thus justifies the necessity of the proper coordination of the syllables and notes. This rule assures this coordination.[95]

In the third section of his discussion, Stoquerus mentions that he will defer his discussion of the middle notes and syllables to his discretionary rules, for although the middle syllables must necessarily be assigned to the middle notes, necessary rules cannot be prescribed for each one of the middle notes and syllables because of the variety of situations that may occur and the choices to be made. The discretionary rules will indicate what can be done most reasonably in face of these situations and choices.

In the final section of his discussion, Stoquerus points to this rule's only exception. That is, if a notated ligature rather than a single note occurs at the beginning or end of a phrase, the first and last syllable of text is set to the entire ligature.[96] This exception is particularly important in regard to the end of a phrase, in which case the final syllable does not go to the last note but to

---

[95]In this respect, Stoquerus's fifth rule is a combination of Zarlino's rule 7 (the first note must carry a syllable) and rule 10 (the last syllable goes with the last note) (see Zarlino, *Istitutioni harmoniche* [1558], pp. 340–41). This rule also contains echoes of Lanfranco's rule 1 (cadences should coincide with textual structure) and rule 8 in part (last note given to last syllable), as listed in Harrán, "New Light," pp. 46–47. It may be noted here that the necessary observance of this rule (and all the necessary rules, for that matter) represents the most basic preparation for the full realization of the Renaissance humanist ideal of the integral relation of the words and music.

[96]In effect, however, the exception to this rule is really only the application of the ligature rule requiring that only one syllable be given to the ligature.

the first note of the ligature. In regard to those final notes that are bound in an implied ligature, however, there are no prescriptions that can be given as absolutely necessary. These will be discussed in the discretionary rules. Here Stoquerus is probably referring to various cadential formulae involving semiminimae followed by a longer note, the text placement of which may be handled variously by the older and modern generations of composers.[97]

Chapter 17: The Practice of the Necessary Rules.

Having discussed each of his necessary rules separately and in detail, Stoquerus now discusses them as a group, bringing them within the broader focus of their practice (*usus*), their practitioners, and the general errors they are intended to correct.

The necessary rules provide the primary benefit of sure directions in setting a text to its melody and a secure knowledge of why the text should be set as prescribed by the rules. This in turn explains Stoquerus's meticulous explanation of each of his rules, particularly in regard to the near metaphysical basis governing their necessity: to set the text in any other way is to be exposed clearly to error.

Stoquerus intends his rules to be of primary benefit to the performer, as indicated in the very first sentence of this chapter. Stoquerus is careful to point out, however, that his rules also benefit the composer,[98] who of all musicians should know the principles of his art and be able to give a rational explanation for doing what he claims he is doing correctly.

These rules also have a remedial value, for they help to remove any errors that may have been made by a composer or scribe and that are often liable to appear in performance. These errors, as Stoquerus points out, can be readily detected and eliminated by anyone who is familiar with the rules.[99] The errors, in general, that these rules are intended to correct are of two kinds: (1) notes that should be kept separate (and therefore given separate syllables) are

---

[97]For a discussion of how the text placement of these implied ligatures might be better handled, see Lowinsky, "Treatise on Text Underlay," p. 245; Reese-Jones, "Textunterlegung," *MGG* 16 (1979): 1845–46 and example no. 4 on the unnumbered pages following the entry; and "Harrán, "New Light," p. 46.

[98]Cf. Lowinsky, "Treatise on Text Underlay," p. 233, and his comment on this chapter, p. 237. Harrán, in "New Light," pp. 30–31, shows that Lanfranco's rules were intended for singers, Zarlino's for composers and singers, and Stoquerus's necessary rules for singers and composers.

[99]The justification for doing so has, of course, already been established by Stoquerus's argumentation in chapter 10 (see pp. 43–44 *supra*).

wrongly combined (and wrongly given one syllable)[100] and (2) notes that should be combined (and therefore given one syllable) are wrongly separated (and wrongly given separate syllables).[101] Since in this chapter Stoquerus is considering his rules more broadly, his two-fold division of the errors that violate them provides a good perspective from which to view these rules as a group, enabling the performer or the composer or the scribe to apply them systematically in order to correct or avoid any common errors.

The polarity of these two general errors and the correction of them by doing just the opposite (combining what should be combined; separating what should be separated) form the context for Stoquerus's concluding references to the dictum that contraries are remedied by contraries[102] and to Aristotle's teaching that a virtue (habit), being the middle position between two opposing vices, is acquired by abandoning one vice and moving in the direction of its opposite vice, with the actual intent of correcting both vices and arriving at the middle (correct) position between the two.[103]

---

[100] This class of errors would include the error against rule 4 of assigning one syllable to two or more notes of the same pitch.

[101] This class of errors would include the error against rule 1 of dividing notes (at the end of a musical unit) to accommodate a surplus of syllables; against rule 2 of assigning more than one syllable to a ligature; against rule 3 of assigning two syllables to a note with a punctus where this clearly cannot be done; against rule 5 (perhaps) of wrongly assigning the last syllable of a textual unit to the last note of a ligature.

[102] This dictum stated by Stoquerus (in indirect discourse) as "contraria contrariis mederi" is also stated "contraria contrariis curantur," for which see Reeb, *Thesaurus philosophorum*, p. 221, and n. 10 in which he traces this dictum to Aristotle *Problemata* 1.58 (i.e., 57), for which see 866b5, where it is stated that some diseases arise from heat and some from moisture, and those diseases arising from heat are cured by moisture and those arising from moisture are cured by heat.

[103] See in *Ethica Nicomachea* 1109a20–b27 (a general discussion) and 1119b20–22a17 (discussion of prodigality, the example Stoquerus uses to illustrate his point here). The application of Aristotle's teaching here to the two classes of errors can be understood as follows: the two classes of errors are the two opposing "vices" (combining what should be separated; separating what should be combined). The good musician is in the middle (virtuous) position and, as such, corrects (that is, avoids) either of these two vices or extremes, combining what should be combined and separating what should be separated: that is, he assigns the right number of syllables to the right number of notes.

Chapter 18: On the Discretionary Rules.

Having discussed his necessary rules, Stoquerus now turns to his discretionary rules. Stoquerus's discussion in this chapter—functioning as an introduction to his discretionary rules in general—proceeds scholastically by definition and distinction. Stoquerus (1) explains his terminology and its implications as to the degree of observance these rules entail and (2) distinguishes these rules from the necessary ones by (a) establishing their origin and (b) indicating how they differ from the necessary rules.

Stoquerus derives the characterization of this second group of rules as "discretionary" (*arbitrariae*) from the term *arbitrium boni viri* as used in Roman legal procedure: a judgment or decision of an honest and upright man, one, that is, who decides on a course of action that is in agreement with right reason.[104] With the use of this term from Roman legal procedure, Stoquerus draws a clear parallel between *arbitrium boni viri* and *arbitrium boni musici*, thereby characterizing these rules as representative of the choices or judgments of a good musician acting in accord with right reason. These rules, then, are *arbitrariae*, or discretionary, in the sense that they represent the reasoned judgments of a good musician confronting the circumstances (textual and musical) each of these rules describes.

These rules, Stoquerus adds, are so in accord with reason that they cannot be changed unless right reason should suggest another course of action ("nisi

---

[104]Stoquerus qualifies the *arbitrium boni viri* as a judgment that agrees with right reason. In Adolph Berger's definition of this term in his *Encyclopedic Dictionary of Roman Law*, Transactions of the American Philosophical Society, n. s. 43, pt. 2 (Philadelphia: American Philosophical Society, 1953), this qualification is not given explicitly but may certainly be presumed. From his dictionary, the following may be informative: s.v. "Arbitrium (arbitratus) boni viri": "the judgment, opinion of an honest, upright man to whom a controversial point has been submitted"; s.v. "Vir bonus": "an honest, upright man (a Roman citizen). In certain contractual relations, particularly in those governed by good faith (*bona fides*), the judgment (*arbitrium*) of a third impartial and honest person was decisive whether a party had fulfilled its obligations or not, e.g., the appraisal of a work done by a contractor or artisan (*locatio, conductio operis*). The moral qualifications of a *vir bonus* were honesty and righteousness." Cf. s.v. "Bonus pater familias": "the average type of an honest, prudent (*prudens*) and industrious (*diligens, studiosus*) man (father of a family), whose behavior in relations with the other citizens is given as a pattern of an upright man and may be required from anyone. Acting contrary to what a *bonus pater familias* would do in a given situation may serve as a basis for measuring his culpability and liability in a specific case."

ratione recta aliud suadente"). Stoquerus explains this by saying that just as customs (*mores*) can change according to time and place, so also can these rules change according to various circumstances. Thus, a course of action that might prove to be good at one time and under a certain set of circumstances might not prove to be so at another, and so must be set aside (laudably even) in favor of some other course of action. The same applies to the customary observance of the discretionary rules: at other times and under other circumstances, right reason might dictate another course of action.

Stoquerus is implying here that among his discretionary rules in general, some of them apply to one set of circumstances (of time and place) and others to another. Stoquerus will delineate this distinction more clearly in the next chapter when he divides his discretionary rules into those of the older generation of composers and those of the newer generation.[105] Stoquerus might also be implying here that even these rules have exceptions and that these exceptions are not violations of the rules but rather a reasonable setting aside of them in favor of better alternatives. In either instance, however, these rules are not changed in order to do something wrong (always a *vitium* incurred by departing from right reason) but to do something better.

With the specific character of his discretionary rules and the rationale for their observance or change in observance clearly established, Stoquerus next demonstrates how their need in addition to the necessary rules arises and how, in turn, they differ from the necessary rules. To this end, he first presents a brief review of the general problems of this third branch of vocal music and then shows how these problems can only be addressed completely by another set of rules different in kind from the necessary rules.

According to Stoquerus, the art of setting the text to the melody involves addressing problems that arise from two factors. The first factor is the necessity of the proper coordination of text and melody. Text setting, therefore, does not separately involve the problems of understanding the text (grammar rules would suffice for this) and knowing how to sing the melody (the solmization rules would suffice); rather, it involves the larger problem of coordinating text and melody, which Stoquerus's rules facilitate by addressing syllables and notes together. The second factor is the simple fact that, given the necessity of coordinating text and melody, text placement is a matter of coordinating not merely an equal number of syllables and notes (one-to-

---

[105]Cf. Lowinsky's discussion of this chapter in "Treatise on Text Underlay," pp. 237–38, where at the end he states that this distinction is contained in the present chapter. Lowinsky's statement may be justified if this distinction is considered as implied.

one or one-to-many on an equalized footing, as in notated ligatures) but also an unequal number of syllables and notes.

The second factor, Stoquerus shows, is addressed in the main by all of his necessary rules but requires still more rules. That is to say, his fifth necessary rule addresses any problem in regard to an equal number of syllables and notes; his other four necessary rules, however, address only in part the problem of an unequal number of notes and syllables and therefore require additional rules. In order to better understand Stoquerus's explanation of what follows this general statement, the following scholastically dichotomized schema (with the rules indicated in parentheses) may be helpful as a guide to his discussion.

Equal number of notes and syllables	(5)
Unequal number of notes and syllables	
Fewer notes than syllables	(1)
More notes than syllables	
Notes of the same pitch	(3,4)
Notes of different pitch	
In notated ligature	(2)
In implied ligature	(discretionary rules)

In regard to an equal number of notes and syllables (i.e., one syllable given to one note), the only problem that can arise is the instance of a ligature, in which case a syllable is always set to its first note only, whether the ligature occurs at the beginning of a melodic segment or at the end, as addressed by the fifth necessary rule. In regard to an unequal number of notes and syllables, problems can arise either from fewer notes than syllables or more notes than syllables. When there are fewer notes than syllables, the first necessary rule guarantees the requirement that every syllable be given no less than one note, thus forestalling a situation in which there might not be enough available notes to carry all the syllables. The problems that arise from the instance of more notes than syllables involve two or more notes of the same pitch or of different pitch. The third necessary rule assures that two notes of the same pitch considered as one note (i.e., a note with a punctus) receive only one syllable. The fourth necessary rule assures that two or more distinctly separate notes of the same pitch each receive separate syllables. Or, in terms of Stoquerus's classification here, a note with a punctus must receive only one syllable; several separate notes of the same pitch may not receive only one syllable. The second necessary rule assures that a series of two or more notes of different pitch, when notated in ligature, receive only one syllable. When, however, a series of notes of different pitch is not notated in ligature but instead as a series of separate notes (and yet would seem to require only one syllable and therefore be understood as an implied ligature), there can be no necessary rule to address this situation because there is no procedure that can be shown to be absolutely necessary. Rather, Stoquerus concludes, new rules are required to address what can be done most reasonably in this situation.

These new rules must be discretionary because, by definition, they address the various ways in which a series of notes of different pitch may according to reason (rather than necessity) be considered to be an implied ligature. Thus, these rules are distinct in kind from the necessary rules and in particular from the necessary rule concerning notated ligatures. Notated ligatures obviously must carry only one syllable, whereas a reasoned judgment must be made in individual circumstances to determine whether or not a series of separate notes may or may not carry only one syllable.

Just as Stoquerus demonstrated the necessity governing each of his necessary rules, he promises now to discuss his discretionary rules singly and in detail and to give the reason why in each rule a series of notes of different pitch should be either grouped together in implied ligature (and given one syllable) or considered as separate notes (and given separate syllables).

At the close of this chapter, Stoquerus promises to give instructive music examples for these rules at the end of his treatise, but these are, of course, missing from the treatise as it stands.

Chapter 19: On the Rules of the Older Composers.

Having justified the need of discretionary rules in addition to the necessary rules, Stoquerus now proceeds to classify the discretionary rules themselves according to the two groups of composers who observed them, after which he presents the rules of the first group. Stoquerus first establishes his rationale for dividing these rules into two groups; then, on the basis of this rationale, he divides his rules into those of the older generation of composers headed by Josquin and those of the modern generation headed by Willaert. Finally, he turns to the rules of the older generation (hence, the title of this chapter) and presents first their origin and then the rules themselves.

In order to establish his rationale for dividing his discretionary rules into two groups of composers, Stoquerus contrasts the necessary and discretionary rules by the way they are known. The necessary rules are known by instinct (*sensui se offerunt*) and are the gut responses, as it were, of even the most untutored musicians. They are therefore "natural" in that they are known by nature (i.e., instinct) and to follow them is simply a matter of doing what comes naturally. The discretionary rules, on the other hand, are grasped by reason (*comprehenduntur ratione*), that is, by the correct judgment of the circumstances these rules address. This ability to reason correctly, considered by Stoquerus as the property of highly talented persons in general and of skilled musicians in particular, accounts for their seeming agreement or resonance with these rules. That is to say, composers' observance of these rules in their works manifests these rules' reasonableness. In this respect, then, the discretionary rules can be called "artificial" (*artificiales*) in reference to the artists (*artifices*) who followed them by using right judgment or reason. And, since Stoquerus can discern two large schools of composers or artists from his particular vantage point in music history, he is now able to divide his discretionary rules into two general groups: those rules of the older generation of composers headed by Josquin and those of the modern generation headed by Willaert.[106]

In order to fully understand Stoquerus's two-fold division of his discretionary rules, it is necessary to recall Stoquerus's perspective on the origin of all his rules, necessary and discretionary alike: they have always existed, though in an unformulated state, prior even to the first composition ever, and only gradually down through the millennia have come to be understood with more refinement as man's aesthetic awareness and reasoning power evolved.[107] In regard to Stoquerus and his rules, this cosmic awareness, as it were, is focused more immediately on the music of his own time, particularly on the music of Willaert's brilliant career—both his earlier music composed in a chiefly Netherlandish, melismatic style until the late 1530s and his later music in a less melismatic, more syllabic Venetian style from the late 1530s to his death in 1562. This later style is his "new music" (*nova musice*) as exemplified in the collection *La Peccorina*.[108] Stoquerus can therefore

---

[106]Ibid., p. 238, comments on Stoquerus's division: "In so doing he shares the historical consciousness of a generation that was keenly aware of the changes of style that occurred in the second half of the sixteenth century. At the same time he goes beyond Zarlino who did not deal at all with the problem from the point of view of the older generation."

[107]See pp. 42–43 and 24 *supra*.

[108]Lowinsky, in "Treatise on Text Underlay," pp. 245–49, presents an enlightening account (an essay in itself) of *La Peccorina* (with all its various spellings), particularly as to its most likely time of publication (between 1546–49), its earlier dates of composition (before or about 1540), its title (after Polissena Peccorina, famous singer and interpreter of Willaert's music), its identity with the *Musica nova* of 1559, and its confirmation of Stoquerus's claim for it as the harbinger of a new musical style marked by a clear observance of all the rules regarding the union of text and melody. For an illuminating discussion of the differences between Willaert's early and later styles, see idem, *Medici Codex*, 3:101–3, and 134–35. For a summary of Willaert's

observe that Willaert in his early style brought to a final stage of expression the musical style of the previous generation (headed by Josquin and continued by his contemporaries) and then embarked on a new style markedly different from his earlier one and extremely contagious to his own contemporaries. In this respect, Willaert's music exemplifies the careful observance of all of Stoquerus's rules—the necessary rules, of course, but more to the point, his entire set of discretionary rules as well. The distinction that Stoquerus draws between the rules of the older generation of composers and those of the modern generation is therefore valid only in respect to the degree to which all these rules were observed by both generations. As Stoquerus contends, Willaert and his generation, in their early style, observed more carefully all the rules the older generation followed, and as the tendency toward a new musical style dawned on their awareness and associations, they also observed more precisely those additional discretionary rules, which were, according to Stoquerus's position, always present in their aesthetic awareness but now come to the forefront of their refined musical judgments. On the other hand, the older generation of composers—Josquin and his contemporaries—adhered fairly exclusively to their own set of discretionary rules and even to the later ones, though but rarely, since those aspects of the new style that would later predominate were as yet in the background of their own stylistic preferences—preferences that favored in their time a freer, more melismatic procedure. On this basis then, Stoquerus divides his discretionary rules into two sets, based on the way in which each set particularly applies to each group, separately (to be sure) but not exclusively.

On the basis of this division of his discretionary rules into two groups and the chronological precedence of the rules of the older generation of composers, Stoquerus now presents the factors that give rise to this first group of rules.[109] His point of departure is, of course, the problem that all of the discretionary rules concern: how to determine when a series of notes should be considered an implied ligature and given one syllable or should be considered a group of separate notes and given separate syllables. Since the problem embraces both the syllables of a word and the notes of the melody, Stoquerus uses these two constituents as the beginning of a chain of dichotomizations that show the logical basis for these rules, which are listed at the end of the chapter. The rules are logically determined within this schema:

Venetian style and its relation to his earlier style, see Gustave Reese, *Music in the Renaissance*, rev. ed. (New York: W. W. Norton, 1959), p. 372.

[109]This section is translated in full in Lowinsky, "Treatise on Text Underlay," pp. 238–39.

Words	(1)
Notes	
not in implied ligature	(2)
in implied ligature	
because of the nature of the punctus	(3)
because of the quality of the notes	
two notes	(4)
several notes	(5)

The "notes" to which Stoquerus refers throughout this section are those notes smaller in value than a semibrevis, that is, minimae and semiminimae. These note values are treated in the final section of Stoquerus's discussion of his necessary rule concerning ligatures in chapter 13, where he indicated that there are groups of two notes smaller than semibreves that are not notated as ligatures but are sometimes intended to be treated as ligatures and given only one syllable.[110] Stoquerus indicated that a discussion of this situation would not apply within the context of the ligature rule, because giving these groups of notes only one syllable is not based on necessity (of nature) but presumably on a reasoned judgment.[111] This section in chapter 13 is then the first hint at the content of these discretionary rules and explains the general focus of the rules governing whether or not syllables are given to minimae and semiminimae.

As to the syllabic makeup of a word, Stoquerus reasons that just as an accented syllable of a word is quantitatively longer and takes more time to pronounce than its other syllables, so also such a syllable can receive more notes. The notes envisioned here are semiminimae, as his first discretionary rule specifies. As to a series of notes, Stoquerus indicates that they may (or may not) be considered an implied ligature. He first addresses the situation in which a series of notes is not to be considered in ligature: when an isolated semiminima is followed by a longer note, each note should receive a separate syllable. This is the substance of his second discretionary rule. As to the possibility that a series of notes may be grouped in ligature, Stoquerus further specifies that this can be determined either from the nature of the punctus preceding the notes or from the character of the notes themselves. In the former instance, a note following the punctus should receive the same syllable given to the preceding note and punctus, since the note following the punctus is part of the mensural completion of the note and its punctus. This is even more

---

[110]Semibreves and notes larger than semibreves, when grouped in ligature, notated or implied, are included in the ligature rule.

[111]See p. 50 *supra*.

binding when two notes equalling the value of the punctus follow the note with a punctus. This latter instance, in particular, is the focus of the third discretionary rule. The possibility of combining a series of notes in an implied ligature can also be determined from the property of the notes themselves (i.e., apart from a situation involving a punctus). As to the property of the notes, Stoquerus makes a further distinction, i.e., whether they are a series of two notes or a series of more than two notes. If the notes (minimae or semiminimae) form a group of two notes, they should receive only one syllable, given to the first note. In the case of two minimae, a syllable is given to the first because it begins the tactus, and in the case of two semiminimae, a syllable is given to the first because it is the first on the arsis or thesis of the tactus. Both these note-groups receive only one syllable because the two notes taken together constitute either a complete tactus (two minimae = a semibrevis, the unit of the tactus) or a complete minima (two semiminimae = a minima). So, in either instance both notes are parts of a whole and should receive only one syllable. This instance of pairs of minimae or semiminimae forms the substance of the fourth discretionary rule. On the other hand, in respect to a series of semiminimae or smaller notes, only one syllable is given to the first of the entire series, since the rest of the notes of the series succeed too rapidly to take additional syllables. This is the substance of the fifth discretionary rule.

This explication of the origin of the discretionary rules of the older generation is not intended by Stoquerus to be explanatory but only to indicate his reasoning of their formulations and number. Stoquerus concludes this chapter with a statement of his five discretionary rules, each of which will be explained more fully in the following five chapters and in the same manner as followed for the necessary rules.

Chapter 20: On Accent.

The first discretionary rule of the older generation of composers states that the accented syllable of a word may be set to several notes, including a series of semiminimae. In order to provide a clear understanding of this rule, Stoquerus discusses four relevant considerations: (1) why the accented syllable of a word may be assigned several notes; (2) what, precisely, is the accented syllable this rule addresses; (3) how this rule relates to the distribution of the other syllables over the other notes; and (4) how this rule works with the other four discretionary rules of the older generation.

Stoquerus establishes his assertion that several notes may be assigned to the accented syllable of a word on the basis of the close relationship between music and oratory.[112] That is, both of these arts are directed toward inducing emotional responses and involve vocal production. Thus, just as in speaking, the accented syllable of a word is emphasized by a longer duration, so also in singing, the accented syllable is emphasized by being given more notes than the unaccented syllables. Stoquerus explores this relationship further by pointing to the integral relationship between text and music, namely, that the musical flow is shaped by the demands of the text and hence is the expression of the very nature and character of the words it expresses.[113] It is therefore only reasonable that the accented syllable of a word be given the proper musical emphasis by being set to several notes or, in particular, as this rule permits, to a series of semiminimae.

In the second section of his discussion, Stoquerus indicates which accented syllable this rule particularly concerns. To establish this, he first points out that there are two kinds of accent: the accent proper to each word (according to grammatical rules) and that proper to each group of words forming a complete thought or *sententia*, i.e., a phrase, clause, or complete sentence. As to the accented syllable of each word, Stoquerus points out that the rules governing accent cannot be fittingly carried over into musical declamation. Stoquerus presumably considers this a too literal approach to textual declamation, in regard to which word-accentuation might sometimes have to yield to musical principles, especially among composers of the older generation.[114] Sentence accent, as Stoquerus explains, is much like the accent of the last word of a phrase, clause, or sentence (each of these constituting a

---

[112]For a discussion of the relationship between music and rhetoric, see George J. Buelow, "Rhetoric and Music," *New Grove Dictionary of Music and Musicians* 15 (1980): 793–803, particularly 793–94, where Buelow traces the Renaissance concept of this relationship to the rediscovery in 1416 of Quintilian's *Institutio oratoria*, to the humanist influence that incorporated elements of music as part of the *quadrivium* into elements of rhetoric as part of the *trivium*, and to the German theorists Listenius and Dressler. For a pertinent statement of Quintilian, see his *Institutio oratoria* 1.10.9–33, especially 22–23, where he discusses the close alliance between music and oratory.

[113]For an excellent account of this close alliance between text and music in the Renaissance, see Lowinsky, "Music in the Culture of the Renaissance," pp. 535–43.

[114]See, for example, Lowinsky's discussion in *Medici Codex*, 3:134–35, of Willaert's early style as manifested in his "Saluto te, sancta Virgo Maria," particularly in regard to the opening setting of *saluto*.

sententia in the broad sense). In this instance, the emphasis of a group of words is located at the final word, presumably because the last word completes the thought, after which there is either a pause before going on to the next word-group or a complete stop ending the composition. Immediately before a pause or the end, the final word of a phrase may therefore be spoken more slowly, with the accent of that word receiving more emphasis than the accents of the other words of the phrase. This is the point of the two examples Stoquerus gives as analogues to musical declamation: in Greek oratory and liturgical chant according to reciting formulae, special emphasis is given, for the sake of a more effective or expressive close, to the accented syllable of the final word of a period (oratory) or of a sentence (of a scripture reading). In the same way, in mensural music the accented syllable of the final word of the entire phrase (*integra sententia*) should be given special attention. Hence, this rule particularly concerns the accented syllable of the final word of a phrase, and it is this syllable that may receive a series of several notes—or, in particular, semiminimae.[115]

Stoquerus concludes this second section by clarifying what he means by a phrase (*sententia*), particularly as it applies to the older generation of composers. Many of these, he points out, either do not know or simply do not care about the implication of a phrase in the grammatical sense of the term (an intelligible group of words) and instead group words together indiscriminately or even use only one word as if it were a complete phrase. In this respect, Stoquerus indicates that it is better to think of a phrase primarily in regard to its meaning in music, that is, as a group of notes ending with a pause or formal cadence, thus expressing a complete musical thought. This, of course, is the common theoretical thought of Stoquerus's time: just as a speech can be subdivided into many intelligible units of thought (*membra seu sententiae*), so also can a musical work have its own sections, marked off one from another by pauses or formal cadences.[116] It is Stoquerus's contention

---

[115]In this respect, this rule is similar to Zarlino's rule 9, which is discussed in relation to Lanfranco's rule 8 as given in Harrán, "New Light," pp. 44–45. For further discussion of this rule, see Lowinsky, "Treatise on Text Underlay," p. 239, and Reese-Jones, "Textunterlegung," *MGG* 16 (1979): 1846.

[116]See Lowinsky, "Treatise on Text Underlay," p. 239, and n. 20, where he translates Zarlino's remark in *Istitutioni harmoniche* (1573), Pt. 3, chap. 51, p. 148: "... the cadence has the same value in music as the period in speech. Indeed, one can call it the period in music." Cf. this same idea in chap. 53 of the 1558 edition, as it appears in Gioseffo Zarlino, *The Art of Counterpoint: Part Three of Le Istitutioni Harmoniche, 1558*, trans. Guy A.

that the learned and careful musicians of the older generation know this close relationship between intelligible units of words and music and divide their text and musical segments accordingly, whereas the careless musicians think primarily in terms of the musical sentence and text it to one, two, or any number of words.[117] All this notwithstanding, whatever segment of a text they do use for a phrase of music can be divided into first, middle, accented antepenultimate or penultimate, and final syllables.

In the third section of his discussion of this rule, Stoquerus indicates how this rule applies in practice. The application of this rule presumes two givens: the accented syllable is that which occurs on the antepenultimate or penultimate syllable of the last word of the phrase, as was established in the second section above; and the first syllable of the first word of the phrase goes to the first note of the musical phrase and the final syllable of the last word to the final note of the phrase, as was established in the fifth necessary rule. Thus, in applying a text to the music, the first syllable goes to the first note, the last syllable to the last note. The middle syllables are set as fittingly as possible to the notes after the first note, after which all the remaining middle notes are set to the final accented syllable. In the event that these notes, or semiminimae, as the case may be, are set to the accented antepenultimate syllable, then the penultimate and final syllables are set to the final two notes. If the penultimate syllable is accented, however, then the antepenultimate syllable is counted among the other middle syllables. Such a method of text placement would allow for an easy comprehension of the text and, with the accented syllable given a melismatic setting, an expressive rendering of the text as well.[118]

Marco and Claude V. Palisca (New Haven, Conn.: Yale University Press, 1968), pp. 141–42.

[117]Stoquerus is echoing Zarlino's advice that the cadence should correspond to the end of a phrase or sentence (Stoquerus's *sententia*). See Marco-Palisca, *Art of Counterpoint*, p. 142. See also Harrán's discussion of this in reference to the prescriptions of Lanfranco and Zarlino (and Vicentino as well) and to their source in Gaffurius, in "New Light," pp. 32–35. Stoquerus's observation that the composers of the older generation did not think primarily in terms of a proper textual division of thought to correspond with their musical division may well serve to distinguish the style of the older composers from that of the moderns. In this respect, Lowinsky observes in "Treatise on Text Underlay," p. 239, that the earlier composers were wont "to repeat single words instead of intelligible parts of a sentence."

[118]For an example of this in practice, especially in regard to a series of semiminimae on the accented syllable at the end of a phrase, see Brunet's "Ite in orbem" in Lowinsky, *Medici Codex*, 5:f. 75v, in the tenor, score 3,

The fourth section of Stoquerus's discussion relates this rule to the other four discretionary rules. In so doing, he essentially recapitulates a point in chapter 19. This rule is one with the others in that it, too, considers which notes are to be gathered in an implied ligature. Indeed, if the notes are distributed properly according to the method described above, there should be a surplus of notes for the accented syllable, in which case they would be considered an implied ligature. This rule differs, however, from the others in that they consider which notes should be grouped in ligature from the nature of the notes themselves, whereas this rule considers the problem from the nature of the words, according to which the accent falls on only certain syllables.

Chapter 21: On a Semiminima Placed before a Note of Larger Value.

In the preceding chapter, Stoquerus discussed the syllable-to-note correspondence in terms of the text, particularly in regard to the suitability of assigning a series of semiminimae to the last accented syllable of a textual unit. In the present chapter and the three to follow, Stoquerus discusses the syllable-to-note correspondence in terms of the notes. These notes, as he pointed out in chapter 19, may be either a series of separate notes that cannot be grouped in an implied ligature, or one that can.[119] This chapter discusses those notes that cannot be grouped in an implied ligature and must therefore be given separate syllables. In turn, this particular syllable-to-note situation is the focus of Stoquerus's second discretionary rule, which states that if a syllable is given to a semiminima, one must also be given to the note following the semiminima.

Stoquerus discusses this rule in regard to (1) its distinction (*differentia*) from the other four discretionary rules, (2) its confirmation (*confirmatio*) by supporting arguments, (3) its further application (*extensio*), and (4) its restriction (*limitatio*). Stoquerus's first consideration is ordered simply toward establishing the *raison d'être* of the rule. While in a broad sense, all the discretionary rules address the possibility of assigning one syllable to a series of notes involving semiminimae, this rule differs from the other four in that they point to situations in which one syllable may be given to such a series of notes, while this rule addresses situations in which a syllable may not be given to the series as a whole (that is, as an implied ligature). These arrangements, discussed in the remaining three considerations, are: a single

---

"Linguis loquentur." See also "novis" immediately following, as illustrative of the use of one word spread over an entire phrase.

[119] See schema p. 65 *supra*.

semiminima followed by a note greater in value (hence the title of this chapter); a semiminima followed by two or more notes equal in value, i.e., semiminimae; and a semiminima followed by a series of notes smaller in value.

All three of these arrangements have in common that a syllable is, in fact, assigned to the first semiminima of the given series for some reason (presumably a good one) on the part of the composer or performer. The first arrangement—a semiminima followed by a longer note—requires a separate syllable on the longer note following the semiminima. Of the three arrangements, this one is the most common, and Stoquerus is simply stating a practice common in syllabic as opposed to melismatic settings of text. Unique, however, to Stoquerus's presentation of this rule are his accompanying reasons. His first reason why the two notes cannot be treated as a ligated series, with a syllable given to the semiminima only, is this: the two notes, not being equal, either fall short of measuring the tactus, i.e., a brevis (a semiminima followed by a minima), or exceed it (a semiminima followed by a semibrevis). Stoquerus seems to be saying here that these notes are not co-equal parts of the same tactus:

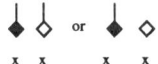

or occur on different tactus:

In either situation, the notes in question should be considered as separate notes ("wholes," perhaps, according to his part-whole argument) and given separate syllables:

His second reason is a simple matter of justice: when a syllable is given, as in this instance, to a faster note, then one should also be given to the slower note following.[120]

---

[120]Since Stoquerus does not specify the kind of note preceding the semiminima, he is presumably referring to the situation of a semiminima both in a context that involves a preceding punctus and in one that does not. (Most likely he is referring to the former, in which a syllable *is*, in fact, given to a semiminima following the punctus of a minima. This would further distinguish this rule from the next, which discusses a context that involves a preceding punctus but in which a syllable is *not* given [for a good reason] to the note or notes following.) Stoquerus's statement of the rule reflects the same idea as Zarlino's rule 6, in regard to which Harrán has shown in "New Light," pp. 40–41, that Zarlino's rules 4, 5, and 6 are all derived from Lanfranco's rule 5 concerning the semiminima following a punctus. Harrán

The second arrangement—a semiminima followed by more than one semiminima—is discussed by Stoquerus as a further application of this rule. If a separate syllable is given to the first two semiminimae of a series of semiminimae, the remaining semiminimae should also each receive a separate syllable:

x   x x x x

In effect, Stoquerus is saying that a series of semiminimae should be treated either as an entire ligature or not, and if not, then the composer or performer must be consistent and assign each semiminima in the series a separate note, and not just the first two.[121] Stoquerus's closing statement in this section points, in fact, to this inconsistency of composers of the older generation in making implied ligatures out of any combination of note values even larger than semiminimae, as he will discuss below in the second section of chapter 27.

The third arrangement—a semiminima followed by a series of smaller notes—is presented by Stoquerus as a restriction (*limitatio*) to this rule. That is, the first of these smaller notes is not equal with the semiminima, just as the larger note following the semiminima is not equal with it. Just as a semiminima and a longer note following each receive a separate syllable, so also should the first smaller note following the semiminima receive a syllable; however—and this is the restriction—, the remaining smaller notes are considered in ligature with the first note of their series but not with the semiminima, and so they receive the same syllable given to the first of the series:

x   x_____

This situation, as Stoquerus is careful to point out, is different from the second, in which the entire series of semiminimae is given separate syllables. That is to say, since the semiminimae of the second situation are all equal, one cannot assign a separate syllable to the first two notes alone and hold the sec-

---

also indicates (p. 40) that in regard to Zarlino's rule 4 (semiminimae and smaller notes in a context not involving a preceding punctus), "innumerable examples of this kind did exist, from the 'forties on, in music under a C mensuration (as in *note nere* madrigals)."

[121]Cf. Harrán's listing and discussion of Lanfranco's rule 6, in regard to its exception, in "New Light," pp. 41–42, in which "... (Italian) works in the style of the French chanson, and, obviously, the French chanson itself, provided exceptions to the rule."

ond syllable over the remaining notes, as is the case with a semiminima followed by a series of smaller notes. As Stoquerus mentioned in the third section of this chapter, all the semiminimae of a series must therefore be given separate syllables. Either they are all considered ligated with the first semiminima, or they are, in fact, a series of separate notes. Stoquerus will address both of these situations more fully in the fourth section of chapter 24, where he compares the fifth discretionary rule with this one.

Chapter 22: On the Punctus Placed before Notes of Smaller Value.

In this chapter, Stoquerus discusses his third discretionary rule of the composers of the older generation, which states that no syllable is given to the two notes following the punctus of a semibrevis or minima if the value of the two notes taken together equals that of the punctus; nor is a syllable usually given to the longer note following these two notes. According to the rule as stated in chapter 19, it is clear that Stoquerus has these figures and their texting in mind:

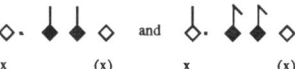

Stoquerus does not include in his discussion here the second part of the rule stating that the longer note following the two notes is generally not given a syllable. Perhaps he considers this self-evident but is also conceding that the older generation of composers dealt freely with this situation.

This rule and the fourth and fifth rules of this set are related in that they all address the problem of assigning one syllable to a series of notes smaller than a semibrevis and considered as grouped in an implied ligature. Such a series, as Stoquerus has already pointed out in chapter 19, can be considered either from the aspect of the punctus preceding the series of notes or from the particular quality of the notes themselves.[122] The third discretionary rule addresses the problem from the aspect of the punctus preceding the series of notes (hence the emphasis on the punctus in the title of this chapter); the fourth and fifth rules address the problem from the aspect of the notes themselves in the series, that is, whether they may be considered as groups of two notes (rule 4) or as a group of several notes (rule 5).

For his discussion of this rule, Stoquerus first gives the rationale (*ratio*) for the rule, that is, the reasons governing the statement of the rule. Then, in

---

[122]See schema, p. 65 *supra*.

light of these reasons, he points out the relation (*collatio*) of this rule with the second necessary rule (also concerning the punctus) and with the fourth and fifth discretionary rules of this set.

With one long sentence, Stoquerus begins the first section (*ratio*) of his discussion with a paraphrase of the third discretionary rule, followed in turn by the statement of the reasons in support of the rule. His paraphrase is clear: two notes that follow the punctus of a semibrevis or minima and together equal the value of the punctus do not receive a syllable but are considered in ligature with the punctus (which of course, in turn, is in ligature with its note).[123]

Stoquerus gives four reasons in support of this rule, with each reason signalled syntactically by *vel quod*. The first, third, and fourth reasons explain the rule from the aspect of the punctus preceding the two notes; the second reason from the aspect of the notes themselves. The three reasons from the aspect of the punctus point to the mensural alliance of the note and its punctus with the two notes following. The first reason associates the two notes following the punctus as "partners" (*compartes*) of the punctus for the completion of the mensuration of either the tempus or of the tactus in regard to the punctus. Thus, for example, two semiminimae following the punctus of a semibrevis complete the mensuration of the next semibrevis of the tempus:

or two fusae following the punctus of a minima complete the arsis of the tactus begun on the punctus of the minima:

The third reason considers the two notes as the smaller-valued division or resolution (*resolutio*) of one note following a note with a punctus and equal in

---

[123]This rule concords with Zarlino's rule 5 as noted by Lowinsky in "Treatise on Text Underlay," p. 239; and Reese-Jones, "Textunterlegung," *MGG* 16 (1979): 1846. For a translation of Zarlino's rule 5 and comment on it, see Harrán, "New Light," pp. 40–41. For examples (among many) of the application of this rule by composers of the older generation, see in Lowinsky, *Medici Codex*, 5: Lhiretier, "Te Matrem Dei laudamus," f. 38r, bassus, score 4, on *curia* (for the transcription, see ibid., 4:88, mm. 135–36); and Willaert, "Regina celi," f. 47v, cantus, score 1, on *celi* (for the transcription, see ibid., 4:114, mm. 3–5).

value to the punctus. Since this one note following the punctus does not usually receive a syllable,[124] as Stoquerus said in chapter 19, neither should the two-note division of this note receive a syllable. The fourth reason is essentially the same as the first, except that it emphasizes the note, its punctus, and the two notes following as links of one mensural chain. Just as the punctus, as part of its note, does not receive a syllable, neither do the two notes, as parts of the mensural completion of the tempus or tactus of the note and its punctus, receive a separate syllable. The second reason—from the aspect of the notes themselves—points to the speed of these smaller note-values, which precludes the enunciation of syllables on them. In presenting all of these reasons, Stoquerus proves his point on both theoretical and practical grounds.

In the second, third, and fourth sections of his discussion, Stoquerus points to the alliance (*collatio*) of this rule with the necessary rule concerning the punctus and with the fourth and fifth discretionary rules. He does this by indicating the correspondence of these rules with the related reasons given above in support of this rule. What he has already stated in the first section is now merely repeated here and applied in reference to these other rules. This alliance recognizes the kinship of all these rules in that they all concern implied ligatures, with only one syllable given to the first note of the ligature—(1) the note preceding a punctus or (2) the first note of a pair or (3) the first of a longer series of semiminimae. In turn, these rules are distinct from the second discretionary rule in which separate syllables can be given to semiminimae not considered in ligature. In combination with the second discretionary rule, this third discretionary rule and the fourth and fifth rules are regularized formulations of Stoquerus's contention that a given series of notes should be considered either as in ligature (rules 3, 4, and 5) or as a group of separate notes (rule 2).

Chapter 23: On Two Minimae or Semiminimae.

Stoquerus now discusses his fourth discretionary rule. According to the distinction made in his discussion of the origin of this set of discretionary rules in chapter 19, this rule and the fifth rule address a context different from that of the third rule. The third rule addresses the matter of assigning

---

[124]This observation is not, of course, a formulated rule in Stoquerus's list but can be considered as an implied rule in relation to this third rule. It would appear that in view of Stoquerus's guarded expression, he is recognizing the validity of both manners of text placement in a situation involving a punctus. Cf. Lanfranco's rule 5 as listed in Harrán, "New Light," p. 40.

syllables to note values smaller than a semibrevis in a context involving a punctus; the fourth and fifth rules address this matter in a context not involving a punctus.[125] The distinction is important because these note values within the context of a punctus (*ex natura puncti*) receive no syllables at all; however, in a context not involving a punctus, these notes may receive syllables. To determine the proper manner of addressing this latter context, Stoquerus looks to the character of the notes themselves (*ex proprietate* or *ex qualitate notarum*) for the proper way in which they may be grouped together in relation to the number of available syllables. These notes may occur as one or more groups of two notes (*binae*) for one or more syllables or as one group of several notes (*plures*) for one syllable only. Stoquerus's fourth rule prescribes how to set one syllable to these smaller note values occurring in sets of two. The rule accordingly states that in the instance of groups of two minimae or semiminimae, a syllable should be assigned to the first note only and held over the second. The following figures and their texting illustrate the application of this rule:

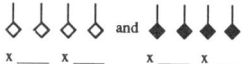

In the first section of his discussion of this rule (*declaratio*), Stoquerus establishes a hierarchical division of the two-note group as determined by the tactus. Of the two notes, the principal one, in the case of minimae, is that which falls on the thesis (*depressione*) of the tactus, and in the case of semiminimae, that which falls on either the thesis or arsis (*elevatio*). In either instance, the second note is considered to be in ligature with the first note and carries the same syllable given to the first note.

In his second section (*ratio*), Stoquerus shows why these two notes should take only one syllable and why that syllable should be set to the first note and not to the second. In order to explain why these two notes should take only one syllable, Stoquerus once again summons his part-whole argument: syllables should be given not to parts but to wholes. This argument, he mentions, provided the basis for his first and fourth necessary rules.[126] In the first necessary rule, two syllables may not be given to one note divided into parts, and in the fourth necessary rule, one syllable may not be given to two notes (of the same pitch) considered as parts of one note. In either case,

---

[125]See schema, p. 65 *supra*.

[126]The argument is given in Stoquerus's discussion of the fourth necessary rule in chapter 15, sections 2 and 4.

each note is considered a whole and receives one syllable. In regard to this rule, the "parts" in question are the two notes taken separately; the "whole" refers to these two notes taken as a group and considered as subdivisions or resolutions of their next higher note-value: the semibrevis in respect to two minimae, the minima in respect to two semiminimae. Thus, either group of two notes, minimae or semiminimae, should receive only one syllable.

Furthermore, of these two notes, the first is the more important and should receive the syllable. This is so, Stoquerus explains, either because of its position as the first note of the group or because of its importance, in contrapuntal theory, for the management of consonance in regard to these smaller note-values.[127] Minimae must be consonant with the other voices on the thesis of the tactus and semiminimae with the other voices on the thesis or arsis of the tactus.[128] This implies, of course, that a syllable should be set to a note consonant with the other voices, and since the first of two minimae is always consonant on the thesis of the tactus and the first of two semiminimae on the thesis and arsis, these notes should receive the syllable.

As to the reason why the second note of the group should not receive a syllable, Stoquerus explains that these notes are of secondary importance in a phrase (*sententia*) in that they follow from the notes placed on the odd beat (*impari loco*, i.e., the first beat) of the tactus, the most important location in the counterpoint. The other notes can be allied with these beginning notes according to a variety of options (passing notes, smaller note-values, etc.). In view of their secondary importance, these notes should not receive a syllable, at least in the context this rule addresses, that is, when two minimae or semiminimae are available for one syllable.

In the third section of his discussion (*extensio*), Stoquerus shows a further application of this rule, presumably in regard to the minima followed by a

---

[127]The two reasons taken together would appear to include both the horizontal and vertical ordering of the melodic lines of a phrase. The discussion of this rule by Reese-Jones, "Textunterlegung," *MGG* 16 (1979): 1846–47 and music example no. 5 on the unnumbered pages following the entry emphasize the horizontal application of this rule.

[128]As taught, for example, by Zarlino, *Istitutioni harmoniche* (1558), chap. 42 (see Marco-Palisca, *Art of Counterpoint*, p. 93).

syncopated semibrevis as part of the superius in the common cadential formula:[129]

| ♩ ◇ ♩ | □

Normally, apart from this cadential situation, an isolated minima and a following semibrevis may each receive a separate syllable. In the above cadential pattern, however, Stoquerus considers the semibrevis as the doubled value of two minimae:[130]

| ◇ ♩ ♩ ♩ | □

Of these minimae, the first is then considered to be in ligature with the first minima of the cadential formula. The first minima is then measured on the thesis of the tactus, and the next minima (the first of the two minimae doubled) is measured on the arsis or even beat (*pari loco*, i.e., the second beat) as the second minima. In this instance, the second minima is considered as an accessory to the first because it completes the tactus and so receives the same syllable as the first minima. The *extensio* of the rule in this pattern is useful because the syncopated semibrevis in the pattern may go without a syllable and thus avoid highlighting a dissonance on the thesis of the tactus beginning on the second half of the semibrevis in the syncope. Stoquerus's explanation of this situation provides the means for understanding why this is so.[131]

In the final section (*limitatio*), Stoquerus emphasizes that this rule is proper only to the older generation of composers, since the modern generation gives separate syllables to all minimae but not to all in a series of semi-

---

[129]This follows the interpretation given to this section by Lowinsky, who also provides a theoretical musical example. See "Treatise on Text Underlay," pp. 239–40. Cf. Harrán's discussion of Vicentino's rule 12 as listed in "Vicentino and His Rules," pp. 628–31.

[130]The semibrevis as consisting of two minimae is given by Zarlino, *Istitutioni harmoniche* (1558), chap. 42 (see Marco-Paliska, *Art of Counterpoint*, pp. 95–97). As can be noted from Zarlino's discussion (concerning syncopation), the division of the semibrevis into two minimae is helpful for explaining on which parts of the semibrevis the dissonance and consonance occur.

[131]Lowinsky's discussion of this part of the rule in *Medici Codex*, 3:106, offers a convincing reason for not giving a syllable to the semibrevis from the aspect of textual declamation: "The character of a syncopated note [the semibrevis] springs from its ambiguous play between pull and stress. This ambiguity is lost when the syncopated note receives a syllable."

minimae (excepting the first of any given series).¹³² He will clarify these procedures when he discusses them in the rules of the modern generation of composers.

Chapter 24: On Several Semiminimae.

In this chapter, Stoquerus discusses his fifth discretionary rule of the older generation of composers. This rule addresses the instance of the availability of one syllable for a series of several semiminimae (more than two) or smaller note values and advises that a syllable be given only to the first note of the series.

Stoquerus begins his discussion of this rule with a *declaratio*, here consisting of a statement of the rule as it pertains to a series of semiminimae and an explanation of what is meant by the "first" semiminima. The rule prescribes that where only one syllable is available for a series of several semiminimae, that syllable is set to the first of the series, with the remaining semiminimae regarded as in ligature with the first.¹³³ Stoquerus's explanation of what is meant by the "first" semiminima distinguishes between the first semiminima as found in a context not involving a punctus and in one that does. In the former, the first note of the series is that which begins on either the thesis or arsis of the tactus. In the latter (i.e., a minima with a punctus), the first semiminima is not the first ostensible semiminima, but rather the punctus itself. In this latter instance, however, the necessary rule concerning the punctus takes precedence, and the syllable is given instead to the minima and held over the punctus and the series of semiminimae as well. Thus, in a context not involving a punctus, a separate syllable may be assigned to the first semiminima, but after a punctus, no separate syllable may be assigned to

---

¹³²In "Treatise on Text Underlay," p. 239, Lowinsky notes that "this rule aids Stocker in distinguishing the modern style of text setting from that of preceding generations." The *limitatio* of this rule does not imply, of course, that the older generation of composers never applied separate syllables to a series of minimae or only one syllable to a series of several semiminimae, but rather that they felt free to mingle a syllabic and melismatic style as it suited them.

¹³³This rule is not presented as such in Zarlino's canon; however, a remote relation to his rule 4 might be noted, for which see Lowinsky, "Treatise on Text Underlay," p. 239. Note, however, the absence of reference to Zarlino's rule in the discussion of this rule in Reese-Jones, "Textunterlegung," *MGG* 16 (1979): 1847. Harrán, in "New Light," pp. 41–42, relates this rule clearly to Lanfranco's rule 6, to which Zarlino's rule 4 might be only remotely related, if at all (ibid., p. 42, n. 63).

the semiminimae other than that given to the minima preceding the punctus. In both instances, however, the tactus is the regulating factor determining the possible placement of syllables, as shown in the following patterns:[134]

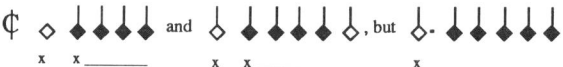

In regard to the rationale (*ratio*) governing this rule, Stoquerus's argumentation is based on his part-whole argument, with the semibrevis and larger note-values considered as the only note values capable of receiving separate syllables in their own right. As Stoquerus has already noted, the assigning of separate syllables to minimae is characteristic of only the modern generation of composers. When these note values are divided into a series of several semiminimae (eight semiminimae to a brevis, four to a semibrevis, or parts thereof), the series should also receive only one syllable. Of the semiminimae in the series, Stoquerus considers the first semiminima as having prime importance in the series, and this for two reasons. The first reason Stoquerus already discussed in the fourth discretionary rule: the first semiminima of the series must above all be consonant in counterpoint with the other voices. The syllable should therefore be placed on the consonance in the series. The second reason, derived from performance practice, concerns the semiminimae considered as ornamentations or diminutions of larger note-values constituting a melodic line, either as a whole or in part, as for example a cadential formula. In this instance, the singer would begin the diminution, in semiminimae, with the same syllable and with the same first note of the unadorned line. The remaining semiminimae in the series would proceed, of course, according to the rules for managing consonance and dissonance with the other parts, but they may be handled in a variety of ways and so do not have to correspond exactly to their longer-note derivations.[135]

---

[134]For examples of the occurrence of both these instances in one convenient location, see in Lowinsky, *Medici Codex*, 5:ff. 46v–47 (the *secunda pars* of Richafort's "Emendemus in melius") *passim*; and the transcription in ibid., 4:111–14. In his discussion of the rule in "Treatise on Text Underlay," pp. 240–41, Lowinsky makes the important observation that "among the new ideas contained in our treatise is the concept of the tactus as influencing the setting of the text." An inchoative form of this concept of the tactus may perhaps be noted prior to Stoquerus in Harrán, "In Pursuit of Origins," pp. 228–30, describing "rule 6" of the anonymous author's treatise.

[135]See Lowinsky, "Treatise on Text Underlay," p. 240. For a detailed account of embellishment in Renaissance performance practice and some relevant treatises, see Imogene Horsley, "Improvised Embellishment in the

Stoquerus concludes the second section of his discussion with a consideration of the relative speed of the series of semiminimae, which prevents each of them from taking a separate syllable. In addition to purely musical reasons for assigning only one syllable to the entire series, there is then also the factor of the aural perception and understanding of the text being sung. Stoquerus's analogy between rapid speaking and rapid singing not only makes his point clear but also emphasizes the importance of the comprehension of the text—the ultimate goal of text placement and reason for these rules as a whole.

In the third section of his discussion (*extensio*), Stoquerus extends his argument concerning the rapidity of semiminimae to include a series of notes smaller than semiminimae (fusae and semifusae, thus answering for these note values as included in the formulation of this rule) and to the longer note following the series (both of semiminimae and smaller notes), as in this figure:

Concerning the longer note following these series, Stoquerus states that it should be included as part of the series, and reasonably so, for the time interval between the final faster note and the longer note is the same as that between the faster notes themselves. Yet, according to Stoquerus, the composers of the older generation frequently disregarded (or did not realize) this obvious conclusion. Stoquerus will discuss this more fully in his rules for the modern generation, who saw the logic of this and carried it out in practice.

Stoquerus concludes his discussion in this chapter by describing the specific domain (*limitatio*) of this rule. To do so, he distinguishes this rule from the second and fourth rules of this set. Basic to his distinction is the consideration of a series of semiminimae as either in ligature or not in ligature. This distinction is determined by the number of syllables available for the semiminimae. Thus, if a large number of syllables is available, then the notes are not in ligature and the second rule is appealed to. This fifth rule, on the other hand, addresses the instance of only one syllable available for the entire series, and in this case, the entire series is considered as in ligature. In turn, this rule is distinguished from the fourth rule, which addresses the problem of fewer than many syllables but more than one syllable available for the series.

Performance of Renaissance Polyphonic Music," *Journal of the American Musicological Society* 4 (1951): 3–19.

In this instance, the series is subdivided into consecutive sets of two-note ligatures, with one syllable assigned to each set. All these distinctions force the conclusion that the rule to be followed is determined by the number of syllables available for the notes in the series.

Stoquerus also notes in this section that the modern generation of composers when writing in C mensuration use semiminimae as equivalent to minimae (in ₵). Whatever these rules prescribe for semiminimae therefore applies on the level of fusae in the C mensuration. Stoquerus seems to be saying that although composers of the newer generation avoided giving more than one syllable to a series of semiminimae, they did do so in a C mensuration and tailored these rules to apply to fusae and smaller note-values. In regard to the older generation of composers, however, this rule is limited to semiminimae in a ₵ mensuration.

Chapter 25: On the Mutual Agreement and Order of the Rules of the Older Composers.

This chapter brings to an end Stoquerus's formal discussion of his discretionary rules of the older generation of composers. Up to this point, he has discussed each rule individually and in detail. Stoquerus's now points to the rather free handling of these rules by the older generation of composers. This freedom may well bewilder the concientious performer confronted with the ideal of these rules as the judgments of a good musician and the reality of the way in which they were practiced by composers. In view of this "diversity of opinions," Stoquerus intends this chapter to be a brief summary of his rules, indicating the various factors that must be taken into account and which rules apply at which points in singing a textual phrase. The title of this chapter indicates Stoquerus's intent to discuss his discretionary rules, but he includes his necessary rules in his discussion as well.

Central to Stoquerus's application of these rules in performance is his division of a textual unit into first, middle, and final syllables, and of a musical unit into first, middle, and final notes. Proper text placement, therefore, consists in coordinating the order of syllables of the given textual unit with the order of notes of the given melodic unit. The rules, both the necessary and discretionary ones, facilitate this coordination and assure a correct placement of the syllables on the notes available for them.

In order to indicate which rules apply at which points in this process of coordination, Stoquerus engages the reader in a kind of practicum, starting with the first syllable and first note, continuing with the middle syllables (including the accented syllable of the last word) and middle notes, and ending with the last syllable and last note. Accordingly, the first syllable of the textual phrase is set to the first note of the melodic phrase, as prescribed by the first part of the fifth necessary rule.

Setting the middle syllables to the middle notes involves several factors. The first is the general and obvious directive that all the middle syllables should be set to the middle notes. To assure that this be done correctly, Stoquerus appeals to his first and fifth necessary rules and his first discretionary rule. The first necessary rule assures that the final note or notes will not have to be divided so as to accommodate syllables that should have been assigned to the middle notes. The fifth necessary rule assures that the order of syllables follows the order of notes; hence, the middle notes should receive the middle syllables. The first discretionary rule assures that all the middle syllables be assigned to the middle notes.

The second factor to be considered in setting the middle syllables to the middle notes is the occurrence of notes with a punctus, ligatures, and successive notes of the same pitch among the middle notes. Notes with a punctus and ligatures may take only one syllable, as prescribed by the second and third necessary rules. Successive notes of the same pitch require separate syllables, by reason of his fourth necessary rule.

The third factor concerns the presence of smaller note values, particularly semiminimae, among the middle notes. In this respect, Stoquerus points to two ways semiminimae may occur among the middle notes: either as an isolated semiminima followed by a longer note or as a series of semiminimae. In the instance of an isolated semiminima followed by a longer note, both notes should receive a syllable, unless the combination occurs as part of a formal clausula. Stoquerus appeals here to his third discretionary rule. This reference is incorrect, since this is the matter of his second, not his third discretionary rule, and the formal clausula exception is mentioned in his discussion of his fourth discretionary rule. On the other hand, it is curious that Stoquerus does not mention here the situation addressed by his third discretionary rule: no syllable is set to two smaller notes equal in value to the punctus after a semibrevis or minima—a common situation among the middle notes.

In the instance of a series of successive semiminimae, Stoquerus advises the performer to note the proportion of syllables to the number of semiminimae in the series and to assign the syllables accordingly: a separate syllable for each semiminima or one syllable for the entire series or one syllable for each group of two semiminimae within the series. In these instances, the second, fifth, and fourth discretionary rules, respectively, are operative.

So far, Stoquerus has allied his rules with all the syllables of a textual unit except the accented syllable of the final word of the phrase. In regard to the accented syllable, there are two options for the performer. First, the accented syllable can be set to all the remaining middle notes of the phrase, by reason of the first discretionary rule, which includes the accented syllable among the middle notes. In this instance, the final syllable or final two syllables, if the antepenultimate syllable is accented, would then be reserved for the final note or the final two notes, respectively, of the phrase. The second option becomes operative if there are so many notes remaining in the phrase that the text can be repeated. In this instance, the accented syllable and the final syllable or syllables are set to the next few notes with no delay on the accented syllable, so that the text or part of it can be repeated along the remaining notes of the phrase. In regard to textual repetition, however, Stoquerus urges caution, prescribing that it be done only for the purpose of an even progression of the text in all the voices or to emphasize the emotional effect of a word or phrase, in much the same way orators repeat words or phrases for rhetorical reasons. Beyond these reasons, however, Stoquerus advises the singer not to indulge in repetition of the text.

The final section of Stoquerus's summary addresses the matter of setting the final syllables of the textual unit to the final notes of the melodic unit. At this stage of the setting of the text, the first discretionary rule and the fifth necessary rule are operative. In the third section of his discussion of the first discretionary rule, Stoquerus mentions precisely that the final note or the final two notes receive the last syllable or the last two syllables after the accented (antepenultimate) syllable. This, in turn, is but another reference to his fifth necessary rule, part of which prescribes that the last syllable be set to the last note. In regard to the last note, Stoquerus recalls for the performer the qualification made in the fourth section of his discussion of the fifth necessary rule: the "last" note may be a ligature, either notated or implied. In both instances, the final syllable is set to the first note of the ligature and held to the end.

It is an advantage of this summary that it provides a synthesis of all the rules thus far, in contrast to the analytical approach determining the order of Stoquerus's rules within each set. Moreover, such a synthesis enables the performer to see these rules applied in practice and illustrates Stoquerus's pedagogical intent governing his treatise.

Chapter 26: On the Discretionary Rules of the Newer Composers.

In this chapter, Stoquerus introduces his set of five discretionary rules of the modern generation of composers. This introduction, in four sections, is comprised of (1) a demonstration of the origin of these five rules "in nature," (2) an explanation of the reason why there can be no more nor fewer than five rules to this set, (3) a comparison of these rules with the discretionary rules of the older generation of composers, and (4) the listing of the five rules of this set.

In order to justify the inclusion of five rules within this set—and his other two sets of rules as well—Stoquerus explains that he is merely recording a grouping of five as constituted by nature herself rather than by his own design. By "nature," Stoquerus means the characteristics or determining properties of the notes and words that give rise to these rules. Any given rule, then, concerning *musica verbalis* as an art addresses the syllable-to-note correspondence in a vocal composition from the requirements (1) of the notes or (2) of the syllables or words or (3) of the notes and syllables or words together. Stoquerus has shown this correspondence in chapter 18 apropos the necessary rules for all composers,[136] and in chapter 19, that of the discretionary rules of the older generation.[137] Stoquerus now shows how these elements enter into consideration in regard to the proper syllable-to-note correspondence as practiced in certain instances by the modern generation of composers. Accordingly, he details the following schema in which the notes and words are first considered separately and then together:

```
Notes and words separately
      notes
            minimae and larger notes                        (1)
            notes smaller than minimae
                  the smaller notes themselves              (2)
                  the longer note following the smaller notes (3)
      words                                                 (4)
Notes and words together                                    (5)
```

Thus, from the aspect of the notes, minimae and larger note-values require separate syllables. This is the substance of the first rule. Note values smaller than minimae, however, do not require separate syllables, nor does the longer note following these shorter values. This is the substance of the second and third rules, respectively. From the aspect of the words, repetition of text should be done cautiously, with repetition of phrases preferred to that of single words. This is the substance of the fourth rule. And from the aspect of the notes and words together, long syllables should be given to long notes, short syllables to short notes. This is the substance of the fifth rule.

Stoquerus maintains that this set of five rules is complete, since nothing can be added to the set that is not already given in the other sets of rules. Nor can anything be removed from this set, since none of them has already been

---

[136]See schema, p. 61 *supra*.
[137]See schema, p. 65 *supra*.

given. The only possible exception is the similarity between the second rule of this set and the fifth discretionary rule of the previous set. Stoquerus explains, however, that the rule among the older generation applied on the condition that they wished to set one syllable to a series of semiminimae. If, however, they wished a different proportion of syllables to semiminimae, they followed their fourth or second rule. The rule is properly given here in this set, however, because the modern composers consistently assigned only one syllable to a series of semiminimae.

The difference between these discretionary rules and those of the earlier generation of composers lies in the extent to which the moderns observed these rules: they regarded them almost as necessary and rarely disregarded them except for a very good reason. As a result, strict observance of these rules by the moderns in their compositions greatly facilitates correct performance in the declamation of their text, quite in contrast to the difficulties encountered in the performance of earlier works, due to the manifold ways in which the text may be set to the music. In this section, Stoquerus's extended simile of a traveller about to set out on a journey—faced with one road and clear directions to his destination or with one among many roads to choose by a random or a reasoned choice—serves effectively to illustrate this difference between the performance of modern compositions and earlier ones.

Yet, as Stoquerus maintains, even these rules of the modern generation must be known by the performer. For, as he continues with his simile, even a traveller faced with only one possible road leading to the city can get lost if he does not know the proper directions. So too, a singer, who does not know these rules, will not necessarily make his way successfully through the compositions of the moderns no matter how natural and necessary their rules for performance may seem. For the benefit of the performer, Stoquerus thus concludes this chapter with the listing of the five discretionary rules as they pertain to the compositions of the modern generation of composers.

Chapter 27: On the Minima and Notes Larger Than a Minima.

The first discretionary rule of the modern generation of composers prescribes that a syllable be given to any minima and to any note larger than a minima. For his discussion of this rule, Stoquerus presents (1) the rationale governing the rule, (2) the reason why this rule is peculiar to this set, (3) a further application of this rule, and (4) its exception.

Stoquerus's rationale for this rule is that the durations of minimae and larger note-values are all long enough to accommodate the articulation of a syllable. For support of this, Stoquerus points out that the original purpose of notated ligatures was to indicate that these notes, which should regularly receive separate syllables (because their duration so permitted), could in a given instance be assigned only one syllable. Since the notated ligatures include combinations only of semibreves and of longer note values, the minima apparently was always intended to carry a syllable. Thus, for Stoquerus, the rationale for this rule is supported by the use of notated ligatures as an exception to the regular practice of giving separate syllables to minimae and notes larger than minimae.[138]

In order to further clarify why the minima also shares in the right ("ius") of larger notes to receive a syllable, Stoquerus appeals to the meaning of the word "minima" itself, which can only be intelligible as "smallest" ("minima") in relation to the notes larger than it. Thus, on a scale of largest to smallest, the minima is the smallest note whose duration is still long enough to carry a syllable. In this sense, then, the minima shares the same privilege or right as the larger notes to carry a syllable, since it occupies the lowest position in the group consisting of the maxima, longa, brevis, semibrevis, and minima.

In the second section of his discussion, Stoquerus points out that this rule properly belongs to the modern generation of composers, since the older generation spread one syllable over any number of notes and note values, treating each grouping as implied ligatures. This observation points to the fundamental difference between the styles of the two generations, with the modern generation preferring a markedly more syllabic style with melismas occurring chiefly on series of semiminimae and smaller note values.[139]

In the third section of his discussion, Stoquerus shows how this rule is extended to apply to semiminimae in both the C and ₵ mensurations. In the C mensuration, the semiminimae function, of course, as minimae and therefore receive separate syllables, just as minimae do in the ₵ mensuration. More important, however, Stoquerus identifies two situations when even in a ₵ mensuration semiminimae may sometimes receive separate syllables. The first situation occurs when part of the entire texture of a composition is pervaded by a predominantly semiminima motion ("omnes voces semiminimas sonant"). The second situation occurs when the semiminimae are spaced

---

[138]Lowinsky, in "Treatise on Text Underlay," p. 241, points to the equivalence of this rule to Zarlino's rule 1. See Harrán, "New Light," pp. 35–38, for a comparison of Zarlino's rule 1 with Lanfranco's rule 2, which also reflects the substance of Stoquerus's present rule.

[139]See the discussion of this rule in Reese-Jones, "Textunterlegung," *MGG* 16 (1979): 1847. For a discussion of Willaert's early style and his later style (the latter as exemplified in his *Musica nova* of 1559), see Lowinsky, *Medici Codex*, 3:101–3.

apart at larger intervals ("intervallis maioribus distantes ponuntur"),[140] with the melodic motion therefore generally disjunct as opposed to the more normal and generally conjunct motion (in which latter case only one syllable is given to the entire series). Both situations are encountered in madrigal and canzona literature, especially when characterized by a parlando style in all the voices and often including successive semiminimae of the same pitch. A figuration such as the following may illustrate both situations:[141]

In the final section of this chapter, Stoquerus repeats the observation he made in the third section of chapter 23: this rule does not apply to the formal clausula:

in which the minima, that is, the first half of the syncopated semibrevis, may often go without a syllable.[142]

Chapter 28: On Semiminimae and Notes Smaller Than Semiminimae.

Stoquerus's discussion in this chapter concerns the second discretionary rule of the composers of the modern generation, which prescribes that only one syllable be set to a series of semiminimae and smaller note values, regardless of the number of these notes in a series.[143] Stoquerus explains (1)

---

[140]I am indebted to Don Harrán for his clarification of these two situations as given in the galley proofs for the chapter on Stoquerus in *Word-Tone Relations*.

[141]For examples, in a convenient location, of such handling of semiminimae in a ₵ mensuration (and a C mensuration as well) by composers of the modern generation, see the facsimiles provided in *Schriftbild der mehrstimmigen Musik*, ed. Heinrich Besseler and Peter Gülke, Musikgeschichte in Bildern, III/5: Musik des Mittelalters und der Renaissance (Leipzig: VEB Deutscher Verlag für Musik, 1973), pp. 132–37.

[142]See pp. 77–78 *supra*.

[143]Reese-Jones, in "Textunterlegung," *MGG* 16 (1979): 1847, indicate, as does Stoquerus, the similarity of this rule to the fifth discretionary rule of the older generation. Lowinsky, in "Treatise on Text Underlay," pp. 241–42, associates this rule with Zarlino's rule 4 with qualification. Harrán, in

the rationale behind the rule, (2) the reason why this rule belongs specifically to this set, (3) the further application of this rule, and (4) its exception.

Stoquerus divides his explanation of the rationale of this rule into two parts. The first part of his explanation shows why no syllable at all is given to semiminimae (and *a fortiori* to notes smaller than semiminimae); the second part addresses the question why a syllable may, however, be given to the first of a series of these smaller notes, particularly semiminimae. The first part of his explanation is contained in the first part of his discussion of this rule in this chapter; the second part appears in conjunction with the explanation of the third discretionary rule in the next chapter.

For his explanation of the reason why no syllable at all may be given to semiminimae and smaller notes, Stoquerus draws from the relatively late appearance of the semiminima in the history of notation, from the meaning of "minima" as a word, and from the relative speed of the semiminimae and smaller notes. As to the relatively late appearance of the semiminima in notation, Stoquerus is probably taking his cue from Gaffurius, who in his *Practica musicae* refers to these shorter notes as introduced by a later generation of composers and chiefly for ornamental purposes.[144] Stoquerus, then, appears to divide the history of notation, as he sees it for purposes of his argument, into two groups. Thus, the first group would consist of the "ancients" ("antiqui"), comprising a group culminating in the notational innovations of the early fourteenth-century French and Italian *ars nova*; the second group would comprise those composers who further expanded these innovations later in the fourteenth and early fifteenth century. For the first group, the minima was the smallest note value in use; for the second, the semiminima and smaller note values were introduced as further subdivisions of the minima.[145] In regard to his argument, Stoquerus relies on the authority of the

---

"New Light," pp. 41–43, finds a clear relation between this rule and Lanfranco's rule 6, to which Zarlino's rule 4 is only loosely related (see p. 42, n. 63).

[144]In Bk. 2, chap. 3, Gaffurius discusses the maxima, longa, brevis, semibrevis, and minima as a group. In chap. 4, he discusses the note values shorter than a minima (see Gaffurius, *Practica musicae*, pp. 74–77).

[145]Margaret Bent, in "Notation (Western, c. 1260–1500)," *New Grove Dictionary of Music and Musicians* 13 (1980): 366, notes: "Semiminims ... which were mentioned by Vitry but not by Italian theorists came into use in later musical sources to divide the minim in half." Richard Hoppin claims that this mention of semiminimae by Vitry "may have been a later addition to his treatise" (*Medieval Music* [New York: W. W. Norton and Co., 1978], p. 356). Cf. Hugo Riemann, *History of Music Theory*, trans. Raymond H. Haggh, 2d ed. (Lincoln: University of Nebraska Press, 1966; reprint ed.,

"ancients," for whom the minima was the smallest note value that carried a syllable. His argument is confirmed by the meaning of the word "minima." Since the minima is the smallest note value whose duration is yet long enough to carry a syllable, the duration of the later and shorter note values is therefore not long enough for a syllable. This, in turn, is confirmed by the consideration that a succession of these smaller notes—each note equipped with a separate syllable—would result in a blurred articulation of the text.

In the second section of his discussion, Stoquerus points to the rightful position of this rule in this set, for, as he explains, the older generation of composers assigned not only just one syllable to a series of semiminimae but also two, three, four or more, and sometimes even just one syllable to each semiminima. Since composers of the modern generation, however, consistently assigned only one syllable to a series of semiminimae, this rule can be regarded as proper to this set.

In the third section of his discussion, Stoquerus points out that this rule extends to minimae in *proportio tripla*, in which minimae are equivalent to semiminimae in a corresponding *integer valor* mensuration and therefore should not receive separate syllables but rather only one syllable for an entire series. When, however, the semiminima functions as a minima (in the C mensuration), as Stoquerus points out in the final section of his discussion, this rule does not apply, and each semiminima is given its own syllable. Stoquerus has already explained this in the previous chapter in the third section of his discussion concerning the first discretionary rule of this set.

Chapter 29: On the Minima or Any Larger Note Immediately Following the Semiminimae.

In this chapter, Stoquerus discusses the third discretionary rule of this set, which prescribes that the longer note following a series of semiminimae receive the same syllable as that set to the first semiminima of the series.[146]

New York: Da Capo Press, 1974), pp. 194–95. For the full account of French and Italian *ars nova* and its later development, see Willi Apel, *The Notation of Polyphonic Music: 900–1600* (Cambridge: Medieval Academy of America, 1953), pp. 338–84.

[146]This rule and the second rule of this set echoes Lanfranco's rule 6 as listed and discussed in Harrán, "New Light," pp. 41–43, and Vicentino's rule 1 as listed in "Vicentino and His Rules of Text Underlay," p. 622. Stoquerus's division of Lanfranco's and Vicentino's rule is prompted, of course, by the division he makes in regard to the origin of these rules in chapter 26 (see p. 85 *supra*). The present chapter is paraphrased and condensed in Lowinsky, "Treatise on Text Underlay," p. 243; its substance is given by

For his discussion, Stoquerus explains the rationale behind the rule and why the rule belongs properly to this set. He then shows how this rule may further apply to the next note after the longer note and, finally, draws a corollary concerning the placement of the last syllable to the last note of a phrase.

In the first section of his discussion, Stoquerus explains why a new syllable should not be given to the first longer note following a series of semiminimae. In the course of his discussion, Stoquerus also explains the second part of the rationale of the second discretionary rule, that is, why a syllable is given to the first semiminima of a series. Stoquerus's explanation of the rationale of the present rule begins with a statement of the rule itself: the longer note immediately following a series of semiminimae receives the same syllable as that given to the semiminimae. The latter half of this statement reflects, of course, the substance of the previous rule: a syllable is given only to the first semiminima in a series. According to Stoquerus, however, a syllable is given to this semiminima in violation of its nature (that is, its short duration). Now since a syllable is given to a note that, contrary to its nature, should not receive a syllable, Stoquerus reasons that, by that same token, a syllable may be taken away from a note that may fittingly (that is, because of its suitable duration) receive one. This is done, Stoquerus explains, in order to balance the inequality of giving a syllable to the first semiminima of the series preceding the longer note. This, however, is not as unfair as it may seem. Stoquerus explains this by pointing out what he has said before: syllables are not given to semiminimae because the syllables are delivered too quickly to allow for their distinct pronunciation. In this respect, however, Stoquerus observes that the distinct pronunciation of a syllable is determined not by the beginning of its delivery but by how long the delivery lasts. Thus, if the delivery of the syllable ends quickly, the syllable is pronounced quickly. In this respect, when a syllable is set to the first of a series of semiminimae (or smaller values), the note in question is not the note on which the delivery begins but the note on which the delivery ends. For Stoquerus, this note is not the last semiminima of the series but the first longer note following the series. Stoquerus seems to have in mind that at the point of arrival at the longer note, the syllable is still moving at semiminima speed[147] because the time interval between the last semiminima and the first longer note is the same as that between the semiminimae themselves. In order to level off this speed

---

Reese-Jones in "Textunterlegung," *MGG* 16 (1979): 1847, with a musical example (no. 6) on the unnumbered pages following the entry.

[147]Cf. Lanfranco's statement under the paraphrase as rule 1 as given by Harrán in "Vicentino and His Rules of Text Underlay," p. 622.

of the syllable set to the series of semiminimae, the syllable should continue along the longer note following the series, thereby prolonging the delivery of the syllable and allowing for its distinct pronunciation. The following figure may serve to illustrate the application of both the second and the third discretionary rules:

With his "argument from swiftness," as it may be termed, Stoquerus therefore justifies why a syllable may be given to the first semiminima (or smaller note) of a series (the second part of the rationale of the previous rule) and why the same syllable should be extended along the first note following the series (the rationale of the present rule).

In the second section of his discussion, Stoquerus justifies his placement of this rule among the rules of the modern generation. He does this on the ground that the composers heeded it with as much care as they did the necessary rules, whereas the composers of the older generation followed or disregarded it at will.

The third section of Stoquerus's discussion concerns two instances in which the syllable given to the first semiminima of a series is extended along the second longer note following the semiminimae. In regard to the first instance, the composer might simply wish, for aesthetic reasons, to prolong the pronunciation of the syllable beyond the first longer note after the semiminimae, as for example:

In regard to the second instance, the composer might want to avoid setting the next syllable on the second longer note falling on the arsis of the tactus. This would apply especially when a minima following the semiminimae falls on the thesis of the tactus and is followed in turn by another minim. In this instance, the composer would complete the tactus with the same syllable and assign the next syllable to the note falling on the thesis of the next tactus, as for example:

This would result in a setting more melismatic than syllabic and in turn accounts for Stoquerus's reference to his fourth discretionary rule of the older generation, which addresses how properly to apply a syllable to a series of two minimae or semiminimae. In this instance, however, the first minima after the semiminimae carries the same syllable given to the semiminimae, according to this rule.

Stoquerus concludes his discussion of this rule by drawing a corollary applicable to the last note at the end of a phrase and preceded by a series of semiminimae. In this instance, the "last" note capable of receiving the last syllable is not the longer note following the semiminimae, but the first semiminima of the series. The longer note following the series is therefore counted among (that is, in implied ligature with) the series of semiminimae, as in these figures:

Chapter 30: On Avoiding Repetition of Words.

In this chapter, Stoquerus discusses the fourth discretionary rule of this set, cautioning chiefly against indiscriminate repetition of individual words, but also of phrases.[148] For his discussion, Stoquerus restates his position already presented in chapter 25[149] but now in a more systematic, that is, scholastic format. Accordingly, Stoquerus (1) gives the rationale for the rule, (2) locates the rule as proper to the modern generation of composers, and (3) indicates its exception.

For the rationale behind the rule, Stoquerus first draws an analogy from faulty intercourse deriving either from stammering or a garrulous person's excessive repetition of the same idea. The analogy is strong but serves to emphasize in particular the listener's discomfort of having to endure the unnecessary repetition of individual words and phrases. As in speech, so also in singing: the listener should be spared the unnecessary repetition of single words and phrases. Stoquerus offers as another reason underlying this

---

[148] A summary of this chapter is given in Lowinsky, "Treatise on Text Underlay," p. 243. This rule is discussed in combination with Stoquerus's previous remarks in chapter 25 in Reese-Jones, "Textunterlegung," *MGG* 16 (1979): 1847–48, and a musical example is supplied (no. 7) on the unnumbered pages following the entry.

[149] See pp. 83–84 *supra*.

rule the example of plainchant, which achieves the ideal correspondence of text and melody with (as far as he can tell) no use of textual repetition.

Stoquerus locates this rule among the modern generation of composers for the simple reason that the moderns were more sparing in their use of repetition of text than were the composers of the older generation.

In the final section of his discussion, Stoquerus draws an analogy from the rhetorical use of repetition and indicates that occasional repetition may be employed for the artistic reason of increasing the emotional impact of an important part (preferably a phrase) of the text.[150] Even in this respect, however, Stoquerus sides with moderation in repetition, since overdoing it can produce the opposite effect for which it is intended.

Chapter 31: On the Observance of the Quantity of Syllables.

With this chapter, Stoquerus's treatise in its extant form comes to an abrupt end, stopping in mid-sentence and followed by the scribal note "Caetera desiderantur" ("The rest is missing"). The organization of the treatise in general and the title of this chapter in particular point to a discussion of the fifth discretionary rule of this set, prescribing that long syllables be set to long notes, short syllables to short notes.[151] The four topics given at the beginning of this chapter point to Stoquerus's organization of his intended discussion: (1) a discussion of the terminology of the rule, (2) its rationale, (3) its reason for inclusion in this particular set, and (4) its exception. Only the topic sentence and beginning of the next sentence is given, suggesting a distinction perhaps between the stress accent common to prose and the quantitative (metrical) accent common to classical poetry.

---

[150]The source for the greater part of Stoquerus's discussion in this chapter can easily be traced to the formulation of Zarlino's rule 8, which in turn is an expansion of Lanfranco's rule 7 as discussed in Harrán, "New Light," pp. 43–44. Vicentino particularly cautions the singer against repetition of single words, even if the composer has so indicated. See his rule 4 as listed by Harrán in "Vicentino and His Rules of Text Underlay," p. 623.

[151]This rule is derived from Zarlino's general remarks on text placement preceding his rules and from the first part of his first rule (see *Istitutioni harmoniche* [1558], Bk. 4, chap. 33). See also Vicentino's rule 5 as listed in Harrán, "Vicentino and His Rules of Text Underlay," p. 624 (here Harrán also notes that this rule is not given by Lanfranco). Reese-Jones in "Textunterlegung," *MGG* 16 (1979): 1848 cite Stoquerus's rule and offer a musical example (no. 8) on the unnumbered pages following the entry.

Stoquerus's treatise at this point is virtually complete.[152] All that is missing, in addition to the body of this chapter, is perhaps a following summary chapter, similar in approach to the chapters following the separate discussions of the necessary rules and the discretionary rules of the older generation of composers. After this, and perhaps an epilogue, would surely have come the musical examples that Stoquerus promised (at the end of chapter 18) for the benefit of the beginner.[153]

The Manuscript

Stoquerus's three treatises survive, as far as is presently known, only in the single manuscript residing in the Biblioteca Nacional of Madrid. The manuscript, in a fine state of preservation from beginning to end, is a scribal copy of the autograph. This is shown by (1) its accomplished humanistic script for the body of the text and Roman lettering for the titles of all three treatises, the chapter titles of *De musica verbali*, and the section headings of the other two treatises; (2) normal scribal errors, chiefly omissions of words and lines that are immediately corrected after the indication of the omission by a line drawn through the misplaced text; and (3) the remark at the end of *De musica verbali*, "Caetera desiderantur." The autograph of the manuscript has not yet been discovered.[154]

The manuscript, in quarto, consists of an unnumbered title page (in large Roman lettering) for *De musica verbali* and forty-nine folios numbered in arabic numerals. The manuscript is written by a single hand and averages twenty-five lines of text per page, with adequate margins on all four sides of text. At various places within *De musica verbali* are seven staves, each intended to illustrate a particular point Stoquerus is discussing. The staves, however, are not filled in with their intended examples. In the absence of the autograph, it cannot be satisfactorily determined whether the examples were omitted by Stoquerus himself (he may have planned to return to them later) or by the scribe.

---

[152]Cf. Lowinsky, "Treatise on Text Underlay," p. 243.

[153]See pp. 14–16 *supra*.

[154]Acting on the possibility that Stoquerus's autograph might be found in the archives of the library at the University of Salamanca where Stoquerus worked in association with Salinas, I inquired of Dra. Teresa Santander, director of the library, if Stoquerus's autograph might in fact be found there. She replied that after a thorough search of the manuscript collection of the library, no work of Stoquerus could be found. She also consulted the *Catálogo de archivo de música de la catedral de Salamanca* (1981) but reported the same negative result. I am grateful to Dra. Santander for making this effort.

The present edition has been made from a microfilm of the Madrid manuscript.[155]

Description and Contents of the Manuscript

M

Madrid, Biblioteca Nacional, MS. 6486

Chartaceous, [i], 49 ff., 21x14.9 cm, in 4°
late 16th century[156]

[ir]   Gasparis Stoqueri Germani de Musica verbali libri Duo.

[iv]   vacat

1r–40v   Verborum notis applicandorum rationem a musicis turpiter ignorari, nec facile sine praeceptis addisci posse. CAP. I. Ociosum me, nec gravioribus additum studiis ad leviora haec ... Quantitas syllabarum aliter in prosa, quam in cantione observatur. In prosa enim. Caetera desiderantur

41r–45v   Gasparis Stoqueri Germani de vera Solfizationis, quam vocant docendae ratione, ad Magistrum Franciscum Salinam Dominum suum. Quam stulte faciant, qui solfizandi rationem pueros ... Sol quidem in cantu naturali, Re vero in B molli, Ut in ♮ duro, quod erat ostendendum

46r   vacat

46v–49r   De Modo, Tempore, et Prolatione. Quae nominibus tria proponuntur ... ut cum velocior fieri mensura deberet, virgula interciderentur

---

[155]I am grateful to Rev. Raymond L. Sullivant, S.J., director of the St. Louis University extension in Madrid, for acquiring for me from the Biblioteca Nacional the microfilm and the description of the manuscript that follows.

[156]This is the revised date. In regard to the original date of the codex, see pp. 5–6 *supra*.

The Edition

The edition aims to present as precise a reading as possible of the text of *De musica verbali*. To this end, any errors and inconsistencies in the manuscript have been emended for the sake of clarification for the reader. The more substantial of these errors and inconsistencies, such as grammatical errors and slips of the pen that affect the sense of the text, are reported in the apparatus; others of less consequence are silently emended. These latter include variants of a purely orthographical nature, simple orthographical errors, capitalization or lower-case lettering at variance with modern principles, and deletions that the scribe himself made. The text of the manuscript is divided into paragraphs and punctuated, where necessary, according to modern principles.

The translation aims to preserve the spirit and flavor of Stoquerus's style in as close a corresponding English style as possible. Stoquerus was given to the use of synonyms, especially verbs and nouns, as a device for variety, and an attempt has been made to achieve the same effect in the translation. Technical and philosophical terms are translated as consistently as possible with their English equivalents, unless a particular context demands otherwise. This also holds true for terminology outside a technical and philosophical context.

The annotations to the translation provide cross-references and elucidation as deemed necessary, especially if a point has not previously been discussed in the introduction.

The present edition is a revision of my Ph.D. dissertation.[157] Some material has been corrected and new material has been added. The translation has been completely revised and the format has been redesigned in accord with the principles of Greek and Latin Music Theory.

---

[157]Albert C. Rotola, S.J., "Gaspar Stoquerus, *De musica verbali*: Critical Edition, Translation, and Commentary" (Ph.D. dissertation, The Catholic University of America, Washington, D.C., 1984).

CONSPECTUS CODICIS ET NOTARUM

Manuscript

M   Madrid, Biblioteca Nacional, MS. 6486 (late 16th century), E-Mn

Notes

arcus et verba om. in schema	arcs and words omitted in illustration
bis	twice
corr.	corrected
delevi	I deleted
fortasse	perhaps
hic	here
in marg.	in margin
om.	omitted
post	after
schema	illustration
scripsi	I have written
sec.	second
spatium est duarum linearum	there is a space of two lines
spatium in	space in
supplevi	I supplied
tit.	title
transp.	transposed

' ' enclose insertions by the scribe
⟨ ⟩ enclose words or figures added by conjecture
⟨***⟩ indicate an omission for which a space has been allowed by the scribe

GASPARIS STOQUERI GERMANI
DE MUSICA VERBALI LIBRI DUO

VERBORUM NOTIS APPLICANDORUM RATIONEM
A MUSICIS TURPITER IGNORARI,
NEC FACILE SINE PRAECEPTIS ADDISCI POSSE

CAP. I

5   Ociosum me nec gravioribus additum studiis, ad leviora haec et ab omnibus fere musicis hactenus neglecta descendere putet, qui, praesenti inspecto opusculo, rei et novitatem et musicorum nostrae aetatis in arte canendi nullo huius libelli adminiculo adiutorum peritiam considerabit. Ego vero, ut olim a nullo fere quod hoc praestantius censeri queat studio abstinui, ita nunc, iis
10 omnibus sepositis, huic uni et multis etiam abiectioribus negociis, fortuna ita cogente, deditum me esse nec diffiteor nec idcirco a quoquam merito reprehendi posse existimo. Nam et quilibet in fortunae statu honeste se gerere, vitaeque actiones pro loco ac tempore mutare sapientis est; et laborem hunc meum viris bonis probari, nec ut inutilem, levitatisve nomine argui posse
15 reor. Musicae enim laudes omnibus fere notissimas hic recensere supervacaneum forte fuerit, maxime cum iis non musicorum tantum, sed et sacrae scripturae, poetarum, historiographorum, aliorumque scriptorum libri refertissimi sint. Quare qui ipsi musicae studere honestum putant laborem simul hunc nostrum ut probent necesse est, quando sine hoc legitimum huius finem assequi
20 nemo potest. Nec enim perfecti musici censendi sunt, qui solfizando (quod

THE TWO BOOKS ON VERBAL MUSIC BY GASPAR STOQUERUS THE GERMAN

CHAPTER 1

THE METHOD OF APPLYING THE WORDS TO THE NOTES IS SHAMEFULLY IGNORED BY MUSICIANS AND CANNOT BE EASILY LEARNED WITHOUT PRECEPTS[2]

Someone who, upon the inspection of the present little work, will consider both the newness of the subject and the skill of musicians of our age in the art of singing (aided by no assistance of this little book) might think that I am unoccupied—or uninvolved in weightier studies—and am descending to these lighter matters neglected by almost all musicians up to now. Just as I formerly withheld myself from almost no study that could be regarded as more important than this one, so now, with all of them set aside, I do not deny that at the behest of fortune I am consigned to this one study and to many affairs even more undistinguished. Nor on that account do I suppose I can be justly faulted by anyone, for to conduct oneself honorably in whatever state of fortune and to change the activities of life according to place and time is the mark of a wise man. I also deem that this labor of mine is approved by good men and cannot be accused of being useless or light. It would perhaps be superfluous to recount here the praises of music so well known to almost everyone, especially since books are filled with them—not only books of musicians but also those of Sacred Scripture, poets, historians, and other writers. Therefore, those who think the study of music is an honorable labor must at the same time necessarily approve of this labor of ours, since without this no one can attain music's rightful end. Musicians should not be regarded as perfect

---

[1] Concerning the division of this treatise into two books, see Introduction, pp. 13–16.

[2] For the commentary on this chapter, see Introduction, pp. 16–17.

vocant) contenti, verborum canendorum rationem prorsus negligunt. Notarum enim figurae ac nomina, quas voces musicales appellant, non nisi verborum exprimendorum causa efficta sunt; ipsaque solfizatio cantantibus idem est, quod iuncus natantibus. Quod si iuncus natandi peritos parum decet, musicae
5 peritos tyrocinii instrumenta nolle deponere, merito demiror. Caeci quidem et infirmi baculo uti, infantes curribus deambulatoriis honeste possunt; si autem hos sani, oculati, ac adulti imitentur, id a turpitudine quomodo abesse queat, non video. Quod si igitur et musicis, verbis cantionum propriis quam solfizatione uti honestius est, et musicae artis tyrones ad hunc tanquam ultimum can-
10 tandi finem tendere aequum est, non levem tentasse rem dicendus sum, qui finem, partem cuiusque rei praestantissimum huic studio adiicere voluerim.

Nec est cur operam hanc nostram quisquam reprehendat, quod multi hanc scientiam absque huius operis nostri inspectione sint consecuti. Constat enim multos quoque orandi peritos solo naturae beneficio et mediocri exercitio
15 absque praeceptis evasisse, nec tamen ideo operam perdidisse, qui de arte oratoria libros scripserunt. Nam et iis qui tardiori sunt ingenio consulendum est, ut quod naturae defectu consequi per se non possunt, id ab arte naturam supplente acquirant. Quique ad facultatem sive orandi, sive cantandi se natos existimant, iidem praeceptis adiuti, proculdubio et citius et perfectius, labo-
20 reque etiam longe minori idem consequuntur. Ideo prudenter Isocrates ad Daemonicum de praeceptis minime contemnendis sic scribit: κατανάλισκε τὴν ἐν τῷ βίῳ σχολὴν εἰς τὴν τῶν λόγων φιληκοΐαν· οὕτω γὰρ τὰ τοῖς ἄλλοις χαλεπῶς εὑρημένα συμβήσεταί σοι ῥᾳδίως μανθάνειν.

Quare si quis cantandi scientiae finem legitimum cito perfecte ac facile
25 consequi optet, operam hanc nostram ne improbet, sed eam alacriter amplexans mediocri meditatione et exercitio comitetur. Ita fiet, ut nec ipsum lectionis, nec me compositionis poenitudo sequatur.

---

17 consequi 'per se' non possunt M ‖ 22–23 τοῖς ἄλλοις]τους αλλους M ‖

who, content with solmization (as they term it), entirely neglect the method of singing the words. Indeed, the figures of the notes and their names (which they call musical syllables) were fashioned for the sole purpose of expressing the words. And solmization itself bears the same relationship to singers as a rush plant does to swimmers. But if a rush plant hardly befits skilled swimmers, I justly wonder when skilled musicians are unwilling to set aside the instruments of initiation. The blind and infirm can honorably use a cane, and infants walkers; but if the healthy, keen-sighted, and adults imitate them, I do not see how this can be free from shame. Therefore, if it is more honorable for musicians to use the particular words of songs rather than solmization, it is also reasonable that initiates in the art of music strive for this as the ultimate end of singing. Therefore, I should not be said to have attempted something light, I who have wished to add to this study its end, the most important part of any subject.

Nor is there any reason why anyone should fault this effort of ours on the ground that many have attained this science without an inspection of this, our work. For it is certain that many have also become skilled in oratory solely by the benefit of nature and a little practice without the aid of precepts; nevertheless, it is certain that those who have written books on oratorical art have not therefore wasted their effort. Provision must also be made for those who are slower in ability so that what they cannot attain by themselves because of a deficiency of nature, they may acquire from art, which supplements nature. And even those who suppose they are naturally suited for the power of speaking or singing are also helped by precepts and without doubt attain the same power more quickly and more perfectly and with even far less effort. Wisely, therefore, does Isocrates write to Demonicus about not disdaining precepts: "Spend your leisure time in the enjoyment of listening in on discussions, for it will turn out that you will learn with ease what others have found out with difficulty."[3]

Therefore, if anyone wants to attain quickly, perfectly, and easily the rightful end of the science of singing, let him not disdain this work of ours, but rather eagerly embrace it and follow it with a little reflection and practice. As a result, he will not regret having read it, nor will I regret having written it.

---

[3] Isocrates *Ad Daemonicum* 18.

MUSICAE DIVISIO

CAP. II

Ne lector rei qua de agitur ignarus aut plus quam hic docetur, aut aliud pro alio expectet, sciat nos hic non de integra musica, sed de certa eius parte acturos, quae ipsum ne lateat praevia musices divisione praecavendum puto.

Est igitur haec biformis, altera theorica, altera practica; et haec rursus vel instrumentalis, vel vocalis. Theorica practicam natura, certitudine, et dignitate antecedit; de qua qui scripserint non desunt. Sed omnes longo intervallo dominus meus Franciscus Salinas superasse videtur. De utraque etiam practica libri complurium extant, sed eam quae humana voce peragitur neglectius tractatam suspicor, maximeque circa finem; quod plane demiror. Constat enim inter omnes finem rei cuiusque partem esse praestantissimam, et natura ab omnibus magis quam caetera, quae ad eandem rem pertinentia ipsum antecedunt, desiderari.

Hanc rursus triplicem Franchinus facit in 3 practicae suae capite. Primamque esse ait, quae solfizando; secundam, quae sonorum tantum modulatione sine verbis ac syllabis: tertiam, quae verborum quorum causa soni effecti sunt, pronuntiatione exercetur. Addit idem Franchinus primam initiandis pueris tradi solere; secundam exercitatorum esse; ad tertiam vero tanquam ad electi modulaminis finem clericos deduci. Haec Franchinus.

Constat autem prima sex syllabarum (quas voces musicales vocant) enuntiatione harum: ut, re, mi, fa, sol, la. Hanc, quae sequitur pars, aut syllabas

---

10 per agitur M II

CHAPTER 2

THE DIVISION OF MUSIC[4]

Lest the reader, ignorant of the subject that is being treated, expect more than what is taught here (or something else instead), he should know that we will not treat here music in its entirety, but a certain part of it. And lest this part escape his attention, I think precaution should be taken by means of a preliminary division of music.

This division, therefore, is of two parts: one is theory, the other, practice. Practice, in turn, is either instrumental or vocal. Theory precedes practice in nature, certitude, and eminence. There is no lack of those who have written on theory, but my master, Francisco Salinas, seems to have surpassed them all by a long distance.[5] There also exist books by very many authors concerning each part of practice; however, I believe that the part that is accomplished by the human voice has been rather negligently handled, especially in regard to its end. I distinctly wonder at this, for it is clear among all that the end is the most important part of any activity and is naturally desired by everyone more than the other things that, pertaining to the same activity, precede it.[6]

Franchinus Gaffurius, in the third chapter of his *Practica musicae*, makes this part in turn threefold. The first part, he says, is exercised by solmization; the second, by the modulation of sounds only, without words and syllables; the third, by the pronunciation of words, on which account the sounds were brought about. Franchinus adds that the first part is customarily handed down in the induction of choirboys; the second is the mark of those already trained; to the third, however, clerics are led—to the end, as it were, of a select modulated line. These things Franchinus states.[7]

Furthermore, the first part consists in the enunciation of these six syllables (which they term musical syllables): ut, re, mi, fa, sol, la. The part that fol-

---

[4]For the commentary on this chapter, see Introduction, pp. 17–20.

[5]Stoquerus refers here, of course, to Salinas's *De musica libri septem*, with which he became familiar while assisting the blind Salinas in its preparation for publication. See Arthur Michael Daniels, "The *De musica libri vii* of Francisco de Salinas" (Ph.D dissertation, University of Southern California, Los Angeles, 1962).

[6]See Introduction, n. 36.

[7]See Franchinus Gaffurius, *Practica musicae* (Milan, 1496; reprint ed., Farnborough: Gregg Press, 1967), Bk. I, chap. 3, ff. A4v–5r. For the full quotation from this section of the *Practica musicae*, see Introduction, n. 37.

omnino omittit, avesque ut instrumenta musica solius soni expressione imitatur, aut et syllabas certas quibuslibet sonis applicat, ut Germani, Tantaritarire; Itali, Fa li la le la; cornicines, Tirili. Tertia nec sine syllabis contingit, nec iis solis, aut certis, sed integris dictionibus decantatur. Haec si apte fiat, mire hominum animos ad amorem, odium, iram, misericordiam, pietatem, etc., pro subiecta verbis materia commovet.

Est et trium harum musicae vocalis specierum primae finis secunda, secundae tertia. Recte autem inter eas medium locum secunda obtinet, quod caeteris ambabus communis; sola quidem sine illis subsistere potest, illae ab hac separari omnino non possunt. Primam satis perspicue permulti nostrae aetatis musici exposuerunt; secunda autem antiquis antequam prima a Guidone inveniretur in usu erat; illi enim (syllabis sonorum nondum inventis) solis utebantur literis, quibus sonos, ut nos nunc lineis ac figuris enuntiabant. Itaque, illi prima nondum nota solis duabus posterioribus utebantur, et secundum perscriptas literas vel sonos tantum vel etiam verba pronuntiabant. Unde et Virgilius eas ambas in Bucolicis duobus verbis coniungit, cum inquit: Numeros memini; si verba tenerem.

Sed ut secunda priorem antiquitate vincit, ita secundam tertia. Eam enim etiam nondum inventis literis extitisse dubium non est: quippe quae ut avium cantus cum ipsa hominum creatione coepit.

Cum igitur haec maxime naturae humanae conveniat, indigni mihi hominis vocabulo videntur, qui, hac relicta, priori soli perpetuo immorantur; quia nec ipsa propter se inventa est, sed ut huic antiquissimae et longe praestantissimae serviret. Hanc ergo scitu dignissimam musicae partem, cuius causa et priores institutae sunt, cuiusque solius cognitio, eo quod sola ultimum finem contineat, perfectum musicum reddit, tractandam suscepimus.

lows this either entirely omits syllables and imitates birds, as musical instruments do by the expression of sound alone, or applies in addition certain syllables to any sounds whatsoever, as the Germans do with Tantaritarire, the Italians with Fa li la le la, and horn players with Tirili.[8] The third part is neither produced without syllables nor with them alone (or with certain ones), but rather is sung with entire expressions. If this is done fittingly, it stirs the minds of men remarkably to love, hate, rage, pity, devotion, etc., in accord with the subject matter of the words.

Of these three species of vocal music, the second is the end of the first, the third the end of the second. Furthermore, the second species rightly obtains the middle position because it is common to both of the others. Indeed, it subsists alone without them, but they cannot be wholly separated from it. Numerous musicians of our age have explained the first species clearly enough; however, the second branch was in practice among the ancients long before the first was invented by Guido. They used letters alone (the syllables for the sounds were not yet invented) to enunciate sounds, just as we now use lines and figures. Hence, since the first species was not yet known, they used only the latter two, and according to the letters written down, they pronounced either sounds alone or the words as well. Whence, Vergil, too, in the *Eclogues*, joins them both together with two words when he says: "I remember the rhythm; would that I retained the words."[9]

Moreover, just as the second species surpasses the former in antiquity, so does the third surpass the second. There is no doubt that it existed even when letters were not yet invented, inasmuch as it originated, as did the song of birds, at the very creation of man.

Since, therefore, this third species especially befits human nature, those who neglect it and linger continually with the former alone seem to me undeserving of the term "man." The first species was invented not for its own sake, but that it might serve this oldest and by far most important species. It is, therefore, this part of music—the part most fitting to know—that we have undertaken to handle. For its sake the former parts were established; and the knowledge of it alone—because it alone contains the ultimate end of music—renders the musician perfect.

---

[8]Perhaps "tantaritarire" is a reference to the Latin term "taratantara," representing the sound of a tuba, and "tirili" a reference to the German term "tirilieren," representing the chirping of birds. In reference to horn players, "tirili" might well be a kind of trill.

[9]Vergil *Eclogae* 9.45.

AN TERTIA HAEC MUSICAE VOCALIS SPECIES ARTE TRACTARI POSSIT

CAP. III

Sunt nonnulli, qui operam hanc nostram improbant, quod nodum in scirpo (ut aiunt) quaeram, eius rei praecepta tradens, quae praeceptis non contineatur, sed aut libere quomodolibet cantoris arbitrio contingat, aut solo usu percipienda artis opere non indigeat. Quorum opinio si vera sit, operam ego atque oleum perdiderim. Mihi vero non tantum est ocii, ut rebus inanibus nulliusque momenti studere queam; quare antequam operis definitionem aggrediar, falsitatem huius opinionis demonstrandam puto, quae quatuor argumentis niti videtur.

Et primo quidem aiunt solfizationem ad textum cantandum ita se habere ut iuncus ad natandum. Et quia iuncus solus ad natandi artem sufficere videtur, ideo nec in hac parte musices alio praeter solfizationem opus esse ingenio.

Secundo omnes alios musicos, solfizatione recte percepta, verborum cantandorum sibi agilitatem ac dexteritatem usu parasse.

Tertio symphonetarum in componendo libertatem obiiciunt. Quomodo enim aliter, inquiunt, canenda sunt verba, quam secundum intentionem autoris? Ii autem varii variis in locis terrarum extant, nullisque astricti regulis unusquisque pro suo arbitrio quibuslibet sonis quaevis verba applicat. Quod si igitur compositores regulas certas non sequuntur, male cantaturos esse constat, qui contra intentionem compositoris secundum certas regulas, quas ille secutus non sit, verba notis applicare conentur.

CHAPTER 3

WHETHER THIS THIRD SPECIES OF VOCAL MUSIC CAN BE HANDLED BY MEANS OF ART[10]

There are some who object to this work of ours on the ground that I am looking for a knot in a bulrush (as they say),[11] handing down precepts for something that is not bound by precepts but either is done by the free discretion of the singer (howsoever it pleases him) or, since it is perceived by practice alone, does not need the work of art. If their opinion is true, then I have wasted my work and oil. I, however, do not have the leisure to study subjects that are useless and of no importance. Therefore, before I proceed to the definition of my work, I think the falsity of this opinion must be demonstrated, which seems to rest on four arguments.[12]

First, they say that solmization bears the same relation to singing the text as a rush plant does to swimming; and because a rush plant alone seems to suffice for the art of swimming, it follows that neither in this part of music is there work for another talent beside solmization.

Second, they say that all other musicians—when they have a correct understanding of solmization—have acquired their ease and competence in singing the words from practice.

Third, they raise as an objection the freedom of *sinfonistae* in the process of composing. How else, they say, are the words to be sung than according to the intention of the author? Moreover, authors differ among each other and exist in different locales, and bound by no rules, each one of them applies any words to any sounds according to his own discretion. If, therefore, composers do not follow certain rules, it is clear that singers would perform poorly who, contrary to the intention of the composer, attempt to apply the words to the notes according to certain rules he himself did not follow.

---

[10]For the commentary on this chapter, particularly in regard to its structure as a *quaestio*, see Introduction, pp. 20–24. For the general structure of a *quaestio*, see also Introduction, p. 13.

[11]The bulrush, a slender marsh-reed, has no knots or branch nodules. Hence the proverb "looking for a knot in a bulrush" suggests finding difficulties where there are none. The proverb is first mentioned in Ennius *Satirae* 70 and is explained as to its botanical aspects by Isidore of Seville in *Etymologiae sive Origines* 17.9.97.

[12]The following four arguments represent the *videtur quod non* of the *quaestio* as indicated by the title of this chapter.

Quarto non parum illorum opinionem confirmare videtur quod in proximo capitulo diximus hanc cantandi rationem antiquissimam esse, et cum ipsa creatione coepisse, cum nullae adhuc artes inventae essent. Quare primam quidem et secundam musicae vocalis species arte constare non negandum est, haec
5 autem tertia hominibus natura dari videtur. Et cum ars naturam imitetur, videntur priores duae, quae vere artificiales sunt, hanc ut mere naturalem aemulari.

Possem ego horum argumenta etiam silens more Diogenis confutare. Is enim olim, cum Zeno motum nullum esse multis argumentis probaturus con-
10 tenderet, tacitus surrexisse fertur, manifesto in ambulationis motu ipsius argumenta falsa esse demonstrasse. Ita et ego, solis compositis hic regulis, falsa eorum argumenta, qui arte et regulis hanc rem constare negant, confutare possem, maxime cum opinionem meam multi excellentissimi musici probent. Nemo enim fere est, qui non de ea sparsim in diversis locis praecepta dederit.
15 Et inter alios Zarlinus multa huius rei praecepta esse ait, maxime scitu necessaria, quorum ipse pauca quaedam in unum caput collegit. Verba eius in eodem cap. 33 institutionum eius harmonicarum haec sunt: Accioche non intravenghi alcuna confusione nell' accordarle figure alle sillabe delle soggette parole, volendo io levare, s'io potrò, tanto disordine, oltra le date regole in
20 diversi luoghi, che sono molte, accordate alle materie secondo il proposito; porrò hora queste, le quali serviranno non solo al compositore, ma anche al cantore. Hactenus Zarlinus. Possem et plurium aliorum testimonia adducere,

Fourth, their opinion seems to gain not a little strength from what we ourself stated in the previous chapter: this method of singing is very old and began at the moment of creation, when as yet no arts were invented. Therefore, it must not be denied that the first and second species of vocal music consist in art; however, this third species seems given to man by nature. And inasmuch as art imitates nature, the first two species, which are truly artificial, seem to emulate this one as something entirely natural.

I could refute[13] the arguments of these men in the manner of Diogenes by also remaining silent. Once when Zeno was striving with many arguments to prove the non-existence of motion, Diogenes is said to have arisen in silence and by his motion of walking about clearly demonstrated Zeno's arguments to be false.[14] In like manner, I too, by composing only rules here, could refute the false arguments of those who deny that this subject consists in art and rules—especially since many excellent musicians approve my opinion, for there is practically no one who has not given precepts for this subject somewhere or other in diverse places. Zarlino, among others, says that precepts for this subject are many and are especially necessary to know. He has grouped a few of these together in one chapter. These are his words in that same chapter 33 of his *Istitutioni harmoniche*: "In order to avoid any confusion in setting the figures to syllables and words, and desiring to end, if possible, all this disorder, I now add these rules to those I have given in other places appropriate to the subject matter. I hope they will be helpful not only to the composer but also to the singer."[15] So states Zarlino. I could also adduce the testimonies

---

[13]Stoquerus now discusses his own position, cast in the form of a general refutation of the above arguments. As such, his position corresponds to the *sed contra* and the *respondeo* of the *quaestio*. After he states his own position (based on authority and reason), he will refute each of the four arguments separately.

[14]This interchange, most likely involving a follower of Zeno, is attributed to Diogenes the Cynic. See Diogenes Laertius *Vitae* 6.39. Zeno's arguments on immotility are summarized in Aristotle *Physica* 239b5–240a19 (see also 233a13–32).

[15]Zarlino, *L'Istitutioni harmoniche*, pt. 4, chap. 33; however, in none of the editions that I have consulted (Venice, 1558, 1562 [reprint of 1558 ed.], 1573, 1589 [reprint of 1573 ed. with small changes], and 1602 [reprint of 1589 ed.]—see Gioseffo Zarlino, *The Art of Counterpoint: Part Three of Le Istitutioni Harmoniche, 1558*, trans. Guy A. Marco and Claude V. Palisca [New Haven, Conn.: Yale University Press, 1968], p. xxiv) does this passage appear exactly as Stoquerus cites it. Stoquerus substituted "accordarle" and "accordate" respectively for Zarlino's "accommodarle" and "accommodate," which appear in all the editions. Moreover, after "accordarle" Sto-

sed sufficit vel unius domini mei D. Francisci Salinae longe in utraque musices parte praestantissimi autoritas, qui me ad has regulas componendas hortatus est, easque etiam publice Salmanticae doceri et exerceri voluit.

    Sed ne sola autoritate fretus vi potius quam ratione victoriam obtenturus videar, propius nunc ad veritatis argumenta accedam. Solfizationem regulis constare non negant; nonne igitur necessario hinc sequitur eam, quam hic tractamus, musicae partem artis minime esse expertem? Propter quod enim unumquodque tale est, illud magis est tale. Inventa autem est solfizatio ut certa verborum canendorum extaret ratio; ergo si solfizatio regulis atque arte perficitur, multo magis haec, cuius causa inventa est, praeceptis continetur. Alioqui sequeretur liberiorem et faciliorem esse verborum cantandorum rationem quam vocum musicalium; quo nihil dici absurdius potest. Accedit huc quod non potest esse minus in abstracto quam in concreto. Sed qui verba canit, solis vocum nominibus, quarum loco verba succedunt, omissis, omnem solfizationis vim ac partem exprimit, nihilque quod in illa observatur negligit. Quare et illius regulas omnes observat, et praeterea alias; alioqui nihil a solfizatione distaret. Solfizatio autem singulis notis suas tribuit voces seu syllabas, nec ulla in his syllabarum quantitas, nec accentus consideratur, nec distinguit figuras plures connexas et colligatas a solutis ac separatim positis, nec veloces a tardioribus.

    Quae et multa alia aliter sese in hac parte habere, suo loco monstrabimus. Sed ne, ut quondam Alexander in nodi Gordiani solutione, rescindere potius

of many others, but the authority of my sole master, Francisco Salinas, most outstanding by far in both parts of music, is sufficient. He encouraged me to compose these rules and wanted them publicly taught and exercised at Salamanca.

But lest I should seem to be on the verge of obtaining victory by authority alone, relying on force rather than reason, let me now more closely approach arguments based on truth. They do not deny that solmization consists in rules. Does it not therefore necessarily follow from this that the part of music we are handling here should by no means be exempt from art? "For that on account of which something is what it is, is that and more."[16] But solmization was invented in order that there should be a certain method for singing the words. Therefore, if solmization is accomplished by rules and art, much more is this third species, for the sake of which solmization was invented, bound by precepts. Otherwise it would follow that the method of singing the words is freer and easier than that of singing the solmization syllables. Nothing could be said more absurdly. In addition, "there cannot be less in the abstract than in the concrete." But one who sings the words—when only the names of the syllables are omitted and the words take their place—expresses the entire force and part of solmization and neglects nothing that is observed in it. Therefore, he observes all the rules of solmization and others as well; otherwise the process would be no different from that of solmization. Solmization grants to each note its own *vox* or syllable, and in these neither the quantity of the syllables nor the accent is considered, nor does solmization distinguish between several figures connected and bound together and those unfastened and put down separately, nor between swift and slower ones.

That these and many other things are different in this part, we will show in their proper place. But lest we seem, like Alexander of yore in the unfasten-

---

querus added "figure," which appears in none of the editions. Most likely Stoquerus added "figure" to supply the referent of "accordarle." Except for these changes, the quotation accords most closely with the 1558 edition (reprint ed., New York: Broude Brothers, 1965), p. 341. The parallel source in the 1589 edition (pp. 440–41) is worded quite differently. This latter consideration would then confirm Lowinsky's dating of the treatise from the early 1570s.

[16]This axiom and the one following are the bases of Stoquerus's arguments from reason. As can be noted in their contexts, they are used as major premises of syllogisms, the method of reasoning Stoquerus uses here to establish his own position. In regard to the axioms themselves, see Introduction, nn. 46 and 47.

eorum argumenta quam solvere videamur, nunc singula eorum argumenta examinabimus, et eorum errores detegemus.

Primumque, cum aiunt solfizationem omnem verborum cantandorum rationem continere, quod subrogatum naturam sapiat eius in cuius locum sub-
5 rogatur, ut in similitudine a iunco allegata ostensum est, ex eoque sequi putant hanc, quod in solfizationis locum succedat, non aliis praeter quam illius uti regulis. Ego vero regulam de subrogato veram tunc esse fateor, cum eadem utrobique est ratio; in diversis autem eandem sequi rationem plane dementis est. Quare si ut in solfizatione sua cuique notarum adderetur syllaba, caete-
10 raque omnia similia essent, non novis opus esset regulis. Sed quia saepe una syllaba pluribus notis subiicitur, nec etiam quaevis syllaba cuilibet notae succedere apte potest, ideo opus est novis praeceptis, quae in hac diversitate quid deceat aperiant.

Secundo, quod vero aiunt plerosque musicos, solfizatione arte percepta,
15 caetera usu apprehendisse, dico non omnes eadem esse naturae foelicitate, maximamque eorum partem verborum applicationem usu aut assequi omnino non posse, aut non pure ac sincere absque omni vitio eam apprehendere; paucis denique illis, qui benigniore natura sint praediti, multo id labore longoque tempore contingere quod praeceptis et cito et facile addiscere potuissent.

20 Tertio, iam quod de compositorum libertate opponunt, dico quamvis non omnes omnes secuti sint regulas, neminem tamen, his omnibus neglectis, quidquam scripsisse; alioqui sequeretur id verbis quibus vellet exprimi omnino non posse. Sunt autem regulae variae: aliae enim necessariae sunt, aliae vero arbitrariae; illas ab omnibus observari dubium non est, has vero
25 quanto magis aut minus observarunt, tanto maiori aut minori cum applausu eorum compositio a vulgi auribus est recepta.

Quarto, respondeo quod sicut loquendi facultas naturalis quidem est, arte autem magis expolitur, ita omnes praedictas species tum ut naturales ac rudes,

ing of the Gordian Knot,[17] to slash through our opponents' arguments rather than unfasten them, we will now examine each of their arguments and expose their errors.[18]

First, they say that solmization contains the entire method for singing the words because "a substitute resembles the nature of that in whose place it is substituted,"[19] as was shown by the comparison drawn from the rush plant. They think it follows from this that because this part takes the place of solmization, it does not use any rules other than those of solmization. I acknowledge that the rule concerning the substitute is valid when the method is the same for both activities; however, to follow the same method in diverse activities is clearly foolish. Therefore, if as in solmization a separate syllable were given to each of the notes and the rest were similar, there would be no work for new rules. But because one syllable is often put under several notes and not just any syllable can aptly succeed to just any note, there is work for new precepts that disclose what is fitting amidst this difference.

Second, they say that most musicians—when they have grasped solmization by art—have apprehended the rest from practice. I say that not all are of the same felicity of nature and that the greatest part of them either are entirely unable to attain the application of words from practice or do not apprehend it clearly and simply and without any defect. And even for those few who are endowed with a kinder nature, they could have learned quickly and easily with precepts what is instead accomplished with much labor and a long time.

Third, they pose the objection concerning composers' freedom. I say that although not all of them have followed all the rules, no one has written anything in complete neglect of them. Otherwise it would follow that such a work could not be wholly expressed with the words he wished. Rules, however, are various; some are necessary, some discretionary. There is no doubt that the necessary rules are observed by all, but in the degree to which they more or less observe the discretionary rules, their composition was received by the public with so much greater or lesser applause.

Fourth, I respond that just as the faculty of speech is indeed natural but more refined by art, so too can all the aforesaid species be considered both as

---

[17]The story of Alexander and the Gordian Knot is found in Plutarch *Vitae*, "Alexander" 18. The saying "to cut the Gordian Knot" suggests any quick and bold solution to a difficult problem.

[18]The four refutations that follow represent the final part of the *quaestio*: Stoquerus's response to the four arguments presented as the negative position at the beginning of this chapter.

[19]For the explanation of this axiom, see Introduction, n. 48.

tum ut artificiales ac politae considerari posse. Nam ut avibus cantus, ita hominibus sonorum ac vocum expressio a natura concessa est. Verborum autem canendorum ratio primo quidem rudior, tanto postea ornatior evasit, quanto ei plus artis a posteris accessit.

5 Quare ita statuendum est, si arte prima vocalis musicae species non careat, plus inesse artis alteri oportere, huic autem tertiae longe plurimum; et si cui prima difficilis videtur, alteram non ea non difficiliorem esse non posse, longe autem difficillimam aestimandam esse hanc tertiam. Difficilius enim finem obtineri constat quam ea, quae eius obtinendi gratia praeparantur. Itaque cum 10 prima species non multo admodum tempore addisci queat, alteram, priore nondum inventa, vix decimo tandem anno a musicae artis studiosis percipi potuisse ⟨Nicolaus⟩ Vicentinus testatur. Manifestum autem est unicuique rei tanto minus inesse artis, quanto facilius efficitur. Quare cum haec illarum finis sit, illisque et tardius et difficilius addiscatur, ab arte abesse dici omnino non 15 potest.

DE MUSICAE VERBALIS DEFINITIONE

CAP. IIII

Parti huic musicae non unum aliquod nomen attributum est, sed ab actione eius prima denominatur, quam Hispani dicunt, cantar la letra; Itali, cantar le 20 parole; Germani, textum canere; sua lingua, den Text singen; Latini, verba canere; Virgilius, Numeros memini; si verba tenerem. Quare hanc musicam verborum seu verbalem appellare licebit, sicut generalem, vocalem. Vox

---

12 Nicolaus]Petrus (*fortasse* Pater) M ‖

natural and unformed and as artificial and refined. Just as song was granted to birds by nature, so too was the expression of sounds and syllables granted to man. The method of singing the words, however, was at first quite unformed but later became more ornate as more art was added to it by later generations.

Therefore, it must be established that if the first species of vocal music does not lack art, there must be more art in the second and most by far in the third; and if the first species seems difficult to someone, the second species cannot but be more so, and this third species must be reckoned as by far the most difficult. For it is clear that the end is obtained with more difficulty than anything preparatory to obtaining it. In consequence, although the first species can be learned in a relatively brief time, the second species, were the first not yet invented, could scarcely have been grasped by students of the art of music by their tenth year—to this Nicola Vicentino attests.[20] Moreover, it is plain that the less art there is in anything, the more easily it is brought about. Therefore, since this third species is the end of the other two and is learned more slowly and with greater difficulty than they, it cannot be said to be wholly without art.

CHAPTER 4

ON THE DEFINITION OF VERBAL MUSIC[21]

No one name has been attributed to this part of music, rather, it is designated by its primary activity, which the Spaniards say is "cantar la letra"; the Italians, "cantar le parole"; the Germans, "singing the text" or, in their language, "den Text singen"; and the Romans, "singing the words" (Vergil says: "I remember the rhythm; would that I retained the words"[22]). Therefore, it will be permitted to call this part "music with words," or "verbal music," just as the general division is called "vocal music." For since "vox" also signifies

---

[20]As noted in the apparatus, I have emended "Petrus" as given in the manuscript to "Nicolaus." It is also possible that the scribe wrote "Petrus" instead of "Pater," a title Stoquerus may have used in reference to Vicentino's priesthood. For Vicentino's statement concerning the difficulties of the first and second species of vocal music, see Nicola Vicentino, *L'antica musica ridotta alla moderna prattica* (Rome: Antonio Barre, 1555; facsimile ed., Documenta musicologica, I/17, ed. Edward E. Lowinsky, Kassel: Bärenreiter, 1959), f. 7v.

[21]For the commentary on this chapter, see Introduction, pp. 24–25.

[22]See n. 9 *supra*.

enim, cum et voces musicales significet, merito generalior verbi appellatione censenda est. Grammatici quoque in sua arte verbum voci ut speciem subiiciunt. Itaque non video cur idem nobis in arte nostra concedi nequeat.

    Cum de nomine constet, nunc quid rei sit accipe. Musica verbalis est,
5 quae docet quae syllabae aut verba quibus notarum figuris recte et sine aurium offensione attribui possint. Nam nec omnes notae syllabas admittunt, et saepe imperitiores barbarismum aliaque vitia committunt, quibus mire auditores offenduntur. Sed de illis hic dicendi locus nondum est. Haec autem ideo iam diximus, ut et definitionis sententia perspiceretur, et usus huius artis quodam-
10 modo aperiretur, qui praecipue is est, ut cantor in verbis canendis quid deceat dedeceatque non ignoret.

MUSICAE VERBALIS DIVISIO

CAP. V

    Verbalis musicae partes duae sunt: verba et soni, seu numeri. Haec enim
15 ambo in hac parte necessario requiri, vel ex illo saepius adducto Virgiliano patet, ubi ait: Numeros memini; si verba tenerem. Obiicere autem hic nobis aliquis possit, quod supra sonorum musicam a verbali seiunximus, easque ambas ut distinctas species musicae vocali subiecimus. Sed advertendum quod ibidem diximus caeteras duas species sine hac subsistere non posse,
20 hanc autem sine illis posse. Sola itaque et separatim (in abstracto, ut vocant)

the musical syllables, it should rightly be considered a more general appellation than "verbum." Even the grammarians in their art put "verbum" as a species under "vox."[23] In consequence, I do not see why the same cannot be granted to us in our art.

Since the name of this part is clear, accept now what it is: verbal music is that which teaches what syllables or words can be attributed to which figures of notes rightly and without offense to the ears. Not all notes admit syllables, and the less skilled often commit a barbarism[24] and other faults remarkably offensive to listeners. But it is not yet the place here to say anything about those matters. This much we have said now, however, so that both the meaning of the definition may be perceived and the purpose of this art be disclosed in a certain manner, which is chiefly this: that the singer not be ignorant of what is proper and improper in singing the words.

CHAPTER 5

THE DIVISION OF VERBAL MUSIC[25]

Verbal music has two parts: words and sounds, or rhythm. Both of these are necessarily required in this part, as is evident from that passage frequently adduced from Vergil, where he says, "I remember the rhythm; would that I retained the words."[26] Someone might raise the objection, however, that above we distinguished music with sounds from verbal music and that we put both as distinct species under vocal music.[27] What we said there should, however, be noted: the other two species cannot subsist apart from this second species, but this species can subsist apart from them.[28] Thus, considered alone and separately (in the abstract, as they term it), it constitutes its own

---

[23]Stoquerus's use of "verbum" to mean "word" corresponds to "dictio" in grammatical terminology. See Introduction, n. 49.

[24]Stoquerus is most likely referring here to a wrong accentuation of a word due to a faulty setting of the word to the notes. For an account of barbarisms in general, see Quintilian *De institutione oratoria* 1.5.5–33.

[25]For the commentary on this chapter, see Introduction, pp. 25–26.

[26]See n. 9 *supra*.

[27]Referring to Gaffurius's division of vocal music and also to Stoquerus's amplification immediately following Gaffurius's division. See chap. 2, 104.15–106.6 *supra* (i.e. p. 104, line 15–p. 106, line 6, and similarly hereafter).

[28]See chap. 2, 106.8–10 *supra*.

considerata propriam per se speciem constituit; concreta autem caeteris ut pars subiicitur. Quare nisi mutilam hanc artem propositi simus, non de verbis tantum, sed et de sonis agere cogimur.

Sed quando et solfizationi hanc partem communem esse diximus, de eaque a multis diligentissime est pertractatum, nihil est quod novi de sonis afferre possimus. Quare ne alieno sudore opusculum nostrum auxisse videamur, ad tyrocinii illa principia, quod ad sonos attinet lectorem remittimus, ex quibus omnem sonorum doctrinam iam hauserit necesse est, qui verbali musicae addiscendae incumbit. Nec enim hic nos tyronibus, sed mediocriter exercitatis praecepta damus, ut in 2 cap. praediximus.

Quando autem de cognoscendo vocum musicalium progressu varii modi traduntur, quorum nec ullus est, qui mihi satisfaciat, controversia haec musicorum in re maxime necessaria mihi omnino tollenda videtur. Quare non prius ad alteram partem transibimus, quam variis ipsorum opinionibus seu modis allatis, et rationem reddiderimus, quare illos improbemus, et novum longeque faciliorem eorum loco restituamus.

DE PROGRESSU SEX VOCUM MUSICALIUM

CAP. VI

Modum inquirendarum vocum musicalium alii alium ponunt. Quos ego hactenus vidi, quinque hic aut sex ponam, et examinabo, ut lectores, cum eos apud alios legerint, quid de iis iudicandum sit, ne ignorent.

species in itself. On the other hand, it is put under the other two species as a composite part. Therefore, unless we intend to propose this art as a mutilated one, we are forced to treat not only words but sounds as well.

Since, however, we said that this second part is common also to solmization[29] and since it has been very carefully handled by many, there is nothing new that we can offer concerning sounds. Therefore, lest we should seem to have enlarged our little work with someone else's toil, we refer the reader, in regard to what pertains to sounds, to those principles of initiation from which one who is intent on learning verbal music must necessarily have already drawn the entire doctrine of sounds. The precepts we are giving here are not for initiates but for those already somewhat trained, as we said before in chapter 2.[30]

Since, however, various ways of recognizing the progression of the musical syllables are handed down—none of which satisfies me—I think I must entirely remove this controversy among musicians about so necessary a subject. Therefore, we will not move on to the second part of verbal music until we have imparted their various opinions or ways, and then we will render the reason why we object to them and restore in their place a new and far easier way.

CHAPTER 6

ON THE PROGRESSION OF THE SIX MUSICAL SYLLABLES[31]

Some authors put down one way of investigating the musical syllables, others another. Here I will put down and examine five or six ways that I have heretofore seen, so that when readers read about them elsewhere, they will not be ignorant in their judgment of them.

---

[29]Ibid.

[30]I.e., apropos of Gaffurius's three-fold division of vocal music, one who is ready to sing words to a melody has already passed through the first stage (solmizing a melody) and the second (vocalizing a melody). See n. 27 *supra*.

[31]For the commentary on this chapter, see Introduction, pp. 26–30.

1. Quidam pueris viginti claves introductorii, quam manum vocant, ediscendas proponunt, et secundum illas voces investigari iubent.

2. Alii septem clavium cognitionem sufficere putant, quod idem sit iudicium de octavis, clavesque acutas tanquam perfectiores, omnesque cuiusque cantus tam ascendendo quam descendendo voces continentes eligunt; et qua voce quando utendum sit in earum singulis simul docent. Verbi gratia: in A-la-mi-re primam vocem la esse cantus naturalis, mi b mollis, re ♮ duri; et ita consequenter de caeteris.

3. Nonnulli vero observarunt voces ex earum ordine rectius ac facilius deprehendi quam clavibus inquiri. Itaque putant, si prima vocum, quae est ut, sciatur, caeteras ipso vocum ordine facile patere. Quoniam vero vox ut non uni tantum tribuitur clavi, sed sicut triplex est cantus, ita et triplex hexachordum, et unam ut in tribus diversis clavibus reperiri necesse est; itaque tres tantum claves illas notandas putant, quibus ut continetur, quae sunt C in cantu naturali, F in b molli, G in ♮ duro.

4. Alii non primam hexachordi vocem, sed eam potius inspiciendam esse putant, quae eius mutationem prima inchoet, ut sunt ascendendo re, descen-

1. Some propose for choirboys the memorization of the twenty letters of the *Introductorium*, a group they call the "hand," and they command that the syllables be traced according to those letters.[32]

2. Others think that the knowledge of seven letters is sufficient, because the judgment is the same in regard to their octaves. They select the *claves acutae*[33] as the more perfect letters and as containing all the syllables of each *cantus*, both in ascent and in descent, and they teach at one and the same time when each syllable should be used in each of the letters. For example, in A-la-mi-re, the first syllable, la, belongs to the cantus naturalis, mi to the cantus b mollis, re to the cantus ♮ durus, and so on consequently for the rest.[34]

3. Some, however, have observed that the syllables are more rightly and easily detected by their order than investigated by the letters. In consequence, they think that if the first of the syllables, ut, is known, the others are easily evident from the order itself of the syllables. Moreover, since the syllable ut is granted not to one letter only, but just as the cantus is threefold so too is the hexachord threefold,[35] it is also necessary that the one syllable, ut, be found in three different letters. In consequence, they think only those three letters that contain ut should be noted. These are: C in the cantus naturalis, F in the cantus b mollis, G in the cantus ♮ durus.

4. Others think that the syllable to be inspected is not the first syllable of the hexachord, but rather the first one that begins its mutation, such as re in

---

[32]By *Introductorium* is meant Guido of Arezzo's hexachord system as handed down through the 16th century. The term is employed *passim* by Gaffurius in his *Practica musica*, Bk. I, chaps. 1–4, and by Zarlino in his *Istitutioni harmoniche*, pt. 3, in reference to the series of seven interlocking hexachords distributed along the letters of the Guidonian gamut. For a full account of the *Introductorium* and its contents, see Marco-Palisca, *Art of Counterpoint*, p. 3, n.1; and Claude V. Palisca, "Guido of Arezzo," *New Grove Dictionary of Music and Musicians* 7 (1980): 807. For a full account of the association of Guido with the hand as a learning device, see Oliver B. Ellsworth, *The Berkeley Manuscript*, Greek and Latin Music Theory, vol. 2 (Lincoln: University of Nebraska Press, 1984), p. 33, n.1.

[33]The *claves acutae* are the letters in the middle range of the gamut, extending from A-la-mi-re to G-sol-re-ut. See Introduction, n. 58.

[34]In this method and the one following, cantus is the span of letters (*claves*) along which the hexachord syllables are distributed; according to this span of letters (C–A, F–D, and G–E) the cantus receives its particular character as natural, soft, or hard.

[35]I.e., just as the cantus is natural, soft, or hard, so by association the hexachord of each cantus is natural, soft, or hard.

dendo la; itaque regulas has de trium hexachordorum commixtione tradunt. In cantu naturali, inquiunt, re cantatur in D, la in A. Cum vero de naturali cantu fit transitus ad b mollem, re cantatur in G, la in D. Cum de naturali ad ♮ durum, re in A, et la in E.

5. Quidam, omissa illa triplicis cantus observatione, ne, multis intentis, cantores tardius voces inveniant, cantum duplicem tantum proponunt; et ita aiunt, omnis cantus aut est b mollis, aut ♮ duri, idque statim initio cantilenae ex b scripto vel non scripto apparet. Quare de duplici hoc cantu regulas has proponunt. In cantu b mollis re in D et G, la in D et A cantandum est. In ♮ duro autem re in D et A, la in A et E.

6. Quidam magis memoria locali iuvari pueros arbitrantur. Itaque tenori deditos exercent per clavem ♮ in quarta linea signata in cantu ♮ duro, naturalisque cantilenas eius generis eligunt, donec iis exercitatus puer optime noverit, clavi sic posita, quae vox in quavis linea ac spacio sit cantanda. Deinde sumunt cantilenas, quae clavem ♮ in linea eadem possideant, sed cantus b mollis. Idem demum experiuntur, eadem clavi in media linea posita, in cantu tam b molli quam ♮ duro. Qui vero voci graviori vel acutiori ut alto ⟨aut⟩ discantu se dedunt, eosdem in clavibus illis vocibus propriis exercent.

---

16 demum 'experiuntur' eadem M ‖ 18 *scripsi* ‖

ascent, la in descent. In consequence, they hand down these rules concerning the mingling of the three hexachords: in the cantus naturalis, re, they say, is sung on D, la on A. But when there is a transition from the cantus naturalis to the cantus b mollis, re is sung on G, la on D; and when from the cantus naturalis to the cantus ♮ durus, re on A, and la on E.[36]

5. Some—omitting the observance of the threefold cantus lest singers, with many things to attend to, discover the syllables more slowly—propose only a twofold cantus. And so every cantus, they say, is either b mollis or ♮ durus; and this is immediately apparent at the beginning of a cantilena from the b being written or not written. Therefore, they propose these rules concerning this twofold cantus: in the cantus b mollis, re is to be sung on D and G, la on D and A; in the cantus ♮ durus, re is to be sung on D and A, la on A and E.[37]

6. Some are of the opinion that choirboys are helped more by local memory.[38] In consequence, they exercise those consigned to the tenor range by means of the C clef on the fourth line, signed in the cantus ♮ durus, and select cantilenas of its natural kind until the choirboy is thoroughly trained in them and knows very well—with the clef thus placed—which syllable should be sung on any line and space. Then, they take cantilenas that possess the C clef on the same line, but in the cantus b mollis. Finally, they attempt the same, with the same clef placed on the middle line, in the cantus b mollis and ♮ durus as well. However, they exercise those who consign themselves to a lower or higher range, as for example alto or discant, in the clefs proper to

---

[36] In addition to simplifying the mutation procedure by using only re for ascent and la for descent, this method also simplifies learning the progression of the remaining syllables along the gamut. These remaining syllables merely continue in order from the hexachord of the mutating syllable, re or la.

[37] This method reflects the change occurring in the mid-16th century from the understanding of cantus as spanning six letters to cantus as spanning the letters of the entire gamut. See Introduction, n. 60. The result of this change is the progression of the syllables along two gamuts or cantus. In the cantus mollis, B is sung as fa; in the cantus durus, B is sung as mi. The mutating syllables, however, and the order of the remaining syllables are the same as in the preceding method.

[38] I.e., by learning only the syllables proper to their vocal range or "place."

Et si qui pluribus vocibus delectentur, iis quae claves, quibus cognatae sint, ostendunt, hoc modo:

7. Nuper autem Salmanticae mihi oblatus liber cuiusdam Hispani, qui solam vocem fa inquiri iubet in clavibus B, C, F, hoc modo: primum fa est in F, idque proprie; alterum in B, si sit assignatum; sin minus, in C; reliqua fa in horum octavis statim patent.

8. Ego hunc nondum visum, cum adhuc in Italia versarer, mihi invenisse videbar, quanquam diverso modo. Non enim solum fa simpliciter et per se inquirendum esse putabam, sed ut per id voces re et la statim paterent, in quorum medio vox fa locatur. Nam si fa in linea consistit, in proximis lineis illud re ac la committantur, aut in proximis spaciis, si fa in spacio collocetur.

---

5 proprie]proprio M ||

these ranges. And if there are some who take delight with several ranges, they show them what clefs are related to the ranges, in this way:[39]

7. Recently a book of a certain Spaniard was brought to me at Salamanca. This person commands that only the syllable fa be investigated on the letters B, C, and F, in this manner: the first fa is on F, and this properly. The second fa is on B if B is signed on the staff; if B is not signed, fa is on C. The other fa's are immediately evident in their respective octaves.[40]

8. Although I had not yet seen this latter way, since I was still sojourning in Italy, I seemed to have invented it by myself, although in a different way. I did not think that fa should be investigated simply and in itself but in order that by means of fa, the syllables re and la would be immediately evident, in the middle of which the syllable fa is located. If fa is situated on a line, let the re and la be conjoined on the adjacent lines, or on the adjacent spaces if fa is positioned on a space.[41]

---

[39]The point of this example seems to be that, given the diversity of ranges in each of the three groups, the progression of the syllables (taking cantus as "scale" and the mutation syllables as re and la) within each section is exactly the same. In the first section, for example, the ascending progression of syllables for all three ranges, starting at the bottom line of the staff, is re-mi-fa-sol-re-mi-fa-re-mi. It is difficult to determine, however, how this was applied in practice.

[40]Perhaps the advantage of this method is that the location of fa on its respective letters facilitates the location of ut-re-mi below fa and sol-la above fa. I have not been able to identify this theorist; however, see Introduction, n. 62.

[41]With this method, Stoquerus appears to indicate an easy way of locating the mutation syllables re and la.

THEOREMATA VERUM VOCUM INVESTIGANDARUM MODUM MANIFESTANTIA

CAP. VII

Antequam variis his de modis quid sentiam, quidque erroris habeant explicem, hypotheses quasdam praemittam, quarum certitudine atque ordine lector et ad veritatis contemplationem deducatur, et, iis concessis, statim quid quibusvis opinionibus huic adversantibus respondendum sit perspiciat.

1. Voces musicales sex esse; literas autem clavium, quae his respondent, septem.

2. Literam octavam eandem esse cum prima; idemque de vocibus dicendum esse, tam ascendendo quam descendendo.

3. Ad implendam diapason, nullam quidem literam, sed vocem unam deficere, ut hic patet:

C	D	E	F	G	a	b	c
ut	re	mi	fa	sol	la		ut

4. Hexachordo deesse semiditonum ad implendam diapason.

---

tit.: investigandarum]investigandorum M ‖

CHAPTER 7

THEOREMS SHOWING THE TRUE WAY OF TRACING THE SYLLABLES[42]

Before I explain my opinion of these various ways and what errors they have, I will advance some hypotheses so that by their certitude and order, the reader may be led to a consideration of the truth; and so that if he agrees to them, he may readily perceive the proper response to any opinions opposed to the truth.

1. There are six musical syllables; however, the symbols of the letters[43] that respond to these are seven.

2. The eighth symbol is the same as the first; the same should be said of the syllables in ascent and descent as well.

3. No symbol is missing for completing the octave, but one syllable is, as is evident here:

$$\{ \begin{array}{|c|c|c|c|c|c|c|c|} \hline C & D & E & F & G & a & b & c \\ \hline ut & re & mi & fa & sol & la & & ut \\ \hline \end{array}$$

4. The hexachord lacks a semiditone to complete the octave.[44]

---

[42]For the commentary on this chapter, see Introduction, pp. 30–36.

[43]In the previous chapter and the one following the present chapter, Stoquerus discusses the various methods of determining the progression of the syllables along the gamut with the terms *clavis* and *vox*, which I have translated respectively as "letter" and "syllable." Presenting his own method in this chapter, Stoquerus uses the terms *clavis*, *vox*, and *litera*. In Stoquerus's method, these terms appear to be used as follows. *Clavis* is the general location for a pitch and potential syllable along the gamut in his system. This location is identified by a letter. *Vox* is the syllable corresponding to a *clavis* and indicates both the syllable itself and its intervallic relation to the other syllables progressing along the gamut. *Litera* is the letter itself considered as a character or written symbol. I have accordingly translated *clavis* as "letter," *vox* as "syllable" (thus preserving a consistency with these terms in the other chapters), and *litera* as "symbol" (as used by Stoquerus). Thus, B, for example, is the name of the letter (*clavis*) indicated by the symbol (*litera*) B for the potential syllable (*vox*) fa or mi.

[44]I.e., a semiditone must be added conjunctly to the hexachord in order to complete an octave.

5. Semiditoni duas esse species, alteram cum semitonium graviorem locum occupet, alteram cum acutiorem, et praedictas sex voces constituere hexachordum maius; itaque ipsis necessario aut septimam vocem aut octavam oportere esse fa, ut hexachordo semiditonum accedat. Atque idcirco septimo loco, cui vox ad implendam diapason deest, fa aut mi collocari posse, caeteras autem voces non posse.

6. Clavem septimam, cui inter ut et la constitutae vox deerat, esse B, quae potentia tam mi quam fa possidet, actu autem ex his alteram, quae, si mi sit cantum ab ea, ♮ durum, sin fa, b mollem dici; naturale vero hexachordum, quod inter B et b diapason versatur, ipsum b non attingit.

7. Ordinem vocum certum esse oportere; ideoque semiditonum post hexachordum ad diapason accedentem non posse cantari per voces ascendendo la-mi-ut, vel la-fa-ut, aut contra descendendo. Itaque quot voces tribuuntur literae B, tot hexachorda ab ea ascendendo aut descendendo constitui ultra praedictum hexachordum naturale, quorum exordium sit ut in tribus diversis clavibus: cantus naturalis in C, ♮ duri in G, b mollis in F, quae 3 et in principio cantilenarum signari solet.

8. Sicut ut triplicatur, ita et caeteras voces triplicari; ideoque et unamquamque literam possidere tres voces, praeter tres literas, quod unumquodque hexachordum literam unam non attingit, ut patuit in prima hypothesi. Et cum praedictae literae trium hexachordorum sint C, F, G, dici septimae hypothesis, literas his proxime subiectas ab earundem hexachordo intactas manere; ideoque duas possidere voces, ut sunt B, E, F.

---

13 tribuuntur]tribunt M ||

5. There are two species of the semiditone: one, when the semitone occupies the lower place, the other, when it occupies the higher place. The aforesaid six syllables form the major hexachord;[45] in consequence, either the seventh or the eighth syllable in relation to them must of necessity be fa, so that the semiditone may be added to the hexachord. Accordingly, on the seventh place, which lacks a syllable to complete the octave, fa or mi can be placed, but the other syllables cannot.

6. The seventh letter, which is formed between ut and la and lacks a syllable, is B. It has the power of both mi and fa but in an actual situation may possess only one of these. If it is mi, the cantus from it is said to be ♮ durus; if fa, b mollis. The natural hexachord, which is situated between the octave B-b, does not reach b itself.

7. The order of the syllables must be certain; hence, the semiditone approaching the octave after the hexachord cannot be sung with the syllables la-mi-ut or la-fa-ut in ascent, or contrariwise in descent. In consequence, for as many syllables granted to the symbol B, there are as many hexachords formed from that symbol in ascent or descent beyond the aforesaid natural hexachord. The beginning of these hexachords is ut on three diverse letters: C of the cantus naturalis, G of the cantus ♮ durus, F of the cantus b mollis. These three letters are customarily signed at the beginning of cantilenas.

8. Just as ut is tripled, so too are the other syllables tripled. Hence, each symbol possesses three syllables, except for three symbols, because each hexachord does not reach one symbol, as was evident in the first hypothesis. And since the aforesaid symbols of the three hexachords are C, F, and G (as stated in the seventh hypothesis), the symbols put immediately below these remain untouched by the hexachords of the same symbols C, F, and G, and therefore possess two syllables. These symbols are B, E, and F.

---

[45]The major hexachord (or major sixth) is formed from four whole-tones and one half-tone, as in the progression ut-re-mi-fa-sol-la (as here, in reference to hypothesis 3), or re-mi-fa-sol-re-mi and fa-sol-re-mi-fa-sol. See Stephanus Vanneo, *Recanetum de musica aurea* (Rome: Valerius Doricus, 1533; facsimile ed., Documenta musicologica, I/28, ed. Suzanne Clercx, Kassel: Bärenreiter, 1969), f. 26r.

9. Si descendatur a B-fa et B-mi ad infimam hexachordorum ipsorum vocem, apparere hexachorda, naturale distare ab hexachordo B-fa per diatessaron, et a B-mi per diapente in grave, ut hic videre est:

```
B       fa    mi
a   la  mi    re
g   sol re    ut
f   fa  ut
e   mi
d   re        Diatessaron  Diapente
c   ut
```

Contraque ab eodem B ad naturale ascendendo, distare naturale a B-fa per
5 diapente, et a B-mi per diatessaron; ipsum vero B-mi a B-fa uno tantum loco in acutum distare:

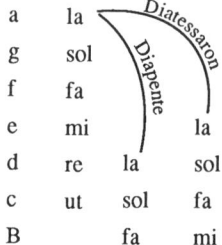

```
a   la              Diatessaron
g   sol       Diapente
f   fa
e   mi              la
d   re   la         sol
c   ut   sol        fa
B        fa         mi
```

10. Sicut hexachordum ab hexachordo distat, ita etiam voces his correspondentes in unaquaque litera a se invicem distare.

11. Quanto unumquodque hexachordum est acutius, tanto vocum eius
10 quamlibet esse inferiorem, et e converso; ideoque cum hexachordum B-mi a B-fa distet in acutum, vox mi a fa in grave distat, ut:

---

arcus et verba om. in sec. schema ‖ B *in sec. schema*]b M ‖ 11 *hic schema om.* M ‖

9. If there is a descent from B-fa and B-mi to the lowest syllable of their hexachords, the hexachords show the natural hexachord as lying a fourth below the B-fa hexachord and a fifth below the B-mi hexachord, as seen here:

		fa	mi
B			
a	la	mi	re
g	sol	re	ut
f	fa	ut	
e	mi		
d	re		
c	ut		

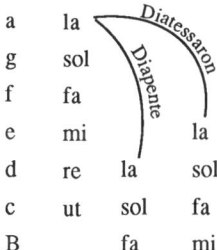

And oppositely, in ascent from that same B to the highest syllable of the natural hexachord, the natural hexachord lies a fifth above the B-fa hexachord and a fourth above the B-mi hexachord; moreover, the B-mi hexachord lies only one place higher than the B-fa hexachord:

a	la		
g	sol		
f	fa		
e	mi		la
d	re	la	sol
c	ut	sol	fa
B		fa	mi

10. Just as one hexachord lies distant from another hexachord, so too do the syllables corresponding to them in each symbol lie distant from one another.

11. By the same degree that each hexachord is higher, any of its syllables is correspondingly lower, and conversely. Thus, since the B-mi hexachord lies above the B-fa hexachord, the syllable mi lies below the syllable fa, as shown here.

12. In literis trium vocum voces proximas esse accidentarias per naturale vero quae ab harum altera quarta, ⟨ab⟩ altera quinta abesse videtur per decimam. Accidentariarum vero superiorem esse B-fa, inferiorem B-mi per undecimam. In duarum autem vocum literis deesse eam, quae non potuisse accedere videtur: ut in E-la-mi non la acutior, in F-fa-ut gravior voce ut, in B-fa-B-mi, quae a fa et mi ab altera quarta, ab altera quinta abesset.

13. Clavibus voces pluras, ordine unam ac certam manifestari; ideoque non claves, sed ordinem in canendo ut faciliorem esse inspiciendum.

14. Ordinem septem vocum septem literis respondentium procedere ascendendo per inferiores duorum hexachordorum literas, descendendo per superiores per septem; et cum septenarius non possit dividi in duas aequas partes, sed in 3 et 4 aequis proximas, ideo et voces ex uno hexachordo 3, ex altero 4 petendas esse, ut septem literarum voces compleantur, hoc modo: ascendendo ut-re-mi, ut-re-mi-fa; descendendo la-sol-fa, la-sol-fa-mi. Et si quatuor praecedant, sequuntur tres, et e contra, ut septenarius impleatur.

---

2 *scripsi* ‖ 2–3 decimam]nonam M ‖ 4 undecimam]decimam M ‖

12. In symbols having three syllables, the closest syllables are accidentals in relation to the natural hexachord,[46] one by the distance of a fourth, the other by the distance of a fifth, as in the tenth hypothesis.[47] The higher of the accidentals is B-fa, the lower, B-mi, as in the eleventh hypothesis. In symbols having two syllables, that syllable is missing which could not be reached: in E-la-mi, there is no syllable higher than la;[48] in F-fa-ut, no syllable lower than the syllable ut; in B-fa-B-mi, no syllable that would be a fourth and a fifth away from fa and mi respectively.

13. Many syllables are shown by the letters; a single and certain syllable is shown by the order of the syllables. Therefore, in singing, it is not the letters but rather the order of the syllables (as easier) that should be inspected.

14. An order of seven syllables corresponding to seven symbols proceeds in ascent along the lower symbols of two hexachords; in descent, along the higher symbols through seven. Since a group of seven cannot be divided into two equal parts, but into three and four, which are proximately equal, three syllables should therefore be sought from one hexachord and four from another so that the syllables may be furnished with seven symbols. Thus in ascent: ut-re-mi, ut-re-mi-fa; in descent: la-sol-fa, la-sol-fa-mi. And if four syllables precede, three follow (and oppositely) so that the group of seven may be completed.

---

[46]In this hypothesis, the "closest syllables" would seem to be those syllables of each symbol that are closest together in their intervallic relation, as for example, sol-fa in C-ut-sol-fa. In turn, these syllables are "accidentals" in respect to their "accidental" hexachords B-fa (B$^\flat$) and B-mi (B$^\sharp$).

[47]Beginning with this hypothesis, Stoquerus's references in M to his previous hypotheses by number in this chapter and the next are consistently less by one. In order to make his original references work, it would be necessary to combine two hypotheses after hypothesis 8 (since the references there are correct), in particular numbers 9 and 10. These, however, are clearly separate in thought and should not be combined. I have accordingly emended each hypothesis number by increasing Stoquerus's references by one number and have noted the original numbers in the apparatus.

[48]I.e., since the soft hexachord has reached its topmost syllable (la) in D-re-la-sol (see the second example in hypothesis 9), there is no further possible syllable from this hexachord that could be included in E-mi-la that would be one degree "higher" than la, as for example la in D-re-la-sol is one degree "higher" than sol, as posited by hypotheses 10 and 11. *Mutatis mutandis*, this same reasoning applies to F-fa-ut and B-fa-B-mi in this hypothesis.

15. Vocum mutationem faciliorem fieri, si iisdem contingat intervallis, quam si variatis; ideoque sicut descendendo fit per tonum in la-sol-fa, la-sol-fa-mi, et in la-sol-fa-mi, la-sol-fa, ita et ascendendo fieri debere. Sed huius contrarium apparet, si principium ab ut sumatur, ut in ut-re-mi, ut-re-mi-fa. Ideoque non per ut, sed per re mutationem ascendendo esse inchoandam, hoc modo: re-mi-fa, re-mi-fa-sol, vel re-mi-fa-sol, re-mi-fa.

16. Mutationem (cum ad naturalem cantum transitur) semper fieri descendendo infra B immediate; ascendendo vero supra B non immediate, quia vox ut inepta est mutationibus per 15, sed, hac sola mediante, in proximi soni voce contingere. Itaque si in B fa cantatur, ab hac inchoando, descendendo fa-la; ascendendo, una voce mediante, fa-sol-re cantari. Sin mi in eadem cantatur, descendendo mi-la; ascendendo mi-fa-re esse canendum.

17. Disdiapason in duo aequa dividi posse. Diapason non posse, sed in diatessaron et diapente dividi. Itaque si usque ad disdiapason ascendatur, mediam mutationem, quae eadem sit cum prima, seu infima, certam esse; intra diapason autem eandem incertam esse. Quod nunc in diatessaron ut re-mi-fa-re, nunc in diapente inchoetur re-mi-fa-sol-re. Itaque deberi diatessaron voces diversas 3: ascendendo re-mi-fa, descendendo la-sol-fa; diapente autem 4, ut

---

9 15]14 M ‖ 15 mediam mutationem]media mutatione M ‖

15. Mutation of syllables is made easier if it takes place on the same intervals rather than on different ones. Hence, just as in descent it is made on a tone in la-sol-fa, la-sol-fa-mi,[49] and in la-sol-fa-mi, la-sol-fa, so too should it be made in ascent. But the opposite of this is shown if the beginning is taken from ut, as in ut-re-mi, ut-re-mi-fa. Hence, in ascent the mutation should begin not on ut but on re, in this way: re-mi-fa, re-mi-fa-sol, or re-mi-fa-sol, re-mi-fa.

16. Mutation (when the transition is to the *cantus naturalis*) always takes place directly below B in descent; however, not directly above B in ascent because the syllable ut is not suitable for mutations by reason of the fifteenth hypothesis, but instead it takes place, with this one syllable intervening, on the syllable of the next sound. In consequence, if fa is sung on B, the descent beginning from this syllable is fa-la; the ascent, with one syllable intervening, is sung fa-sol-re. But if mi is sung on the same B, the descent should be sung mi-la, the ascent, mi-fa-re.

17. The double octave can be divided equally in two; the octave cannot, but rather into a fourth and a fifth. In consequence, if an ascent is made all the way to the double octave, the middle mutation,[50] which is identical with the first or bottom one,[51] is certain. Within the octave, however, the same middle mutation is not certain, because in the case of the fourth, the mutation begins re-mi-fa-re, but in the case of the fifth, re-mi-fa-sol-re. In consequence, the fourth ought to be given three different syllables: re-mi-fa in ascent, la-sol-fa in descent; the fifth, however, four different syllables: re-mi-fa-sol in ascent,

---

[49]The opening statement of this hypothesis does not apply in this descending progression, because the mutation occurs in the area of a half-tone (fa-la from B^b-A or F-E). Since this is the only instance where the statement does not apply, the statement stands as a generally true principle. The idea behind this hypothesis is that the mutation on a whole tone is easier to sing. See Eberhard Preussner, "Solmizationsmethoden in Schulunterricht des 16. und 17. Jahrhunderts," in *Festschrift Fritz Stein*, ed. Hans Hoffmann and Franz Kuehlmann (Braunschweig: Henry Litolff, 1939), pp. 117–18.

[50]The "middle mutation" is the one occurring between the two octaves. I have emended *media mutatione* of M to *mediam mutationem* in order to suit the syntax.

[51]The "first" or "bottom" mutation is the one leading into the first octave from the one preceding it.

ascendendo re-mi-fa-sol, descendendo la-sol-fa-mi. Et cum diapason componatur ex diatessaron et diapente, si tres voces diatessaron praecedant, statim sequi quatuor voces diapente, et hanc rursus tres, et ita deinceps alternatim.

18. B autem scripto, fa cani; eodem non scripto, mi esse canendum, secundum versiculum.

Corollarium

Ex his sequitur, inspecto B, statim apparere septem vocum ordinem, quibus repetitis quandiu velis in infinitum tam descendendo quam ascendendo procedere queas, ut in sequenti figura videre est:

IMPROBATIO VARIORUM MODORUM DE VOCUM PROGRESSU A DIVERSIS AUTORIBUS TRADITORUM; ET ERRORUM, QUOS CONTINENT, DEMONSTRATIO

CAP. VIII

Vero modo, quo vocum progressus intelligitur, tradito, restat ut respondeamus contrariis.

Quod igitur ad primum: insanire mihi videntur, qui singulas singularum vocum claves observari iubent, quando id nec facile, nec cito fieri possit. Quis enim in tanta clavium, earundemque vocum multitudine facile internoscat, quam clavem quaeque signatura obtineat, et qua eiusdem clavis voce pronuntianda sit? Etsi maxime id fieri possit, quomodo tam cito fiet, quam saepe cantandum usu venit, ut cum minimae, semiminimae, et fusae occurrunt? Adde quod nec raro aliter quam vocibus docetur cantandum est, ut re in Gamma ut, etc.

---

6 corollarium]correlarium M ‖ 9 *hic schema om.* M ‖ 16 videntur]videtur M ‖

la-sol-fa-mi in descent. And since the octave is comprised of a fourth and a fifth, if three syllables belonging to the fourth precede, then four syllables belonging to the fifth directly follow; in turn three syllables follow this, and so on, in alternating succession.[52]

18. If B is written, then fa is sung; if B is not written, mi is sung, according to the versicle.[53]

Corollary

It follows from these hypotheses that by inspecting B, the order of seven syllables is immediately manifest. And by repeating them for as long as you wish, you can proceed endlessly in ascent as well as descent, as seen in the following figure:[54]

CHAPTER 8

THE REJECTION OF THE VARIOUS WAYS HANDED DOWN BY DIFFERENT AUTHORS CONCERNING THE PROGRESSION OF THE SYLLABLES, AND THE INDICATION OF THE ERRORS THEY CONTAIN[55]

Now that the true way for understanding the progression of the syllables has been handed down, it remains for us to respond to those ways that are contrary to it.

In regard to the first way, therefore, I think they are insane who command the observance of each letter of each syllable, since this cannot be done easily or quickly. For who, amidst such a profusion of letters and corresponding syllables, can easily determine what letter each note has and with which syllable of that letter it is to be pronounced? And even if this could be done most easily, how could it be done as quickly as singing often requires in practice, as when, for example, minimae, semiminimae, and fusae occur? In addition, the syllable to be sung is not infrequently at variance with what is taught with the syllables, as for example re on Gamma ut, etc.

---

[52]For an example illustrating this hypothesis, see Introduction, p. 35.

[53]I have not been able to locate a versicle stating the exact substance of this hypothesis.

[54]The figure is not given in the manuscript.

[55]For the commentary on this chapter, see Introduction, pp. 36–38.

2. Qui vero septem claves observari iubent, ob eandem clavium ac vocum multitudinem reprehendendi videntur; nec enim intelligunt illi claves a veteribus variis vocibus constantes institutas fuisse non tam ut quid canendum quovis loco esset sciretur, quam quare quidque canendum esset. Quid autem canendum sit, facilius ex vocum ordine, quam ex clavibus perspicitur.

3. Nec immerito reiiciuntur, qui vocem ut observandam docent. Nam praeterquam quod tres claves notari iubent, quibus facilius ac citius unicum B invenitur, cur eam vocem mutationi admiscent, quae mutationem nunquam ingreditur, ut in proximo capite theoremate 15 ostensum est.

4. Nec idcirco ii probandi sunt, qui voces re et la, quae primae mutationem inducunt, observari iubent; nam et voces plures et claves complures notari iubent, quibus facilius unicum B et unica eius vox observatur, quae semper certa est, per theorema ultimum capitis septimi.

5. Quare multo magis reprehensibiles videntur ii, qui praeter haec et varietatem cantuum notari volunt.

6. Longe hic maiorem memoriam et exercitationem requirunt, qui claves, quae variae variis in locis signari solent, considerari mandant, cum tanta res et fundamento prorsus careat, soli fidens locali memoriae.

7. Qui vero fa inspici iubent, in eadem cum superioribus vitia incidunt; nam nec fa illud unicum est, et claves plures. Qua ratione nec ei amplius inquisitioni assentior, quam olim me probasse dixi, cum in Italia adhuc versarer. Facilius enim et velocius unicum B unicamque eius vocem invenias et observes, quam tantam vocum ac clavium multitudinem. Facilius item et citius ex ordine vocum, quam ex clavibus voces patent, ut theoremate 13, cap. 7 ostendimus.

---

5 quam 'ex' clavibus M ‖ 9 15]14 M ‖ 24 13]12 M ‖

2. Those who command that seven letters be observed should be faulted by reason of the same profusion of letters and syllables. They do not understand that the letters consisting of various syllables were established by the ancients not so much to know what syllable should be sung at any particular place as to know why each syllable should be sung there.[56] What should be sung, however, is more easily perceived by the order of the syllables than by the letters.

3. And they are not undeservedly rejected who teach that the syllable ut be observed, for apart from the fact that they command that three letters be noted—a single B is found more easily and quickly than these—why do they involve the syllable with mutation that never begins a mutation, as was shown by theorem 15 in the previous chapter?

4. Nor on that account, however, should they be approved who command that the syllables re and la be observed as the starting syllables of mutation, for they command that more than one syllable be noted, as well as several letters. But the one letter B and its one syllable is observed more easily than these, for it is always certain by reason of the last theorem of the seventh chapter.

5. Much more at fault, then, are they who want, in addition to these letters, a variety of *cantus* to be noted.

6. Those who recommend that the clefs be considered, each of which is usually variously signed on the staff, require much more memory and practice, since such a method has absolutely no foundation, relying as it does on local memory alone.

7. Those, however, who command that fa be inspected fall into the same faults as those above, for that particular fa is not a single one, and its letters are several. For this reason, I do not agree with that fuller investigation that I said I once approved when I was still sojourning in Italy. For you will find and observe a single B and its single syllable more easily and swiftly than such a profusion of syllables and letters. In turn, the syllables are more easily and quickly evident from their order than from the letters, as we showed in theorem 13 of the seventh chapter.

---

[56]See Introduction, n. 63.

VOCUM DIVISIO REPREHENSA

CAP. IX

Omnes fere musici hactenus voces diviserunt in superiores et inferiores: superiores appellantes eas, quibus in descensu cantus utimur; inferiores, qui-
5 bus in ascensu. Nos, ordine situs considerato, vel etiam acumine ac gravitate, alias aliis esse superiores et acutiores, et contra, non negamus. Sin usus varietatem spectes, qua fit ut non iisdem ascendentes utamur quibus descendentes, omnino falsum esse dicimus, quod omnes hactenus caeci caecos sequentes opinati sunt.
10 Nam nec tribus tantum in ascensu vel in descensu utimur, nec illis tribus, quibus asserunt. Nam descendendo tam quatuor, la sol fa mi, quam tribus, la sol fa, utimur; theorema 14, cap. 7. Ascendendo vero non his tribus, ut re mi, sed re mi fa utimur; theorema 15, eodem cap. 7. Nec magis illis tribus utimur, quam quatuor, re mi fa sol; dicto theorema 14, cap. 7. Quare duabus tantum
15 vocibus illa divisio convenire videtur, quam illi omnibus tribuerunt. Descendendo enim solo la, ascendendo vero non nisi re utimur; fa autem tam ascendendo quam descendendo, ut ascendendo, re-mi-fa; descendendo la-sol-fa-mi. Mi vero licet ascendendo semper usu veniat, ut in re-mi-fa, et re-mi-fa-sol; tamen et descendendo eodem nonnunquam utimur, ut in la-sol-fa-mi.
20 Contraque sol descendendo quidem semper, ut in la-sol-fa, et la-sol-fa-mi; nonnunquam vero et ascendendo, ut in re-mi-fa-sol.

Quare constat vocum illam secundum ascensum ac descensum in duo membra divisionem falsissimam esse; veriusque tot membra fieri oportuisse quot erant voces. Utimur enim alia descendendo, ut la, alia ascendendo, ut re,
25 alia neutro modo, uti ut, alia utroque, idque aut pariter, ut fa, aut impariter, et hoc item bifariam, alia enim semper ascendendo utimur, nonnunquam vero

---

12 14]13 M ‖ 13 15]14 M ‖ 14 14]13 M ‖ 17–18 la-sol-fa-mi]mi-la-sol-fa M ‖

CHAPTER 9

THE DIVISION OF THE SYLLABLES FAULTED[57]

Practically all musicians up to now have divided the syllables into higher and lower ones, calling the "higher" ones those we use for song in descent, the "lower" ones those we use in ascent.[58] Taking into consideration the order of this arrangement, or even the height and depth of pitch,[59] we do not deny that some syllables are higher in arrangement and in pitch than others, and the opposite. But if you take into account the variance in practice whereby we do not use those same syllables for ascent and descent, we say that what everyone—like the blind following the blind—has up to now thought is entirely false.

We do not use only three syllables in ascent or in descent, nor do we use those three that they assert. In descent we use four, la-sol-fa-mi, as well as three, la-sol-fa (theorem 14, chapter 7). Moreover, in ascent we do not use these three, ut-re-mi, but rather re-mi-fa (theorem 15, in the same chapter 7). Nor do we use those three more than these four, re-mi-fa-sol (as stated in theorem 14, chapter 7). Therefore, the division they granted to all the syllables seems fitting for only two syllables, for in descent we use only la, in ascent, only re. We use fa, however, in both ascent and descent: in ascent, re-mi-fa; in descent, la-sol-fa-mi. And although mi always comes into practice in ascent, as in re-mi-fa and re-mi-fa-sol, nevertheless, we sometimes also use it in descent, as in la-sol-fa-mi. On the other hand, we always use sol in descent, as in la-sol-fa and la-sol-fa-mi, and sometimes we also use it in ascent, as in re-mi-fa-sol.

Therefore, it is clear that the division of syllables into two members according to ascent and descent is most false. More truly, there should have been as many members as there were syllables. We use one syllable, la, in descent; another syllable, re, in ascent; another syllable, ut, in neither way; another syllable for both, either equally, fa, or unequally; and this in turn we use in two different ways: we always use one syllable, mi, in ascent, and

---

[57]For the commentary on this chapter, see Introduction, pp. 38–40.

[58]See Introduction, n. 65.

[59]"The order of this arrangement" refers to the division of the syllables into two general groups: the three higher or upper syllables of the hexachord, and the three lower syllables. In turn, the syllables of the higher group are higher in pitch (*acumen*) than are the syllables of the lower group. The use of these groups for ascent and descent is explained in the following paragraphs.

etiam descendendo, ut mi, alia contra semper descendendo, nonnunquam etiam ascendendo, ut sol.

    Nec quemquam moveat, quod ut tam ab ascensu quam a descensu exclusimus, quod ea ratione ab omni cantus usu prorsus reiici videatur. Loquimur enim hic de vocum mutatione, qua fit, ut vocum aliae ascensui videantur, aliae descensui aptiores. Cum vero mutatione opus non est, omnis haec vocum differentia tam ab aliis quam a nobis tradita tollitur, omnibusque vocibus aeque et ascendendo et descendendo utimur.

DE ALTERA MUSICAE VERBALIS PARTE. ET UTRUM VERBA SECUNDUM INTENTIONEM SYMPHONISTAE PROFERENDA SINT NECNE

CAP. X

    Hactenus de priori parte musicae verbalis, hoc est, de sonis; nunc de altera agemus, ut quomodo sonis verba applicanda sint cognoscatur. Qua de re, regulas me daturum promisi.

    Sed de his dubitari potest an symphonistae intentionem praecedant, an comitentur vel sequantur. Nam si praecedunt, sequetur plus autoritatis esse regulis hisce, quam ipsi cantilenae autori, quippe qui et ipse his regulis subiectus esset, et eas in componendo sequi cogeretur. Sin autem comitentur, non etiam praecedunt, videtur sola ipsius voluntas pro regula habenda; sicut mal-

---

1–2 descendendo (*sec.*) ... ascendendo]ascendendo ... descendendo *transp.* M ‖ 3–4 exclusimus]excluimus M ‖

sometimes also in descent; but another syllable, sol, we always use in descent, and sometimes also in ascent.

Let it disturb no one that we have excluded ut from ascent as well as from descent, as if on that account it would seem to be altogether rejected from all practice of song. We are talking here about mutation of syllables, whereby some syllables seem more suitable for ascent, some more for descent. But when there is no need for mutation, this entire distinction of syllables handed down by others as well as us is removed, and we use all syllables equally in ascent and in descent.

CHAPTER 10

ON THE SECOND PART OF VERBAL MUSIC AND WHETHER OR NOT THE WORDS SHOULD BE DELIVERED ACCORDING TO THE INTENTION OF THE *SINFONISTA*[60]

Up to now we have treated the first part of verbal music, that is, the part concerning sounds. Now we will treat the second part so that the method of applying words to sounds might be known. Apropos of this, I promised that I would give rules.

In regard to these rules, however, it can be a matter of doubt whether they precede the intention of the *sinfonista* or whether they accompany or follow it.[61] If they precede his intention, it will follow that these rules will have more authority than the author of a cantilena himself, who indeed would himself be subject to these rules and forced to follow them while composing. But if they accompany rather than precede his intention, then it seems his will alone should be acknowledged as rule. Such is the case with bad rulers or tyrants:

---

[60]For the commentary on this chapter, see Introduction, pp. 40–44. Cast in the form of a *quaestio*, this chapter serves as the introductory chapter of "Book II" of the treatise, which concerns the rules of *musica verbalis* (see schema, pp. 14–15). That *musica verbalis* is an art with its own set of rules is the substance of "Book I" of the treatise. In chapter 3, also cast in the form of a *quaestio*, *musica verbalis* is established as an art. The employment of the *quaestio* in these two chapters is significant in that it answers convincingly two important questions challenging, ultimately, the validity of Stoquerus's treatise—the distinctness of *musica verbalis* as an art ("Book I") and the authority of its rules in regard to performance and composition ("Book II").

[61]This paragraph functions as a fuller statement of the *quaestio* and points to the consequences of the positions in regard to the origin of the rules of *musica verbalis*.

orum principum seu tyrannorum non ratio, sed voluntas et effrenata desideria legem constituunt, secundum illud: Sic volo, sic jubeo; sit pro ratione voluntas. Quod si hoc concedimus, concedendum quoque erit regulas de hac re componi non posse. Nam voluntates hominum variae sunt, secundum illud Comici: Quot capita, tot sententiae; frustraque rationem inquiremus in iis, quae, ratione duce, composita non sint. Sin regulas sequi affirmandum est, sicut regulae grammaticae sequuntur autores Latinae linguae, et ex eorum scriptis collectae sunt, sequitur ut quoque ex praecedentis quaestionis affirmatione plus autoritatis esse in symphonetis quam his regulis.

Plerique forte hic dicent eas non praecessisse, sed aut simul extitisse, aut nuper collectas fuisse. Quomodo enim praecessisse dicas, quae nusquam visae fuerunt? Verisimilius autem videtur eas simul cum ipsa compositione extare; atque ita quot cantilenae extant tot cantandi esse regulas ac normas; regulamque regularum esse unam intentionem, voluntatem atque arbitrium autoris, qui cantilenam effinxerit. Ipsa enim cuiusque artificis in sua arte autoritas pro regula ac lege habetur, ut iureconsulti asserunt in l. 7 ff de statu hominum.

Et correlativorum eadem est ratio, ut cantus et cantoris. Qua re non aliter cani a cantore oportet, quam ipsa cantilenae natura postulat. Natura autem

---

2 sit 'pro' ratione M ‖ 3 conce'den'dum M ‖ 4 voluntates]voluntas M ‖

not their reason but their will and unbridled desires constitute the law, according to the statement: "As I wish, so do I command. Let will be regarded as reason."[62] If we concede this, however, it must also be conceded that rules for this subject cannot be composed, for the wills of men are various, according to the statement of the comic poet: "So many heads, so many opinions";[63] and in vain will we search for reason in those things that were not composed under the guidance of reason. But if it is to be affirmed that rules follow the intention of the *sinfonista*, just as grammar rules follow the authors of the Latin language and are collected from their writings, it follows likewise from the affirmation of the preceding question that more authority lies with the *sinfonistae* than with these rules.

Perhaps many will say here that the rules did not precede but either existed simultaneously or were recently collected.[64] For how can you say that they preceded since they have nowhere been seen? Rather, it seems more likely that they exist simultaneously with the composition itself, and thus there are as many rules and norms for singing as there are cantilenas in existence and the rule of rules is the one intention, will, and discretion of the author who fashioned the cantilena. For the authority itself of any artist in his own art is acknowledged as rule and law, as the lawyers assert in law 7 of "On the Condition of Men" from the *Pandectae*.[65]

Moreover, "the basis of correlatives is the same"[66] as that of the song and the singer. Hence, the singer should sing in no other way than the nature of the cantilena demands. But the cantilena's nature is that which was determined

---

[62]Juvenal *Satirae* 6.223.

[63]Terence *Phormio* 454. Cf. Cicero *De finibus* 1.5.15.

[64]This section is the *videtur quod non* of the *quaestio* and advances three positions: (1) rules do not precede compositions, but rather (2) accompany or (3) follow them.

[65]Justinian *Corpus juris civilis: Pandectae* [*Digesta*] 1.5.7. In Stoquerus's citation, *l* is the abbreviation for *lex*, here *lege*. The abbreviation *ff* stands for the Greek letter *pi*, which in turn is the abbreviated reference for the *Pandectae* or *Digesta*, the second major section of the *Corpus juris civilis*. The law (no. 7) as given there guarantees the legal protection of an infant during its period of gestation in its mother's womb. By analogy, Stoquerus seems to imply that a composition during its period of gestation (while it is being composed) in the artist's mind is protected from any extrinsic restrictions (rules).

[66]On this axiom, see Introduction, n. 69. The axiom is used here as the major premise of a syllogism.

illius ea est, quam in ipsa compositione sortita est a compositore. Ideo ipse ille
pro regula et autor regulae vel regularum cantionis suae habendus.

Praeterea, qui conveniunt uni tertio, inter se conveniunt; sed cantor et
symphoneta in cantilena conveniunt, hic scripto seu stylo, ille voce repraesen-
tando; ergo et inter se conveniant necesse est, ut quicquid in componendo
secutus est, et fieri voluit symphoneta, id sequatur quoque et imitetur in
canendo cantor. Qua ratione sequitur nullas regulas extare, sed ipsum symphonetam et compositionem eius, quae scriptis expressa est, loco regulae
habendam esse, ut sicut scriptum est, ita et cantetur.

Sin regulas quasdam esse cantandi contendamus, tamen rationi magis consentaneum est eas sequi compositiones quam antecedere, veluti de grammatica
diximus; quanquam interea minus illis autoritatis est quam grammaticis; illi
enim ut anterioribus metam, quam non transilirent, ponere non potuerunt,
posterioribus tamen componendi rationem ab ipsis praescriptam transgredi
non licet. Hae autem regulae, si maxime modum quendam cantandi ea, quae
hactenus composita sunt, tradere possint, non tamen tanti momenti fore
videantur, ut iis futuri symphonetae astringantur, nec libere quovis modo, ut
qui illos antecesserunt, componere possint. Et si quid in quavis cantilena sive
antiquis sive recentioribus his regulis parum conveniat, id secundum illas
emendatius canere non licere videtur, quando cantores et fidicines et caeteros
sic symphonetas sequi oportet, ut rursus ipsos choraedi sequuntur. Qui hoc
facturus sit, non iam cantoris, sed symphonetae officio fungatur, sicut si actor
in comoedia quidpiam immutet, non actoris, sed poetae munere fungatur, vel
etiam quod iudicium exquisitum diligentis symphonetae praeferendum sit
rapto ac momentaneo cantoris iudicio.

Ego vero his omnibus contrarium sentio, putoque regulas has nec cum
cantilenis simul oriri, nec eas secutas esse, sed ante extitisse quam quicquam
scribi coeperit; ideoque non minus sed etiam plus autoritatis eis deberi quam
regulis grammaticae; ita ut cantori etiam nonnunquam, ne eas transgrediatur,
aliter quam scriptum sit canere liceat. Nam et arte hanc musicae partem contineri, et praeceptis regi dicendum est; quando ipsam musicam artem esse non

---

17 videantur]videatur M ‖ 23 fungatur]fungitur M ‖ 28 deberi]debere M ‖

in the composition itself by the composer. Therefore, he himself takes the place of the rule and is to be acknowledged as the author of the rule or rules of his song.

In addition, "those who relate to a third thing relate also to each other."[67] But the singer and the *sinfonista* relate to the cantilena, the latter by writing or style, the former by vocally reproducing it. Therefore, they must relate to each other so that whatever the *sinfonista* followed in composing and wished to effect, the singer should also follow and imitate in singing. On which account, it follows that no rules exist; rather, the *sinfonista* himself and his composition, which is expressed in writing, are to be acknowledged as taking the place of a rule. So, just as the composition is written, so is it sung.

But if we maintain that there are some rules of singing, it is nevertheless more in agreement with reason that they follow compositions rather than precede them, just as we said of grammar. Yet even in this instance, these rules have less authority than grammar rules. For although grammar rules could not set a boundary for previous writers that they could not overstep, later writers are nevertheless not permitted to transgress the method of composing prescribed by them. Even if these rules could very well hand down some way of singing pieces that have been composed up to now, they would not seem to be of such importance that future *sinfonistae* would be restricted to them and be unable to compose as freely as their predecessors. And if some passage in an old or recent cantilena is less in accord with these rules, it seems impermissible to sing it emended according to them, since singers, lutenists, and others must follow the *sinfonistae*, just as dancers, in turn, follow them. Whoever would do this would no longer function as a singer but as a *sinfonista*, just as an actor altering something in a comedy would function not as an actor but as a poet. In addition, the deliberate judgment of a careful *sinfonista* is to be preferred to the quick and spontaneous judgment of a singer.

I, however, hold an opinion opposite to all these positions and think that these rules neither originate simultaneously with the cantilenas nor follow them, but existed before anything began to be written.[68] Therefore, not less, but more authority ought to be given to them than to rules of grammar, so much so that the singer may even be permitted at times to sing differently from what is written, lest he transgress these rules. For it must be said that this part of music is bound by art and governed by precepts, since we do not deny that music itself is an art. However, "the basis is the same concerning

---

[67]On this axiom, see Introduction, n. 70. This axiom, too, is used as the major premise of a syllogism.

[68]This section is Stoquerus's own position in regard to his rules and functions as the *sed contra* and initial *respondeo* of the *quaestio*.

negamus; eadem autem ratio est de parte, quae de toto, 1., quae de tota, ff, de rei vendicatione. Sin autem partem hanc artis expertem dicemus, sequetur nec musicam recte et simpliciter artem dici posse, sed secundum quid.

Eademque haec ars seu regulae praecesserunt compositores seu cantilenas.
5 Sunt enim sententiae communes natura mentibus omnium insculptae, quibus contingit ut et scriptores diversorum locorum similiter scribant, scriptaque unius a pluribus approbentur. Sicut enim leges illae facile admittuntur, quae regulis seu notitiis honestorum ac turpium naturaliter mentibus insitis omnium ⟨consonant⟩, quaeque illis repugnant, non consensu voluntatum communi,
10 sed aut largitionibus aut poenis ad tempus defenduntur; ita et numerorum et sonorum rationes certique canendi modi et huiusmodi multa mentibus insculpta sunt a natura, quibus quanto quidque magis consonat, tanto maiore cum applausu a pluribus et recipitur, contraque quanto quid ab illis recedit, tanto minus gratum est, aliisque minus ab illis deviantibus postponitur. Hinc
15 fit ut scripta doctorum indoctis praeferantur, et in illis etiam recentiores antiquioribus, quod horum alii aliis ad commune aurium iudicium magis accesserunt, ut suo loco videbitur.

His ita praemissis, facile est errores contrariarum opinionum dignoscere. Non igitur obstat quod hae regulae visae antea non fuerunt. Nam et leges seu
20 praecepta morum et vitae honestae agendae ante Decalogum visae non fuerunt; extiterunt tamen. Itaque non solum Decalogi transgressores a Deo puniuntur,

---

6 contingit]contigit M ‖ 9 *scripsi* ‖

the part as that concerning the whole," as in the law from the *Pandectae* that begins, "That which applies to the whole . . . ," from "On the Claiming of Property."[69] But if we say that this part of music does not involve art, it will follow that music cannot be said to be an art correctly and simply, but rather in respect to something.

Moreover, this same art or rules preceded composers or cantilenas. For there are common phrases inscribed by nature in the minds of all, whereby even writers from diverse places write alike and the writings of one are approved by many. Just as those laws are easily accepted that are consonant[70] with the rules or ideas of the honorable and dishonorable that are naturally inherent in the minds of all—and those that are contrary to those rules or ideas are defended for a time not by the common consent of wills, but by rewards or penalties—so too the methods of both rhythms and sounds and certain ways of singing and many other things of this kind are inscribed in minds by nature, and the more anything is consonant with these, the more it is received with applause by the many; and contrariwise, the more anything departs from these methods, the less pleasing it is and is considered inferior to other things deviating less from these methods. As a result, the writings of the learned are preferred to the unlearned, and even among the learned, the more recent ones are preferred to the older ones because some of them come closer than others to the common judgment of the ears, as will be seen in its proper place.

On the basis of the arguments I have advanced, it is easy to discern the errors of the opposite opinions.[71] That these rules had not been seen before does not therefore present an obstacle. The laws or precepts of customs and living honorably had not been seen before the Decalogue; they nevertheless existed. In consequence, not only are the transgressors of the Decalogue

---

[69]Justinian *Corpus juris civilis: Pandectae* [*Digesta*] 6.1.76. This law (no. 76) assures that the principles that guarantee the claiming of an entire piece of property apply also to the claiming of a portion of the same. By analogy, if music as a whole is an art and governed by rules, then any part of it (*musica verbalis*) is an art and therefore also governed by rules. On the axiom "eadem est de parte, quae de toto," see Introduction, n. 71. Stoquerus is possibly incorporating this axiom to strengthen his reference to the *Pandectae*.

[70]I have inserted *consonant* in the Latin text in order to complete the syntax of the relative clause, which lacks a verb to govern *regulis seu notiis*. By analogy with *consonat* in l. 12 *infra*, *consonant* seems to be a reasonable choice.

[71]Stoquerus now responds to each of the three positions of the *videtur quod non* of the *quaestio*. Accordingly, this section functions as the final part of the *quaestio*.

sed et illi, qui Decalogum antecesserunt, naturalium praeceptorum violatores aeternis poenis subiiciendi a Paulo memorantur ad Rom. 1. Et iureconsulti ius in scriptum et non scriptum, quod consuetudinem nuncupant, dividunt: Institut. de iure naturali gentium et civili. Ita et regulae hae nihil aliud docent nisi quod communi consuetudine observatur et naturali illi aurium iudicio maxime consentit.

Quod ad secundam opinionem attinet, qua ex praescripto cani videtur, ipsiusque scriptoris autoritas, voluntas, et scripta regulae loco esse defenduntur, frustraque alias, quae non sint, regulas quaeri, respondetur ad primum: autoritatem quidem cuiusque artificis pro lege haberi; sed ex eo non sequi alias non extare leges. Imo vel eam ob causam ipsi tantum autoritatis accedit, quod legum ac praeceptorum veritatis seu rectae rationis magis quam quisquam alius artis eius ignarus est observator. Quare plus autoritatis debetur regulis illis naturalibus, quam vel scriptori vel scriptis eius, quando horum autoritas ab illis dependet.

Secundo, non obstat regula de simili correlativorum natura; imo prorsus convenit ut sequatur cantor naturam cantionis, si tamen bona. Sed quae sit illius natura, et an bona necne sit, ideoque sequenda vel corrigenda sit, dubitari potest regularum, quibus ea res docetur, ignaris.

Quod tertio obiicitur, symphonetam et cantorem, si in uno tertio, hoc est, in cantilena, conveniant, inter se convenire oportere, itaque tunc recte canere quemque videri, si intentioni symphonistae quam maxime accedat, et e contra, respondetur: et symphonetam et cantorem debere convenire in quodam tertio, quae sit recta ratio, vera norma ac modus canendi et componendi, a quo si symphonista in cantilena composita recesserit, supplendus est eius defectus a cantore secundum datas regulas, si commode id fieri possit, et sic recte inter se convenient. Est enim cuiusque symphonistae intentio, quam fieri potest, optime componendi; quod si contra faciat, id praeter intentionem eius ex ignorantia regularum accidit. Quare si conveniunt in illo tertio, in quo eos convenire decet, inter se quoque convenient; sin minus, nec inter se convenient, quando conveniunt in eo, in quo convenire minime volunt, contraque ab eo

---

3 quod]quam M ‖ 5 observatur]observatae M ‖

punished by God, but those violators of natural precepts who lived before the Decalogue are also to be subject to eternal penalties, as they are recalled by Paul in the first chapter of his letter to the Romans.[72] Lawyers, too, divide the law into written and unwritten law, which they call "custom" ("On the Natural and Civil Law of Nations" in the *Institutes*[73]). In like manner, these rules teach nothing other than what is observed by common custom and what most conforms to that natural judgment of the ears.

As to what pertains to the second opinion—that singing is done according to prescript; that the authority, will, and writings of the writer himself are defended as taking the place of rule; and that it is useless to look for other rules that do not exist—the following is said in response. First, indeed the authority of any artist is acknowledged as law, but it does not follow from this that other laws do not exist. Rather, the very reason why the artist has such authority is that he observes the laws and precepts of truth or right reason more than anyone else ignorant in his art. Therefore, more authority ought to be given to those natural rules than to the writer or his writings, since their authority derives from these natural rules.

Second, the rule concerning the similar nature of correlatives does not present an obstacle. Rather, it is wholly agreed that the singer follow the nature of the song, provided, however, that its nature is good. But what its nature is and whether or not it is good and therefore to be followed or corrected can be a matter of doubt to those ignorant of the rules by which this matter is taught.

To the third objection—that the *sinfonista* and singer must relate to each other if they relate to a third thing, that is, to the cantilena; and that therefore a singer would sing correctly if he approach as closely as possible the intention of the *sinfonista* (and the opposite)—the following is said in response. Both the *sinfonista* and the singer ought to relate to a third thing, which is right reason, the true norm and way of singing and composing. If the *sinfonista* has diverged from this in his composed cantilena, its deficiency must be supplemented by the singer according to given rules, if it can be done conveniently, and thus they will relate correctly to each other. For the intention of any *sinfonista* is to compose in the best possible manner. But if he does just the opposite, the result is unintentional, owing to ignorance of the rules. Therefore, if they relate to a third thing to which it is proper for them to relate, they will also relate to each other. But if not, then they will not relate to each other, since they are relating to that to which they least wish to relate, and, oppo-

---

[72]Rom. 1.18–32.

[73]Justinian *Corpus juris civilis: Institutiones* 1.2.3. Cf. ibid. 1.2.9.

aberrant, in quo convenire maxime optant. Bonum enim naturaliter omnes desiderant: Arist., 1. Ethico.

Iam qui autoritatem his praeceptis derogant, quod innumeros musicos sequentia nova sint, necdum usu recepta, iis respondemus non esse haec praecepta nova, nec post tot musicos, ut putant, sequi, veluti grammaticis accidit. Aliter enim de linguis ac de musica iudicandum est. Haec enim, ut caeterae mathematicae scientiae, ubique locorum eodem modo se habet; linguae autem, pro varietate locorum ac gentium, variae et pene infinitae sunt; ideoque de iis non secundum unam ac communem quandam rationem regulae fieri possunt, sed quod usu receptum est ab iis, qui grammatici vocantur, annotatur.

Secundo, nihil derogat nobis, quod futuri symphonetae his non astringuntur. Non enim ego quicquam hic novi ac peculiare effingo, cui ipsos astringam, sed primas ipsorum notitias communiter omnibus insitas. Itaque si ab his regulis recessuri sint, non solum non imitaturi sunt optimos scriptores, sed a recta ratione quasi se ipsos abnegantes recessuri sunt.

Tertio, quare nec illud obstat, quod de actoribus comoediarum dictum est, et similibus, quod scilicet non liceat autoris errata corrigere. Nam si id actor facere possit, doctiorque ipso poeta sit, licebit ei tanquam poetae; ita et cantorem interdum symphonetam agere licet, ut evitet enormia vitia, quae cantaturo occurrunt.

Quarto, nec id facere impeditur, quod ex improviso hoc facere non liceat, iudiciumque praemeditatum symphonetae subitis ac temerariis iudiciis praeferendum sit. Quid enim si symphoneta regulas ignoraverit? Etsi enim omnes natura notae sint, aliae tamen aliis notiores sunt. Et omnium scientiarum fere semina nobis a natura indita sunt, quae tamen, nisi usu et meditatione excolantur et exerceantur, non apparent.

Cum igitur aliae aliis notiores sint, uti diximus, iam videamus oportet quid sit quod sciverint, quidque ignoraverint, ut, secundum ea, regularum ordinem distinguamus in notissimas et minus notas, quarum hae arbitrariae sint, illae necessariae.

sitely, they are departing from that to which they most want to relate. For "all naturally desire the good" (Aristotle, first book of the *Nicomachean Ethics*[74]).

We now respond to those who weaken the authority of these precepts on the grounds that they are new, following as they do after countless musicians, and that they have not yet been received into practice. These precepts are not new nor do they follow, as my opponents think, after so many musicians, as happens for example with grammar rules. Languages and music must have different criteria for judgment. Music, like the other mathematical sciences, is the same everywhere, but languages are various and almost infinite, owing to their local and national diversity. Hence, rules for languages cannot be made according to a single and common method. Rather, that which has been received into practice is reported by those who are called grammarians.

Second, that future *sinfonistae* are not restricted by these rules does not weaken our position. I am not fashioning anything new and subjective here so as to restrict them, but rather their own first ideas inherent in all alike. In consequence, if they diverge from these rules, not only will they not imitate the best writers, they will also diverge from right reason, abnegating as it were their innermost selves.

Third, what was said about comic actors and the like—namely, that it is not permissible to correct the writer's errors—does not thereby present an obstacle to our position. If an actor is able to do this and is more learned than the poet himself, he may be permitted to function as the poet. In like manner, the singer is permitted at times to function as the *sinfonista* in order to avoid any egregious faults that occur before singing.

Fourth, neither is the singer hindered from doing this because supposedly he is not permitted to do this on the spot and the deliberate judgment of the *sinfonista* should be preferred to sudden and rash judgments. What if the *sinfonista* was ignorant of the rules? Even though all the rules might be naturally known, some are nevertheless more known than others. And though the seeds of practically all the sciences are implanted in us by nature, they will nevertheless not appear unless they are cultivated and exercised by practice and reflection.

Therefore, since some rules are more known than others, as we have said, we must now see what it is that composers knew and of what they were ignorant, and accordingly separate the order of rules into best-known rules and less-known rules. Of these, the latter are discretionary, the former are necessary.[75]

---

[74]See 1094a1–2; also 1172b9.

[75]This distinction between rules that are necessary and those that are discretionary will be explained more fully in the next chapter.

DE REGULARUM IN NECESSARIAS ET ARBITRARIAS DIVISIONE

CAP. XI

Sicut in homine in quantum homine actionum aliae necessariae sunt, aliae arbitrariae, ita in eodem in quantum musico, quaedam necessario fieri contingit, quaedam vero pro animi arbitrio nonnunquam observari, nonnunquam vero negligi. Cuius rei ratio est quod illarum causa a natura dependet, quae immutari, nisi a Deo, non potest. Harum autem executio imperio subiacet voluntatis, quae libera est. Homo igitur in quantum homo necessario comedit, bibit, dormit, digerit, videt, audit, loquitur; naturae enim haec sunt opera; voluntatis autem et pro illius arbitrio mutabilia sunt hoc vel illud edere, ambulare, loqui, canere. Eodem modo et de homine musico etiam censendum, quaedam enim agere cogitur, quaedam vero nunc agit, nunc omittit.

Sed dicet hic aliquis in homine quidem posse contingere, ut opera quaedam eius necessaria sint, quaedam vero libera; in musica autem id locum non habet, quod ut canere voluntatis est, ita omnis canendi ratio et varietas a voluntate dependere videtur; ideoque nec canendi regulas nec quicquam aliud observatu necessarium in musica occurrere. Verum hoc unico praeceptoris Alexandri responso dilui potest. Jussus enim Alexander citharam tangere, cum dixisset quid referre si aliter tangeret, praeceptor respondisse fertur parum interesse futuro regi, futuro autem musico multum. Ita et nos dicimus

CHAPTER 11

ON THE DIVISION OF THE RULES INTO NECESSARY AND DISCRETIONARY RULES[76]

Just as in man *qua* man, some activities are necessary and some are discretionary, so also in the same man *qua* musician, it happens that some activities take place necessarily whereas others are sometimes observed or sometimes neglected at the discretion of the mind. The reason for this is that the cause of the former activities derives from nature, which cannot be transformed except by God; the execution of the latter, however, is subject to the command of the will, which is free. Man *qua* man, therefore, necessarily eats, drinks, sleeps, digests his food, sees, hears, and speaks, for these are operations of nature. But to eat this or that, to walk, speak, and sing are operations of the will and are changeable at its discretion. The same is to be reckoned of man *qua* musician, for there are some things he is forced to do, but some things he does at one time and omits at another.

But someone will say here that in man it might well happen that some of his operations are necessary and others are free; in music, however, this does not apply, because as singing is an act of the will, so every method and variety of singing seems to derive from the will. Hence, in music there occur neither rules for singing nor anything else of necessary observance. This position, however, can be refuted by the single response of Alexander's teacher: When commanded to play the cithara, Alexander asked what it would matter if he were to play other than instructed. His teacher is said to have replied that it made little difference to a future king, but very much to a future musician.[77] Similarly, we too say that how you sing makes no difference to

---

[76] For the commentary on this chapter, see Introduction, pp. 44–46. It may be recalled here that Stoquerus is basing his division of the rules into necessary and discretionary ones on the division made in the scholastic philosophy of human nature between those acts of man that are done by the instinctual part of his nature (therefore, necessarily) and those that are done by the volitional part of his nature (therefore, discretionarily). By analogy, man as a musician acts instinctually by observing the necessary rules and volitionally by observing the discretionary rules. Stoquerus will delineate further the volitional aspect of the discretionary rules in chapter 18.

[77] This interchange between Alexander the Great and his teacher is reported in Claudius Aelianus *Varia historia* 3.32. Cf. Curtius *Historiae Alexander Magni* 1 (now lost but presented in summary in *History of Alexander*, 2

humanitatis non interesse quomodo cantes, musicae autem permultum. Quare et cum homo in quantum homo canere quovis modo possit, in quantum vero musicus non item, regulis aperiendum est quid futuro musico necessario observandum sit, quidque contra liberum ipsi relinquatur.

Sunt igitur quatuor vel quinque, quae necessario ab omnibus observantur.
1. Ne paucioribus notis plures syllabae annumerentur.
2. Punctum eandem sibi cum nota sua syllabam vendicare.
3. Ligaturae quoque non nisi una syllaba est, quae primae notae attributa, in quasvis producenda est.
4. Pluribus notis in uno eodemque loco positis cuique sua debetur syllaba.
5. Primae notae prima syllaba, ultimae ultima cuiusque sententiae assignanda est.

Hae sunt, quas puto transgredi musico nulli licere, quas, quod explicatione indigent, prius exponendas censeo, quam ad arbitrarias transeam.

---

7 *fortasse* punctus ... vendicat ‖ 8 ligaturae quoque non nisi]ligaturam quoque, cum nisi M ‖

your humanity, but very much to your music. Therefore, since man *qua* man can sing in any way he chooses, but not so *qua* musician, there must be rules to disclose what a future musician must of necessity observe and what, on the other hand, is left free for him.

There are, accordingly, four or five rules that are necessarily observed by all:

1. A larger number of syllables should not be put to a smaller number of notes
2. The punctus claims the same syllable as its note[78]
3. The ligature also has only one syllable, which is attributed to the first note and must be held over however many that remain[79]
4. When several notes are put down in one and the same place, each one ought to be given its own syllable
5. The first syllable must be assigned to the first note of a phrase, the last syllable to the last note.

These are the rules that I think no musician may transgress. Since they need explanation, I reckon that they should be discussed in detail before I pass on to the discretionary rules.

---

vols., trans. John C. Rolfe, Loeb Classical Library [Cambridge: Harvard University Press, 1946], 1:10).

[78]The Latin statement of this rule appears to be indirect discourse with a verb such as *dico* understood. I have indicated an alternate possibility in the apparatus.

[79]The original statement of this rule appears, at first sight, to continue in indirect discourse. This would explain *ligaturam quoque*. If *vendicare* is carried over into this rule, the rule can be translated, at the start at least, as "the ligature also claims the same syllable . . ."; however, in continuation, *cum nisi una syllaba est* is meaningless ("unless when there is one syllable"). It is quite possible that the scribe miscopied *cum nisi* for *non nisi*, which makes sense ("only one syllable"). Indeed, Stoquerus employs this expression in his discussion of the ligature rule in chapter 13 (see 166.4, 9–10, and 11–12 *infra*). Nevertheless, *ligaturam quoque, non nisi una syllaba est* still does not make sense. I have accordingly emended the text into a grammatically independent rule, with *ligaturae* functioning as a dative of possession (or reference) construed with *est*, and *non* replacing *cum* to complete the sense.

EXPLICATIO PRIMAE REGULAE

CAP. XII

Cum praecipue cavendum sit ne pauciores sint notae quam syllabae, tria in hoc consideranda puto.

1. De quibus notis haec regula intelligitur.
2. Quot modis in illud peccetur.
3. Quod inconveniens inde sequatur, si non sit observatum; deinde quid de contrario eius iudicandum sit, cum notae plures sint quam syllabae.

⟨1.⟩ Notae syllabis non omnes aptae videntur, sicut ligaturae ⟨et⟩ puncta. His igitur numerum notarum augeri putandum non est, ut in proximis duabus regulis docetur. Nec observata regula videtur, si, his computatis, tot sint notae quot syllabae. Idem fere de semiminimis, et longe magis de caeteris, quae minoris sunt valoris, intelligendum est. Nam nec hae syllabis semper aptae videntur; sed de his plura suo loco dicemus.

⟨2.⟩ Peccatur in hanc regulam duobus modis; aut enim in cantione vitium est, aut in cantante; in cantione rarius ut in illo:

---

9 *bis scripsi* ‖ 15 *scripsi* ‖

161

CHAPTER 12

THE EXPLANATION OF THE FIRST RULE[80]

Since one must take special precaution that there not be fewer notes than syllables, I think three things should be considered in this regard:[81]
1. What notes the understanding of this rule involves
2. In how many ways one offends against it
3. What problem follows if it is not observed; then, what should be the judgment in regard to its opposite, that is, when there are more notes than syllables.

1. Not all notes seem suitable for syllables, as for example ligatures and puncti. These therefore are not to be considered as increasing the number of notes, as is taught in the next two rules.[82] Nor does this rule seem to be observed if, even with these taken into account, there are as many notes as syllables. The same is to be understood for most semiminimae and, much more so, for notes of smaller value, for neither do these always seem suitable for syllables. We will say more about these, however, in their proper place.[83]

2. One offends against this rule in two ways, for the fault is either in the song or in the singer. Less frequently, the fault is in the song, as in this example:[84]

---

[80]For the commentary on this chapter, see Introduction, pp. 46–47.

[81]This outline of the discussion to follow shows, of course, Stoquerus's use of the scholastic method of division, by which a topic is discussed as to its pertinent aspects (see Introduction, p. 12). Stoquerus will employ similar divisions in his discussions of all his rules.

[82]Chapter 13 will discuss the ligature rule, which prescribes that only one syllable be set to a ligature and that syllable to the first note only; chapter 14 will discuss the rule concerning the punctus, prescribing that the punctus receive the same syllable as the note to which it is attached.

[83]I.e., in the discretionary rules.

[84]The example most likely would have shown syllables set by a composer to notes that could not legitimately take them, such as are mentioned in the preceding paragraph.

Cantoribus autem non raro accidit, ut contra praeceptum ⟨quintum⟩ de quo infra. Plures a principio notas paucioribus syllabis tribuentes, postea deficiant, paucioribusque notis quam syllabis relictis, aut syllabarum aliquot omittere cogantur, aut notas divisione plures facere, aut denique iis notis syllabas
5 adiicere, quibus id satis commode fieri vix potest. Exempla:

⟨3.⟩ Recte igitur hoc praeceptum necessariis annumeravimus, quando neglectum mutilam cantilenam reddit; at non idem de contrario eius dicendum est. Etsi enim paucioribus syllabis plures ascribi notae absque vitio vix queunt, ideoque id ab Adriano eiusque discipulis summe vitetur, antiquiores
10 tamen ab eo non abstinuerunt. Aliter enim de superfluis quam de necessariis iudicandum, nam illa sine corruptione subtrahi, et addi, et auferri possunt, haec non item. Quare haec necessaria adesse oportet, illa necessario tolli non opus est.

---

1 quintum *supplevi* ⟨***⟩ M ‖ 6 *scripsi* ‖

Not infrequently, however, the error lies with the singers, as for example against precept five,[85] which will be discussed below. By granting many notes at the beginning to fewer syllables, they later come up short and, left with fewer notes than syllables, are forced either to omit some syllables or to make more notes by division or, finally, to put syllables to those notes to which this hardly can be done conveniently. Some examples:

3. We have rightly, therefore, put this precept among the necessary ones, since its neglect renders a cantilena severely damaged. The same should not be said, however, of its opposite precept.[86] Even though many notes can hardly be allotted without fault to fewer syllables—and for this reason it was studiously avoided by Adrian Willaert and his disciples—the older composers nevertheless did not refrain from doing so. Unnecessary matters and necessary matters require different judgments: while the former can, without any deleterious effect, be lessened, increased, and even done away with,[87] the latter cannot. Therefore, these necessary precepts must be at hand, but the discretionary ones do not have to be necessarily removed.

---

[85]In the manuscript, a space for the (later) identification of this rule has been provided, as noted in the apparatus. Stoquerus is most likely referring to the fifth necessary rule, which, as he indicates, will be discussed below, that is, in chapter 16. The fifth rule assures the proper distribution of the syllables of a text over all the notes of a phrase. Indeed, the remainder of this paragraph points to a faulty allotment of syllables to notes in a given segment of a composition, and the example, probably a hypothetical one, would have illustrated this.

[86]I.e., that a smaller number of syllables can be set to a larger number of notes. This "rule" can be considered as a general formulation that Stoquerus specifies later in his discretionary rules. Thus, as he discusses in the remainder of this paragraph, even though Willaert and his generation preferred not to do this (they preferred a more syllabic style), the generation of composers before him felt no compulsion to do likewise and freely assigned a few syllables to many notes (they preferred a more melismatic style), a setting of text that had its own problems, of course, but did not render a composition damaged (*mutila*) or result in any deleterious effect (*corruptio*).

[87]Stoquerus is probably referring in general here to the degree of observance given the discretionary (unnecessary) rules by composers of both the older and newer generation. Thus, as the next sentence seems to conclude, all

Accidit autem duplici de causa ut plures quam verba requirunt, notae ascribantur. Aut enim necessitas cantionis vel invitos cogit, aut dulcior harmonia in pluribus notis consistens nunc symphonetam, ut eas scriptis mandet, adducit, nunc cantores, ut ex paucioribus plures efficiant, invitat.

Necessitate cantionis fit ut nonnunquam vel fuga, vel temporis implendi, vel alterius vocis assequendae gratia, notas aliquot praeter verborum necessitatem adiungamus. Iucundioris autem harmoniae causa a symphonistis quidem contingit ut aut gravioris sententiae vel vocis animis magis imprimendae gratia, numerum notarum adeo augeant, ut vel paucioribus syllabis plures notae efferantur, vel etiam verba eadem repeti sit necesse; aut etiam nulla sententiae et verborum ratione innita, ipsa melodia, aliquot ultra numerum syllabarum notis adiectis, longe vel plenior vel auditu gratior reddatur.

Cantoribus vero nunc ut libere fugiant notas, nonnunquam vel plures in pauciores contrahere, vel contra, pauciores in plures dividere concedi posse videtur; partim vero, ut suavior harmonia aures oblectet, notas paucas in longe plurimas minimi valoris discindere, quod Hispani glossare, Itali diminuere, Germani, sumpta metaphora a pictoribus, colorare vocant. Quod et quomodo et ubi fiat interest.

---

13 libere]libet M ||

It happens for two reasons that more notes are allotted than the words require. Either the necessity of the song forces it (though the *sinfonista* and the singers are unwilling), or a sweeter harmony consisting in many notes induces the *sinfonista* to commit them to writing or entices the singers to make more notes from fewer ones.

The necessity of the song—for reasons of imitation[88] or completing a tempus or catching up with another part—requires that we sometimes incorporate a few more notes than the words necessitate. For a more agreeable harmony, however, *sinfonistae* may so increase the number of notes for the purpose of further impressing a weightier phrase or word on the mind that, as a result, either many notes are spread over fewer syllables or it may be necessary for the same words to be repeated. Or, even apart from any intrinsic reason of a phrase and words, the melody itself sounds much fuller and nicer with the addition of more notes than the number of syllables.

So that they might freely provide imitation, singers, too, may at times be allowed either to compress many notes into fewer, or, oppositely, to divide fewer notes into many. On the other hand, so that a more charming harmony might delight the ears, they may be allowed to divide a few notes into a great many more notes of smaller value, a practice that the Spanish call "glossare," the Italians, "diminuere," and the Germans, "colorare"—a metaphor borrowed from painters.[89] How and when this is done is a matter of importance.

---

composers must follow the necessary rules, but the older generation of composers did not have to necessarily avoid setting fewer syllables to many notes, even though (from Stoquerus's vantage point) the newer generation generally preferred not to do so.

[88]"Fuga" seems to be used here as a general term for "imitation," as Lowinsky indicates in his commentary on this rule (see Edward E. Lowinsky, "A Treatise on Text Underlay by a German Disciple of Francisco de Salinas," in *Festschrift Heinrich Besseler*, ed. Ernst H. Meyer [Leipzig: VEB Deutscher Verlag für Musik, 1961], p. 236). In this respect, cf. *fugiant*, 164.13 *infra*.

[89]For a detailed exposition of the terms *glossare*, *diminuere*, and *colorare*, and a collocation of pertinent treatises and musical examples, see Imogene Horsley, "Improvised Embellishment in the Performance of Renaissance Polyphonic Music," *Journal of the American Musicological Society* 4 (1951): 3–19. See also the discussion of Lasso's "Susanne un jour" and the music example (including Giovanni Bassano's ornamentation of the melody) in Gustave Reese, *Music in the Renaissance*, rev. ed. (New York: W. W. Norton, 1959), pp. 393–94 and n. 78a.

DE LIGATURIS

CAP. XIII

Declaranda imprimis quatuor videntur:
1. Cur ligaturis non nisi una syllaba sit tribuenda.
2. An id perpetuo stricte sit observandum.
3. An primae ligaturarum sua semper debeatur syllaba.
4. De pluribus ligaturarum speciebus.

1. Sicut pluribus unisonis et voce continuatis et una aliqua notae figura coniunctis et in unum sonum quodammodo contractis, non nisi unam syllabam attribui oportere in proxima regula diximus, ita et etiam sonis intervallo distantibus ⟨et⟩ certa aliqua figura colligatis, quas ligaturas vocant, non nisi una syllaba assignanda est. Cur autem symphonistae ligaturas instituant, eadem ratione iam indicatum videtur, qua diximus in praecedenti capite, pluribus notis interdum unam syllabam adiici. Si plures syllabas attribuamus, essentiam eius destruamus necesse est, ut non nisi nomine ac figura videatur, re autem ipsa ligatura non sit. Quare eius natura unam tantum syllabam necessario requirit.

2. Nec regulam evertit, quod commissi erroris corrigendi causa nonnunquam ligaturae violenter (ut de simplicibus quoque notis dictum est) a quibusdam dividuntur. Nam quod vi et necessitate cogente accidit, non trahendum est in consequentia.

---

6 primae]prima M || 11 *scripsi* ||

CHAPTER 13

ON LIGATURES[90]

Four things, it seems, should especially be made clear:
1. Why only one syllable should be granted to ligatures
2. Whether this should be strictly observed at all times
3. Whether the first note of ligatures ought always be given its own syllable
4. On the several species of ligatures.

1. Just as we said in the next rule[91] that only one syllable should be assigned to several unisons that are sung without a break, joined together into one figure of a note, and compressed into one sound, so too only one syllable should be allocated to sounds that are distant by an interval and are ligated in a certain figure, which they call ligatures. Why *sinfonistae* establish ligatures seems to be already indicated by the same reason we gave in the preceding chapter: occasionally one syllable is put to several notes.[92] If we assign several syllables to a ligature, we must needs destroy its essence, with the result that it is a ligature in name and figure only but not a ligature in fact. Therefore, by its very nature, a ligature requires by necessity only one syllable.

2. The fact that ligatures are sometimes violently divided by some (as was said also in regard to simple notes[93]) in order to correct an error that has been committed does not overthrow the rule, for what happens at the behest of force and necessity should not be carried over into conclusions.[94]

---

[90]For the commentary on this chapter, see Introduction, pp. 48–50.

[91]I.e., the "next" or second rule, which Stoquerus has already stated (*diximus*) in the order of rules given at the end of chapter 11 and which prescribes that the punctus receive the same syllable as the note to which the punctus is added. See Introduction, n. 80.

[92]See the third section of chapter 12 *supra*, which discusses the situation opposite to that of the first rule, namely, that fewer syllables can be given to several notes.

[93]See 164.14–15 *supra*.

[94]This sentence seems to be a statement regarding legitimate departures from rules in general. Applying it to this rule, Stoquerus is saying that although a ligature must be separated and given more than one syllable because of a notational error by the composer (or scribe), the rule as it stands is valid. Thus, what must be done out of necessity should not be used as a basis for concluding that the rule itself is overthrown. That is, the necessity of not following the rule is extrinsic to the necessity itself of the rule. The rule simply does not apply in this instance.

3. Imo interdum nec primae quidem ligaturarum ulla attribuitur syllaba, ut:

Cuius rei ratio est, quod re ipsa plures esse ligaturae videntur quam figuris exprimuntur. Nam si, maxima omissa, quae rarior, conferamus reliquas tres, ◊ , □ , ◌ , quarum unaquaeque prior esse potest, qualibet ex iisdem
5 sequente, novem combinationes contingent, cum non nisi quinque earum figurae existant, ut in sequenti typo apparet:

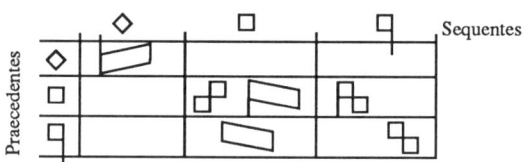

Quare in praecedenti exemplo prima ligaturae figura exprimi non potuit. Verum, cum usu non nisi quinque ligaturarum species receptae sint, non facile admittendae sunt caeterae. Unde longe magis reprehendendi videntur, qui ne
10 eas quidem quae extant figuras in cantilenis inserunt, notisque simplicibus pro ligaturis utuntur. Qua de re accidit ut contra rationem saepe quotlibet et quaslibet notas uni syllabae soli attribuant. Sed hoc nec symphonetis facile est imi-

---

in schema: ▱] ▯ M ||

3. Furthermore, occasionally no syllable at all is assigned to the first note of ligatures, as for example:[95]

The reason for this is that there are more ligatures in fact than are expressed by figures. If, omitting the maxima, which seldom occurs, we combine the remaining three figures, ◇ , ◻ , and ⊐ , each of which can be first, with any one of them following next, nine combinations will result, although only five figures of these exist, as is shown in the following illustration:

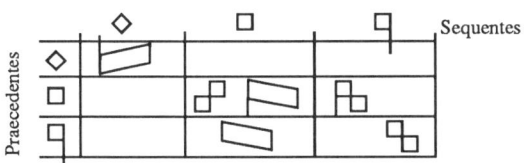

Therefore, in the preceding example, the first note of the ligature could not be expressed by a figure.[96] Indeed, since only five species of ligatures have been received into practice, the rest should not be readily allowed. Even much more to be faulted are those who do not incorporate in their cantilenas even those figures that do exist and use simple notes in place of ligatures. The result is that, contrary to reason, they often assign only one syllable to any number and kind of notes. But *sinfonistae* should not readily imitate this practice; and

---

[95] An example and explanation of this section is presented in the Introduction, pp. 49–50. This section is significant because Stoquerus distinguishes between two kinds of ligatures: (1) notated ligatures (*figurae*) and (2) ligatures in fact or in essence (*re ipsa*), i.e., unnotated ligatures or combinations that do not exist in notated forms (as shown by the blank boxes in the illustration) and yet are intended to carry one syllable.

[96] I.e., the example would show a notated ligature as part of an unnotated or implied ligature, the first note of which carries a syllable that is then continued along the notated ligature. In this instance, the first note of the notated ligature (*prima ligaturae*) cannot be combined with the note carrying the syllable to form an established notated ligature (*figura*).

tandum, et cantoribus quomodo id diiudicent, et quomodo in hac tanta diversitate se gerant, infra suo loco declarabitur.

⟨4.⟩ Sunt et aliae ligaturarum species praeter praedictas novem combinationes, quae singulis figuris non sunt expressae, quod in iis notis consistunt, quae semibrevibus minores sunt, in quibus nonnunquam duae eiusdem generis notae figuris separatae, et simplices re ipsa colligatae, et uni syllabae attributae reperiuntur. Verum hoc, cum non sit proprium, necessariaque ratione careat, locum hic habere non videtur.

DE PUNCTIS

CAP. XIIII

1. Olim pro notis punctum ponebatur.
2. Plura punctorum genera.
3. Ratio cur ⟨nulla⟩ ei ⟨separatim⟩ syllaba sit attribuenda.
4. An contra fieri possit.

---

3 *scripsi* ‖ 13 *bis scripsi* ‖

how singers are to discern this and conduct themselves amidst such diversity will be explained below in its proper place.[97]

4. In addition to the aforesaid nine combinations, there are also other species of ligatures that are not expressed by single figures, because they consist of notes smaller than semibreves. Among these, sometimes two notes of the same class are separate in figures, and although they are simple notes, they are in fact ligated and are found attributed to one syllable. This situation, however, does not seem to have a place in this section, since it is not proper to it and lacks a necessary reason.

CHAPTER 14

ON PUNCTI[98]

1. Formerly, the punctum[99] was put down instead of notes
2. The several classes of puncti
3. The reason why a separate syllable should not be attributed to the punctus[100]
4. Whether the opposite can be done.

---

[97]This will be explained in the discretionary rules, which, as Stoquerus will explain, are based on reasoned judgments in individual instances.

[98]For the commentary on this chapter, see Introduction, pp. 50–52.

[99]In this chapter and in the remainder of the treatise, Stoquerus uses the masculine *punctus* and the neuter *punctum* (both of the second declension) with no apparent distinction (except perhaps here and in its corresponding discussion below). I have not thought it necessary to regularize Stoquerus's usage, for the sole reason—perhaps—of preserving the flavor of his inconsistency. In the translation, however, I have thought it better to be consistent and preserve the distinction between *punctum* as applied to plainchant and *punctus* as applied here to mensural music. Cf., however, Sebald Heyden's usage in *De arte canendi* (Nürnberg: Johannes Petreius, 1540; reprint ed., Monuments of Music and Music Literature in Facsimile, II/139, New York: Broude Brothers, 1969), pp. 50–52; and Johannes Tinctoris's in *Dictionary of Musical Terms [Terminorum musicae diffinitorium]*, translated with Latin text on facing pages by Carl Parrish (New York: The Free Press of Glencoe, 1963), p. 50—indications that this distinction was not always terminologically drawn.

[100]Since the statement as given in the manuscript indicates the opposite of the rule itself, I have emended the text as indicated to conform to Stoquerus's discussion in section 3 *infra* (see in particular 172.11–12).

1. Punctum antiquis pro notis erat, antequam plures notarum figurae invenirentur; una simplici figura puncti, omnes sonos designabant, sicut etiam in cantu plano adhuc fieri videmus. Quare regula haec non nisi in cantu mensurali locum habebat.

5 2. Nec inibi de quovis puncto intelligenda est. Nam cum punctus alius sit perfectionis, alius divisionis, alius alterationis, alius augmentationis, nos de solo augmentationis puncto loquimur, quod ille solus notae vim obtinet. Nec vero de valore eius constat, nisi ex nota, cui apponitur, eius namque dimidiam partem repraesentat; ideo et mediae illi ascribitur, quod media eius parte illam
10 auget.

⟨3.⟩ Quare cum notae, cui adiicitur, pars sit, nulla ei separatim syllaba tribui potest; nam ut in prima regula patuit, parti non alia quam toti syllaba debetur.

⟨4.⟩ Quamvis autem interdum puncta signentur, ubi commodius notae
15 exprimerentur, ut:

Tamen in dubio, cum de hoc errore non satis constat, regula potius sequenda est. Nam duplici de causa punctis in cantionibus utimur, partim textus gratia,

---

2 puncti, [qua *delevi*] omnes M ‖ 11 *scripsi* ‖ 14 *scripsi* ‖

1. Before the several figures of notes were invented, the punctum functioned as notes for the ancients. They designated all sounds by means of the one simple figure of a punctum, just as we see done even now in plainsong. Therefore, this rule had a place only in mensural song.

2. But even in this respect, this rule is not to be understood in regard to any punctus whatsoever. For although the punctus is of various kinds—the *punctus perfectionis, divisionis, alterationis,* and *augmentationis*—we are speaking of the *punctus augmentationis* alone, because it alone obtains the force of a note. Nor, indeed, is its value clear, except from the note to which it is attached, for it represents a half part of the note. Thus the value of a half is allotted to it, which increases the note by its half part.

3. Therefore, since the punctus is a part of the note to which it is added, no syllable should be granted to it separately. For as was evident in the first rule,[101] no syllable other than that given to the whole ought to be given to a part.

4. Occasionally, however, puncti are indicated where notes would be expressed more suitably, as for example:[102]

Nevertheless, in case of doubt, when this error is not sufficiently clear, the rule is rather to be followed. There are two reasons why we use puncti in songs: partly for the sake of the text, partly for the sake of the counterpoint.

---

[101]I.e., in the discussion of this rule as presented in chapter 12, in particular section 2, where Stoquerus points out that singers who wrongly distribute too few syllables to notes at the beginning of a phrase are forced (using one possible—and wrong—solution) to divide the notes at the end in order to accommodate the remaining syllables (see 162.1–5 *supra*). Thus, single notes (wholes) are divided into separate notes (parts) and are wrongly given separate syllables. Stoquerus will use this part-whole argument again in chapter 15 *infra*. The argument is simple: a part cannot be made a whole (by division, as in this rule, in which a whole [a single note] is divided into parts that, by being assigned separate syllables, are in effect made wholes) and a whole cannot be made a part (by compression, as will be seen in the discussion of the fourth rule in chapter 15 *infra*).

[102]The example here would have shown an exceptional instance in which a punctus should be expressed as a separate note in order to correctly accommodate a syllable. See Introduction, n. 87.

partim contrapuncti. Et licet textus causa videatur interdum commodius punctum a nota separari, tamen cavendum est ne altera adhuc maneat ratio, et latens aliqua sub puncto dissonantia clarius per notam expressam aures offendat. Itaque tutius semper in dubio regulam sequemur, nec punctum separatum a nota sono exprimemus.

DE PLURIBUS EODEM LOCO

CAP. XV

1. Convenientia. 2. Differentia. 3. Confirmatio necessitatis. 4. Dubium si loco differenti. 5. Limitatio regulae.

1. Convenit haec regula cum superioribus, quod uni sono vel notae una syllaba tribuenda est, et per consequens, pluribus plures.

⟨2.⟩ Differt autem, quod ibi una nota in plures dividi prohibetur, hic vero plures in unam contrahi. Ut enim ille, qui uni notae plures syllabas adiicit, eam in plures vere dividit, ita etiam, e converso, si pluribus notis unam attribuat syllabam, plures notas in unam contrahit, ut figura quidem sola plures appareant, re autem ipsa omnino plures ⟨una⟩ efficiantur.

3. Necessario autem illis plures syllabae assignantur, quod singulae ut totum considerentur, sin contra fieret, partes esse viderentur, et confusae potius quam distinctae.

---

12 *scripsi* ‖ 16 *scripsi* ‖

Yet even though it might occasionally seem more suitable that a punctus be separated from its note for reasons of text, nevertheless one must take care that the other reason is not still in force and some latent dissonance under the punctus offend the ears by a more clearly expressed note. In consequence, it will always be safer in case of doubt if we follow the rule and not express a punctus separate from its note in sound.

CHAPTER 15

ON SEVERAL NOTES IN THE SAME PLACE[103]

1. Agreement. 2. Difference. 3. Verification of necessity. 4. A question if the notes are in a different place. 5. Limitation of the rule.[104]

1. This rule agrees with the above rules because one syllable should be granted to one sound or note, and consequently, several syllables should be granted to several notes.

2. This rule differs from them, however, because there one note is prohibited from being divided into several notes, whereas here several notes are prohibited from being compressed into one. Just as one who adds several syllables to one note in effect divides it into several notes, so conversely, one who attributes one syllable to several notes compresses several notes into one; so although by figure alone several notes are shown, in fact, however, several notes in all are made one.[105]

3. Moreover, several syllables are necessarily assigned to those notes, for each of the notes would be considered as a whole. But if the opposite is done, they would seem to be parts and blurred together rather than distinct.[106]

---

[103]For the commentary on this chapter, see Introduction, pp. 52–55.

[104]By "limitation" Stoquerus indicates that this rule (and, as will be seen, most of his others as well) has its limits or boundaries. Any exception to a rule, therefore, lies outside the boundaries of a given rule.

[105]Stoquerus seems to be saying here that although the notation shows two or more notes of the same pitch, the setting of only one syllable to them reduces them, in essence, to one note. It is according to this interpretation of this sentence (in particular, from "ut figura . . . .") that I have supplied *una* to Stoquerus's text.

[106]See n. 101 *supra*.

4. Sed videamus utrum idem iuris sit in pluribus notis intervallo distantibus, quod sane rationi consentaneum videtur, eo quod hic totum prohibetur fieri pars, sicut in prima et secunda regula, pars prohibita est fieri totum. Totum vero et pars non modo in uno eodemque loco, ut in prima et tertia, sed
5 et in diversis locis considerantur, sicut in secunda regula in ligaturis. Quare aeque vitiosum videtur, si notas plures eodem in loco, quam si in diversis locis sitas in unam contrahas; ex his enim ligaturam, ex illis unam simplicem efficies. Sed ut fatemur pluribus notis etiam intervallo distantibus plures syllabas tribui debere, ita contra necessario id fieri negamus. Fit enim nonnun-
10 quam ut plures diversae notae colligandae sint, quarum figura non extat, ut supra in de ligaturis diximus.

4. But let us see whether the same thing is a matter of law in regard to several notes distant by an interval. This certainly seems to be in agreement with reason, in that here the whole is prohibited from being made a part, just as in the first and second[107] rule the part was prohibited from being made a whole. Indeed, the whole and the part are considered not only in one and the same place, as in the first and third rules, but also in diverse places, as in the second rule on ligatures.[108] Therefore, it seems equally faulty if you compress into one note several notes situated in the same place or in diverse places.[109] From the latter notes, you will make a ligature, and from the former, a simple note. Just as we acknowledge, however, that several syllables ought to be granted to several notes distant by an interval, so contrariwise, we deny that this should necessarily happen. It sometimes happens that many diverse notes should be ligated for which a figure does not exist, as we said above in the chapter "On Ligatures."[110]

---

[107]The context of this sentence ("here" refers to the rule under discussion, i.e., the fourth rule, regarding successive notes of the same pitch) suggests that the "second" rule refers to the rule concerning the *punctus augmentationis*, which is second in Stoquerus's listing of the rule at the end of chapter 11. In the sentence to follow, Stoquerus refers to the order of his rules according to the order of discussion in chapter 12 (rule 1), chapter 13 (the "second" rule regarding ligatures), and chapter 14 (the "third" rule, regarding the *punctus augmentationis*).

[108]I.e., in all three rules, the part cannot be made a whole (by division).

[109]This situation is the converse of those in the previous sentence, i.e., the whole cannot be made a part (by compression). With the two sentences taken together, Stoquerus argues that just as a notated ligature cannot be divided (a part cannot be made a whole), neither can a series of separate notes of the same or different pitch be combined (a whole cannot be made a part).

[110]See in chapter 13 *supra*, section 3 (168.1–170.2).

5. Nec et haec ipsa, qua de agimus regula, tam necessaria est, ut omni prorsus careat exceptione. Fit enim nonnunquam ut duabus notis eodem loco positis, quarum prior sit semiminima vel et minoris valoris, aut posteriori tantum, aut potius neutri syllaba tribuatur:

Exemplum prioris:

Exemplum posterioris:

Sed hoc accipiendum tunc fieri posse, cum priorem altera similis valoris praecedit, ut ei colligata videatur; ideoque peculiarem syllabam non vendicat; altera autem eam ob causam syllaba destitui potest, quod semiminimam sequitur, de quo infra in regula decima. Quod autem diximus, oportere priorem exhibere ante se alteram similis valoris, id etiam de punctis intelligendum; sufficit enim vel punctum similis valoris antecedere, ut:

5. Nor is this rule that we are treating so necessary that it entirely lacks any exception whatever. It sometimes happens that when two notes are put down in the same place, the first of which is a seminima or a note of smaller value, a syllable is granted to either the second note only or rather to neither note.

Example of the former instance:[111]

Example of the latter instance:

But this should be taken to be possible only when another note of like value precedes the first note so that it seems to be ligated with it and thus it does not claim its own syllable. For the same reason, however, the second note can be left without a syllable because it follows a semiminima, which instance will be discussed below in the tenth rule.[112] Our statement, however, that the first note should display before it another one of like value must also be understood in regard to puncti, for it suffices that just a punctus of like value antecede the first note, as for example:

---

[111] This example would show a syllable given to the second note only. The next example would show a syllable given to neither note. These two examples and the third one intended in this chapter are discussed in the Introduction, pp. 53–55.

[112] The tenth rule (i.e., discretionary rule 5 of the composers of the older generation) is discussed in chapter 24 *infra*. Stoquerus's remark in the present chapter is directed to section 3 of discretionary rule 5, which cautions against assigning a syllable to the first longer note after a series of semiminimae. See Introduction, n. 90.

Sin contra nec nota, nec punctus similis valoris antecedat, solaque semiminima ponatur, syllaba ei necessario secundum praecedentem regulam tribuitur.

DE SYLLABARUM ORDINE CUM NOTARUM ORDINE CONFERENDO

CAP. XVI

1. Divisio syllabarum. 2. Ratio necessitatis. 3. Quid inde colligendum. ⟨4. Limitatio.⟩

1. Syllabarum ut et notarum alia prima, alia media, alia ultima est. Mediae autem syllabae hic accipiendae sunt, quaecumque inter primam et ultimam intercedunt. Itaque quod ad hanc regulam attinet, tam penultimam, quam antepenultimam sub mediis comprehendimus.

2. Necessario autem evenit ut primae notae prima syllaba et sic deinceps reddantur, ob necessitatem tum primae regulae, tum ordinis. Nam secundum primam regulam non sunt pauciores notae quam syllabae, suaque cuivis sylla-

---

6–7 *scripsi* ∥

But if, on the other hand, neither a note nor a punctus of like value antecedes and the semiminima is put down alone, a syllable is granted to it necessarily, according to the preceding rule.[113]

CHAPTER 16

ON COMBINING THE ORDER OF THE SYLLABLES WITH THE ORDER OF THE NOTES[114]

1. The division of syllables. 2. The reason for the necessity. 3. What is thence to be gathered. 4. Limitation.[115]

1. Of syllables as well as notes, some are first, some are middle, and some are last. Middle syllables are here to be taken as whatever ones come between the first and last syllable. In consequence, as far as this rule is concerned, we include under the middle syllables both the penultimate and antepenultimate syllable.

2. That the first syllable is rendered to the first note, and so on, is a necessary result that follows from both the necessity of the first rule and the order of syllables and notes. According to the first rule, there are not fewer notes than syllables and each syllable ought to be given its own and at least one

---

[113]I.e., the rule concerning the *punctus augmentationis* discussed in the preceding chapter (14). The reference is unclear, however, since there seems to be nothing in the discussion of the rule that suggests anything like the situation described here. More likely, the reference is to the present rule itself as it stands "preceding" the discussion of the *limitatio*. Indeed, the conditions presented here are different from the conditions under which the *limitatio* is operative. That is, the semiminima (or a smaller note-value) is preceded by a note of different value or perhaps by no note at all (if, for example, the semiminima is the first note set to a textual unit) or by a punctus of different value. Thus, the semiminima would stand alone and, as the first of two notes of the same pitch, would be given a syllable by reason of the present rule under discussion. In turn, and also by reason of the present rule, the second note would also be given a syllable. See the examples given in the Introduction, p. 55.

[114]For the commentary on this chapter, see Introduction, pp. 55–57.

[115]I have added this fourth topic to conform it to Stoquerus's numbering and discussion of it in the body of this chapter, where he indeed discusses the limitation of the observance of this rule to simple notes. An exception occurs in regard to notated ligatures, in which instance the first and last syllables are set to the first notes of their respective ligatures.

bae nota, et ad minimum una debetur. Quo ita stante, cum notae verba imitentur, necessario sequitur, ut quo ordine scripta sunt verba, eodem eis et notae attribuantur. Itaque ex necessitate primae syllabae prima nota, ultimae ultima, et mediis mediae debentur.

3. Sed cum mediae plures sint, necessariae de singulis regulae tradi non possunt; sed ex arbitrariis regulis, quid in his rationi maxime conveniat, docebimus.

4. De prima quoque et ultima syllabis certa quidem est regula quoad simplices notas, hoc est, si unam aliquam notam primam, unamque ultimam statuas. Cum vero ligaturae accedunt notae, hoc est, quae figura sua exprimitur, eousque primam pertinere putandum est et quousque figura docet; ultimam quoque ibi incipere, ubi figura ligaturae inchoat. In iis autem ligaturis, quae figura non exprimuntur, sed in notis dissolutis et forma discretis consistunt, nihil quod necessario et perpetuo observetur praecipi potest; sed in arbitrariis quid fieri maxime conveniat, aperiemus.

DE USU NECESSARIARUM

CAP. XVII

Usus harum regularum praecipuus est, ne quis incertus in canendo vagetur, rationemque cur sic et non aliter canendum sit ignoret. Ideoque non inutile fore duxi, si, in singularum regularum explicatione, necessitatis causam aperirem, ut regulis canendi modus traderetur; et diligenti earum expositione, similiter quare eo modo canendum esset necessario sequeretur, ita ut qui contra

---

6 conveniat]conveniet M ‖ 22 esset]esse M ‖

note. This being the case, since the notes imitate the words, it necessarily follows that the notes be attributed to the words in the order in which the words are written. In consequence, the first note ought by necessity to be given to the first syllable, the last note to the last syllable, and the middle notes to the middle syllables.

3. But since there are several middle syllables, necessary rules for each one of them cannot be handed down; rather, we will teach from the discretionary rules what is most agreeable with reason for these syllables.

4. In regard to the first and last syllables, the rule is certain insofar as simple notes are concerned, that is, if you set one note to the first syllable and one note to the last syllable. But when the notes are added in ligature (that is, which is expressed by its own figure), one must think that the first syllable extends as far as the figure teaches; the last syllable also starts where the figure of the ligature begins. In regard to those ligatures that are not expressed by a figure but instead consist of notes that are unconnected and discrete in form, nothing, however, can be prescribed that can be necessarily and always observed. Rather, we will show in the discretionary rules what is done most agreeably.

CHAPTER 17

THE PRACTICE OF THE NECESSARY RULES[116]

The practice[117] of these rules is of paramount importance, lest one waver in a state of uncertainty in singing and be ignorant of the reason why singing must be done according to these rules and not otherwise. And so I thought it would be of no little use if in my explanation of each one of the rules, I would disclose the reason for their necessity so that a way of singing would be handed down in the form of rules. By a careful exposition of them, it would likewise necessarily follow why singing must be done in that way so that anyone who would do otherwise could clearly be accused of error. Not only is

---

[116]For the commentary on this chapter, see Introduction, pp. 57–58.

[117]As can be noted in the discussion to follow, Stoquerus's necessary rules provide sure directions for the performer and composer in setting text to melody, and his explanation of each of them in separate chapters provides the reason why they are necessary and, correspondingly, why one should sing or compose according to them. In addition, the rules and his explanations are especially helpful for the performer because they provide the justification for correcting errors that may have been made by the composer or scribe.

ageret plane erroris argui posset. Nec vero recte canendi tantum ratio his regulis continetur, sed et componendi, et errores tam in componendo quam canendo commissos tollendi. Componendi quidem, quia turpe nimium est symphonetae, si adversus musicae principia delinquat. Et si quis dicat has
5 regulas adeo naturales videri, ut vix fieri possit, ut ab iis quisquam in componendo aberret, at nihilominus turpe erit artifici, si artis suae principia ignoret, nec eorum, quae recte agere se putat, rationem cur recte fiant afferre queat.

Quod si autem symphonistae vel librariorum sive imperitia sive incuria aliqua commissa sint vitia, ea a regularum perito facile et apprehendi, et tolli
10 poterunt. Omnia enim haec vitia in duo genera inclusa videntur: quod aut male connectuntur, quae singula per se separatim poni oportebat, aut connectenda quae erant, contra quod eorum natura patitur, distrahuntur.

Vitia quoque, quae in canendo frequenter accidere solent, commode his regulis tolluntur. Nam cum hae regulae observatu plane necessariae sint,
15 sequitur errores adversus eas commissos intolerabiles esse, et omnino corrigendos esse.

Vulgatum autem est contraria contrariis mederi. Et in Ethicis Aristotiles docet prodigum ad liberalitatis virtutem amplectendam nulla via facilius duci et assuefieri, quam si contrario vitio, hoc est, avaritiae, studeat. Versatur autem
20 omne ut scribentis ita et canentis vitium aut in vitiosa connectione, aut in distractione. Quare si quid male connectendo seu colligando peccetur, id sequentium notarum connexarum distractione erit tollendum.

---

1 posset]posse M ‖ 12 quod]quam M | *post* distrahuntur, *spatium est duarum linearum* ‖

the method of correct singing contained in these rules but also those of correct composing and of removing errors that are committed both in composing and in singing. I say, "of correct composing," for it is utterly shameful for a *sinfonista* to err against the principles of music. And if anyone says that these rules seem so natural that it can hardly be possible for anyone to depart from them in composing, it will nonetheless be shameful for an artist to be ignorant of the principles of his art and be unable to present for the things he thinks he is doing correctly the reason why they are done correctly.

If, however, any faults are committed due to lack of skill or carelessness on the part of the *sinfonista* or scribes, these faults will be easily apprehended and removed by one skilled in the rules. All these faults seem to be grouped into two classes: either those things are badly connected that as such should have been set down separately, or those things that should have been connected are disconnected, contrary to what their nature allows.[118]

Faults that are wont to occur frequently in singing are also suitably removed by these rules. Since these rules are clearly necessary in observance, it follows that errors committed against them are unacceptable and should be entirely corrected.

It is a commonplace that "contraries are remedied by contraries."[119] Aristotle teaches in his *Ethics* that by no other path is a wasteful person led more easily and accustomed to embrace the virtue of due generosity than by inclining oneself to the contrary fault: avarice. Now every fault of a writer as well as a singer involves either a faulty connection or disconnection. Therefore, if an offense is due to a bad connection or grouping, it will have to be removed by the disconnection of notes that in sequence are connected.[120]

---

[118]This sentence provides a helpful perspective in which to view the violations of these rules. See Introduction, nn. 100 (as to the first kind of fault) and 101 (as to the second kind of fault).

[119]For this dictum (traceable to Aristotle) and the next reference to Aristotle's treatment of wastefulness (prodigality) in his *Ethica*, see Introduction, nn. 102 and 103. The references function as authoritative supports for Stoquerus's discussion. In regard to the spelling of "Aristotiles," see Prosdocimo de' Beldomandi, *Contrapunctus*, ed. and trans. Jan Herlinger, Greek and Latin Music Theory, vol. 1 (Lincoln: University of Nebraska Press, 1984), p. 27, n. 1.

[120]This sentence might also be translated: "Therefore, if an offense is due to a bad connection or grouping, it will have to be removed by a disconnection of the following connected notes." Interpreted in this way, and in view of the dictum and Aristotle's teaching on wastefulness, it would mean that a (wrong) combining of notes that should be separated (they are given one syllable) is remedied by its contrary: a (wrong) separation of the next note or

DE ARBITRARIIS

CAP. XVIII

Hactenus de regulis necessariis locuti sumus, quae ex ipsa cantus et notarum natura depromptae, mutari non possunt; nunc de arbitrariis dicendum.
5 Non autem ideo arbitrarias has appellamus, quod ab omni prorsus necessitate absint, et ex mero arbitrio et voluntate musicorum dependeant, ut si libeat iis, utantur, sin minus, negligant. Sed arbitrii voce hic fere ut iureconsulti utimur, quibus arbitrium non quodlibet, sed boni viri iudicium est, hoc est, quod cum recta ratione consentiat. Ita et hic arbitrarias vocamus, quae quidem etsi neces-
10 sariae non sint, quod non semper a musicis observatae videntur, arbitrio tamen non prorsus libero sed boni musici relinquuntur. Regulae enim a recta ratione nuncupantur. Ideo sicut necessarias mutari, nisi alia necessitate superveniente, non posse demonstratum est, ita et hae, nisi ratione recta aliud suadente, mutari nequeunt. Sicut enim voluntariae hominis actiones laudabiles

CHAPTER 18

ON THE DISCRETIONARY RULES[121]

Up to now, we have been speaking about the necessary rules, which, drawn as they are from the very nature of song and notes, cannot be changed. Now we must talk about the discretionary rules. We do not, however, call these rules "discretionary," because they are entirely without any necessity and derive from the random discretion and will of musicians to use them if they so please, but if not, to neglect them. Rather, we use the term "discretion" here almost as lawyers do, for whom "discretion" is not just any judgment whatever, but rather the judgment of a good man, that is, a judgment that concurs with right reason.[122] So here too we term those rules "discretionary" that, even though they are not necessary (because they do not always seem to be observed by musicians), are nevertheless left not to entirely free discretion, but rather to that of a good musician. For rules take their name from right reason.[123] Hence, just as it was demonstrated that the necessary rules cannot be changed unless another necessity supersedes them,[124] neither can these rules be changed unless right reason suggests something else. Just as the voluntary actions of man cannot be praiseworthy unless they corre-

---

notes that should be combined (they are given more than one syllable, as for example dividing one note into two parts or splitting a ligature [cf. 160.15–162.5 *supra*). In turn, the experience of having to wrongly separate subsequent notes that have been correctly combined (two notes as parts of one note or the notes of a ligature) because of a previous mistake of wrongly combining will lead one (according to Aristotle's teaching in the *Ethica*) to attend more carefully to the necessary rules, so that he may reach the point of correctly combining and correctly separating.

[121]For the commentary on this chapter, see Introduction, pp. 59–62.

[122]See Introduction, n. 104. For "right reason" as used in scholasticism, see also Introduction, n. 73.

[123]I.e., "regula," etymologically derived from "regere" (to rule or direct), is a directive. Ideally speaking (as Stoquerus here is so doing), a rule, then, is a reflection or statement of reason (*ratio*) that is directed (*recta*) by objective judgments. See Bernard Wuellner, S.J., *A Dictionary of Scholastic Philosophy*, 2d ed. (Milwaukee: Bruce Publishing Company, 1966), s.v. "rule."

[124]Stoquerus here is referring to the limitations or exceptions to the rules. For example, a ligature cannot be broken except in the clear exception of correcting a notational error by a composer or scribe (see 166.18–21).

esse non possunt, nisi cum recta ratione congruant, a qua si discedant, statim virtutis nomine amisso, vitium incurrunt, et publice ab omnibus reprehenduntur; ita et si contra has arbitrarias regulas temere quidquam fiat, vitio non caret. Hae enim cum recta ratione maxime consentiunt, ita ut quicquid contra
5 illas fiat, contra rationem fieri videatur; ideo et ab omnibus musicis observatae, nec facile neglectae inveniuntur, nisi ratione contraria obviante.

Nam et virtutum rectae regulae sunt, contra quas si quis delinquat, illico vitii arguitur; at contra saepe pro loco aut tempore mores mutantur, regulaeque illae virtutum pro variis circumstantiis occurrentibus nonnunquam etiam cum
10 laude negliguntur; ita igitur et de his regulis censendum est eas non nisi raro admodum ob certas circumstantias mutationem admittere, ut suo loco aperiemus. Caeterum, ut planius harum regularum fons et origo cognoscatur, et quare eandem cum necessariis naturam non sapiant, et ab iis separandae sint, paulo rem subtilius considerandam, et exactius distinguendam puto.
15 Dubium igitur omne, quod circa hanc artem versatur, duplici ex causa oriri videtur. Primum, quod verba notis succedere oportet. Secundum, quod non una syllaba uni vel pluribus sonis, nec contra unus sonus uni vel pluribus syllabis, sed plures syllabae pluribus sonis succedunt. Nam si de verbis solis

spond to right reason (and if they depart from it, they immediately lose the name of virtue and take on that of fault and are publicly reprehended by all), so too, whatever is done rashly against these discretionary rules is not without fault. For these rules are so consistent with right reason that whatever is done against them seems to be done against reason. And so, even these rules are observed by all musicians and are not found to be easily neglected unless an opposite reason intervenes.

Virtues have right rules, and anyone who acts against them is straightway accused of fault. According to time and place, however, customs often change and those rules of virtues are sometimes neglected—even praiseworthily—because varying circumstances occur. Even these rules, therefore, must be reckoned as admitting of change, but only rarely because of certain circumstances, as we shall disclose in its proper place. To continue, in order that the source and origin of these rules might be more distinctly known, and why they do not betray the same nature as the necessary rules and should be separated from them, I think our subject should be considered a little more carefully and distinguished more finely.[125]

Every problem, then, that involves this art seems to arise from two reasons. First, the words must go with the notes; second, one syllable does not go with one or several sounds nor, on the other hand, does one sound go with one or several syllables, but rather several syllables go with several sounds. If it were a matter of treating the words alone, the precepts of gram-

---

[125]As can be noted in the discussion that follows, Stoquerus uncovers the origin of the discretionary rules by the scholastic method of distinction by dichotomization. Their separation from the necessary rules may be set out in the following outline (with the necessary rules indicated in parenthesis) that represents a slight enlargement of the schema as given in the Introduction, p. 61:

Words and notes proceed together:
    Equal number of notes and syllables   (5)
    Unequal number of notes and syllables
        Fewer notes than syllables   (1)
        More notes than syllables
            Notes of the same pitch
                A note and its punctus   (3)
                Two (or more) separate notes   (4)
            Notes of different pitch
                In notated ligature   (2)
                In implied ligature   (discretionary rules)
                      Based on reason
                      Shown by authority

ageretur, grammaticae praecepta lectori sufficerent; sin de sonis tantum, solfizationis quoque praecepta cantorem ambigere nihil sinerent. Sin his similiter concurrentibus, unum uni, vel unum pluribus ex aequo tribuendum esset, dubitari non posset quid et quantum cuique esset applicandum; sed cum pluribus sonis plures syllabae numero inaequales tribuendae sint, ambigi necesse est quid cui et quantum tribuendum sit. Quorum illud in posteriori regularum necessariarum explicatum est, hoc vero in reliquis quatuor ex parte declaratum est, sed pluribus adhuc indiget.

Nam si plures syllabae et notae in cantionibus numero pares concurrerent, nullum praeter illud, quod ultima regula dissolvi diximus, dubium oriri posset. Sed quia inaequales numero concurrunt, dubium aut circa defectum notarum, aut circa earum supra numerum syllabarum excessum oritur. Circa defectum cavetur regula prima; reliquae igitur omnes regulae, tam tres illae, quae sequentur, necessariae, quam eae, de quibus acturi nunc sumus, arbitrariae, circa notarum excessum versantur, quando uni syllabae plures soni addicti sunt. Illi igitur soni aut aequales seu unisoni erunt, aut intervallo distantes; in unisonis vero alterum sonum aut nota, aut puncto exprimi necesse est. Certum est igitur, quod si puncto notetur, eandem cum nota sua, cui punctus appositus reperitur, syllabam sortitur, per tertiam. Sin utrique, aut plures unisoni notarum figuris signantur, unicuique propria debetur syllaba, per quartam. Si tandem illi soni intervallo distant, tunc si ligaturarum forma expressi sint, regulam secundam necessariarum sequemur. At si ligaturarum figura, qua dignoscantur, non extat, eodemque modo colligandi notantur, quo illi, qui singuli singulis syllabis adduntur, nihil fere est quod necessario sequendum demonstrari queat. Opus igitur est novis regulis, quibus aperiatur quid maxime verisimile et probabile sit, quod ab omnibus observetur.

Constat igitur arbitrarias regulas versari circa cognitionem earum notarum, quae, plures cum sint, nec ligaturae forma signantur, uni tamen syllabae, perinde ut illae, sunt attribuendae. Quare recte diximus supra in de ligaturis, ligaturarum alias esse et figura et re simul, alias re tantum, quarum illae sensu

---

15 versantur]versatur M ‖ 17 puncto]puncta M ‖

mar would suffice for the reader; and if it were a matter of treating only the sounds, the precepts of solmization would leave the singer no room for uncertainty. But if, when the words and sounds proceed in similar fashion, one had to be granted to one or, equally, one to many, there could be no doubt as to what and how much should be applied to each. But when several syllables, unequal in number, are to be granted to several sounds, it is necessarily uncertain what is to be granted to what and how much. Of these situations, the former was explained in the last of the necessary rules, and the latter was explained in part in the other four rules. Yet, there is still a need for several rules.

If several syllables and notes proceeded in matching number in songs, no problem could arise other than that which we said was solved in the last rule. But since they proceed in unequal number, a problem arises either around a deficiency of notes or around a surplus of them beyond the number of syllables. A deficiency of notes is guarded against by the first rule; all the remaining rules, therefore—both those three necessary rules that will follow[126] as well as those discretionary rules that we will soon treat—involve a surplus of notes, when several sounds are given to one syllable. Those sounds will either be equal or unisons, or distant by an interval. In regard to unisons, the second sound must be expressed by either a note or a punctus. It is certain, therefore, that if a punctus is noted, it is allotted the same syllable as the note to which the punctus is found to be attached, according to the third rule. But if both or several unisons are indicated by the figures of notes, each unison ought to be given its own syllable, according to the fourth rule. And finally, if these sounds are distant by an interval and if they are expressed by the form of ligatures, we will follow the second necessary rule. But if a figure of ligatures by which they might be recognized does not exist and they are noted for ligating in the same way as those individual sounds that are given to individual syllables, there is almost nothing that can be demonstrated that must necessarily be followed. There is work, therefore, for new rules by which it may be shown what is most likely and approvable, which may be observed by all.

It is clear, then, that the discretionary rules concern the knowledge of those notes that, although they are many, are not indicated by the form of a ligature but nevertheless are to be attributed to one syllable, just as are ligatures. Therefore, we rightly stated above in the chapter "On Ligatures" that some ligatures are such both in figure and in fact and others are such only in

---

[126]I.e., necessary rules 3, 4, and 2 cited next in this same paragraph.

patent, hae ratione inquirendae sunt; et de illis in secunda regula necessariarum actum est, de his nunc agendum erit; nec hae ipsa naturae necessitate, sed ratione et autoritate nituntur. Quare sicut in illis singulis necessitatem demonstravimus, ita in his rationem assignabimus quare plures aliquot notae simul colligatae vel sint, vel non sint.

Autoritate autem exemplorum id ostendi non est necesse; nam si unum aliquod exemplum clari autoris adducam id quod semel factum probatur, in omnibus et semper ita se habere non sequitur; sin infinita, quae extant, exempla ascriberem, opus nimium cresceret. Quare cum exempla passim obvia sint, nullis hic nisi declarationis causa exemplis utemur. In fine autem praxim regularum in paucis cantilenis aperiemus, quibus tyrones instituti, facile ipsi exempla colligere, et similiter examinare poterunt. Quare continget, ut brevi omnium cantandorum et modum et rationem perdiscant.

DE REGULIS ANTIQUORUM

CAP. XIX

Arbitrariae regulae probabiles quoque et verisimiles dici possunt, quod, ut diximus, recte rationi congruentes, ad veritatem proxime accedant; sed et artificiales nominari recte possunt, contraque superiores naturales, quod illae natura notae vel indoctis patere videantur, hae autem rudes quidem et amusos latere possint; illae enim etiam sensui sese offerunt, hae autem comprehenduntur ratione, qua maxime praediti ingeniosi homines et huius artis periti in eas

fact. The former of these are evident by perception; the latter must be investigated by reason. The former were treated in the second necessary rule; the latter will now have to be treated. These are not based on the necessity itself of nature but rather on reason and authority. Therefore, just as we demonstrated the necessity in the former rules taken individually, so too in the latter rules we will assign a reason why some groups of notes are or are not ligated together.

It is not necessary, however, that this be shown by the authority of examples, for if I adduce just one example of a famous author that proves something was done once, it does not follow that such is the case always and in all situations. But if I were to insert the infinite examples that exist, this work would become excessively large. Therefore, since examples are readily available here and there, we will use no examples here except for the sake of clarification. At the end, however, we will disclose the practice of the rules in a few cantilenas.[127] Instructed by these examples, initiates will easily be able to collect examples on their own and likewise examine them. Therefore, it will happen that in a short time they will learn thoroughly the way and reason of singing everything.

CHAPTER 19

ON THE RULES OF THE OLDER COMPOSERS[128]

The discretionary rules can be said to be approvable and also likely, because, as we have said, in their correct correspondence with reason, they closely approach the truth.[129] They can, however, also rightly be named "artificial," in contrast to the above "natural" rules, because those rules are known by nature and seem to be evident even to the untaught, while these could escape the unformed and unmusical. The former present themselves to perception, while the latter are grasped by reason. Men talented and skilled in their art, because they are outstandingly gifted with reason, have evidently

---

[127]This section is of course missing from the treatise as it stands. In the event that the entire autograph will someday be discovered, this section will be one of the most valuable items of interest.

[128]For the commentary on this chapter, see Introduction, pp. 62–66.

[129]Cf. 186.7–188.6 and 190.25–26 *supra*.

omnes consensisse videntur. Itaque non immerito et ab artificibus artificiales dicentur, et secundum illos dividentur. Quare in duos ordines dividendae sunt, sicut et artificum duplex est genus.

Nuper enim Adrianus Vuillartius non infeliciter novam musicem exorsus
5 videtur, in qua vagam illam antiquorum libertatem omnino tollit, certisque sese regulis ita astringit, ut eius cantiones et magna cum voluptate, et absque omni, quod ad verborum rationem attinet, difficultate canantur. Eum neoterici nunc omnes sequuntur. Quare sicut Iusquinus princeps antiquioris illius musicae esse videtur, ita Adrianus et illius finis et pater seu princeps atque
10 autor novae huius, quam nunc omnes imitantur, extitit. Nam et veterum praecepta multis cantilenis in publicum aeditis secutus est, et tandem exactius de praeceptis iudicans novam reperit, eamque et alios docuit, ut Orlandum, Cyprianum, etc., et ipse eam plurimis cantionibus partim Latinis, partim Italicis expressit, quarum quae extant vulgo ⟨ab⟩ Italis vocantur Le pecorine, a
15 pellibus ovium, quibus illigari consueverunt.

---

14 *scripsi* ||

concurred in them all. In consequence, they will not unreasonably be said to be "artificial" (from "artisans") and divided with reference to them. Therefore, they should be divided into two orders, just as the class of artisans is twofold.[130]

Recently, Adrian Willaert seems to have not unsuccessfully originated a new music[131] in which he wholly removed that erratic freedom of the older composers and restricts himself to certain rules so that his songs are sung with great enjoyment and with no difficulty at all as to the method of the words. All the modern composers now follow him. Therefore, as Josquin seems to be the leader of that older music, so Adrian existed both as its end and as the father or leader and author of this new music, which all now imitate. He followed the precepts of the past composers in many of his published cantilenas and eventually, through a more precise judgment in regard to the precepts, found a new music and taught it to others, such as Orlando di Lasso, Cipriano de Rore, etc. He himself expressed it in many songs, some in Latin and some in Italian, of which those that exist are commonly termed by the Italians "Le pecorine," from the sheepskins with which they were customarily bound.[132]

---

[130]This is yet another instance of Stoquerus's use of dichotomization to advance his thought. Here, his division of the rules in general into natural (the necessary rules) and artificial (discretionary) ones sets the scene for his further division of the discretionary rules into two classes: those observed by the artists of the older generation (Josquin et al.) and those observed by the artists of the newer generation (Willaert et al.).

[131]The context of this passage suggests that "new music" (*novam musicem*) refers to Willaert's new musical style as shown in his works (dating from the late 1530s) marked by a closer attention to text-music coordination. "New music," then, contrasts Willaert's new style with the style of his "older music" (*antiquior musica*) mentioned below, the style of Josquin and his contemporaries brought to completion by Willaert before he embarked on his new style. Of course, Willaert's new style is shown in his works published in his *Nova musica* of 1559 (see Lowinsky, "Treatise on Text Underlay," p. 247), but as can be noted at the end of this passage, Stoquerus refers to this collection by the title *Le pecorine*.

[132]The etymological explanation of this title shows that Stoquerus was not aware that it referred instead to Polissena Peccorina, the famed interpreter of Willaert's music in Venice (where his new style was forged), and was named after her as the title (*La Peccorina*) of an earlier edition of the *Nova musica* published sometime between 1546 and 1549. See Lowinsky, "Treatise on Text Underlay," pp. 247–49. See also Introduction, n. 108.

Nec vero hoc ita accipiendum est, quasi ille et recentiores caeteri antiquorum praecepta tanquam inutilia reiecerint, novaque, quae ab ipsis observata non sint, invenerint; imo nihil excogitarunt, quod ab illis non sit similiter custoditum. In hoc autem solo ab ipsis differunt, quod nimiam ipsorum licentiam
5 sustulerunt, seque elegantioribus praeceptis magis astrinxerunt. Quanto enim unusquisque artis sese cuiusque praeceptis magis subdit, tanto eius opera maiorem assequuntur laudem. Quare ordinem temporis hic sequemur, et prius regulas antiquorum ponemus; deinde eas subiiciemus, quas perelegantes quidem, illi raro admodum secuti, saepiusque nimia vagae libertatis cupiditate
10 neglexerunt; neoterici autem fere ut necessarias perpetuo custodiunt.

Diximus vero omnem ambiguitatem restare circa notitiam plurium notarum, quae uni alicui syllabae tribuendae viderentur. Quae ligaturae non tam forma quam re ipsa dici possint. Harum igitur coniectura partim ex verbis sumi potest, partim ex notis. Ex verbis quidem, accentui ut longior in pronun-
15 tiatione mora debetur, ita et plures in canendo notae tribui possunt.

In cantu vero quaedem notae ob dissimilitudinem non posse cohaerere, et colligari videntur; ideoque separatim integras per se debere intelligi, ut si semiminimae detur syllaba, eamque maior aliqua sequatur, non intelligitur maior illa praecedenti semiminimae esse connexa, sed peculiarem sibi sylla-
20 bam postulabit.

Quae vero contra colligari apte possint, partim ex puncti natura, partim ex notarum qualitate deprehenduntur. Ex puncto: nam si semibrevi aut minimae punctus apponatur, quia punctus cum sua nota tempus aut mensuram non

But this should not be taken to mean that he and the other recent composers rejected as useless the precepts of the older generation of composers and invented new ones that were not observed by them. On the contrary, they thought up nothing that was not likewise heeded by the older composers. They differ from the older composers only in that they removed their excessive license and restricted themselves to finer precepts. For the more anyone subjects himself to the precepts of any art, the greater praise his works attain. Therefore, we will follow a chronological order here and first put down the rules of the older generation of composers. Then, we will put under them those rules that, refined as they are, these composers rarely followed and more often neglected in their over-eagerness for erratic freedom. The modern composers, however, heed them continually, almost as if they were necessary.

We said that every uncertainty rests around the awareness of more notes that should seemingly be granted to some one syllable.[133] These notes may be said to be ligatures, not so much in form as in fact. The determination of these notes as ligatures, therefore, can be made partly from the words, partly from the notes.[134] In regard to the words, just as an accent ought to be given more length in pronunciation, so it can also be granted more notes in singing.[135]

Moreover, some notes in song because of their dissimilarity seem unable to cohere and be ligated, and so they ought to be understood to be separately distinct in themselves. For example, if a syllable is given to a semiminima and a larger note follows it, the larger note is not understood to be connected to the preceding semiminima, but rather will demand its own special syllable.[136]

On the other hand, those notes that can suitably be ligated can be detected partly from the nature of the punctus, partly from the quality of the notes. From the punctus:[137] if a punctus is attached to a semibrevis or minima, the note following the punctus is sometimes reckoned to be a part of the punctus

---

[133] See 188.15–190.6 *supra*.

[134] Here begins another chain of dichotomizations by which Stoquerus determines the discretionary (or artificial) rules of the older generation of composers. For the schema showing this, see Introduction, p. 61.

[135] This is the substance of the first discretionary rule, which will be explained in chapter 20 *infra*.

[136] This is the substance of the second discretionary rule, which will be explained in chapter 21 *infra*.

[137] What follows is the substance of the third discretionary rule, which will be explained in chapter 22 *infra*.

implet, pars eiusdem sequens nota nonnunquam censetur, ita ut eandem cum nota et puncto syllabam obtineat. Id vero longe firmius observatur, si sequens illa nota non unica sit, sed duae puncti valori aequipollentes, quod tunc ob nimiam illarum velocitatem, syllabae ipsis separatim tribui vix possunt, ita ut plerumque illud etiam in eam, quae illas sequitur, notam extendatur. Quod vero ad notarum proprietatem attinet, aut illarum binae singulis syllabis tribuendae occurrunt, aut plures. Si binae, sciendum est illi imprimis syllabam esse tribuendam, quae prima minima vel semiminima occurrit, quaeque mensurae initium est, aut si sint semiminimae, quae prior in sublatione vel depressione tactus occurrit. Sequens enim prioris pars esse censetur, vel potius ambae partes ad constituendum integrum tactum, vel ⟨minimam⟩; itaque sicut semibrevi una debetur syllaba, ita, si illa in duas minimas resolvatur, poterit priori attributa syllaba in sequentem simul produci. Similiter et de semiminimis dicendum; nam cum in duas semiminimas resolvatur minima, ambae ut partes unam sicuti totum earum syllabam possidebunt.

Denique cum plures notae uni syllabae adiiciendae sese offerunt, usitatissimum quidem est pluribus semiminimis et caeteris, quaecumque minoris valoris sunt quam minima, non nisi unam primae apponendam tribuere syllabam, quod caeterae ob velocissimum cursum syllabas non facile admittunt.

---

11 minimam]semiminimam M ‖

because the punctus and its note do not complete a tempus or measure. As a result, it obtains the same syllable as the note and its punctus. This is observed even more strictly if the note that follows the punctus is not a single note but two notes equal to the value of the punctus, because in this instance, syllables can hardly be given to those notes separately because of their excessive swiftness—so excessive, in fact, that the observance is very often extended even to the note following those two notes. In regard to the property of the notes, either two or more of these occur to be granted to individual syllables. If there are two,[138] it must be known that a syllable should be granted to that note in particular which occurs as the first minima or semiminima and which begins the measure. If they are semiminimae, a syllable must be given to the one that occurs first on the arsis or the thesis of the tactus, for the note that follows is reckoned to be a part of the prior note, or rather both notes are judged to be parts for constituting an entire tactus or minima.[139] In consequence, just as a semibrevis ought to have one syllable, so too, if it is resolved into two minimae, the syllable attributed to the first minima can be held out along the second as well. This should likewise be said of semiminimae, for since a minima is resolved into two semiminimae, both, as parts, will possess one syllable, as does their whole.

And finally, when several notes offer themselves to be added to one syllable,[140] it is very common to grant only the one syllable attached to the first note to several semiminimae and the other notes smaller in value than a minima, since the others, because of their very swift course, do not easily admit syllables.

---

[138]What follows is the substance of the fourth discretionary rule, which will be explained in chapter 23 *infra*.

[139]The manuscript reads *semiminima*, which Lowinsky notes is a slip of the pen (see "Treatise on Text Underlay," p. 238 and n. 17). I.e., two minimae (as parts of a semibrevis) constitute a tactus, and two semiminimae (as parts of a minima) constitute a minima.

[140]What follows is the substance of the fifth discretionary rule, which is explained in chapter 24 *infra*.

Quare quinque antiquorum regulae colligi possunt.
1. Quod syllabae cuiusvis penultimae vel antepenultimae, quae accentum possidet, plures semiminimae addi possunt.
2. Quod semiminimae soli positae plerumque syllaba adiicitur; et si semiminimae, etiam sequenti primae addenda est.
3. Si punctum minimae vel ⟨semibrevis⟩ sequantur duae notae, puncto simul sumptae aequivalentes, nulla ipsis separatim syllaba datur, et plerumque nec notae, quae illas immediate sequitur.

2–3 syllabae ... semiminimae]semiminimae ... syllabae *transp*. M ‖ 5 primae]prima M ‖ 6 semibrevis]semiminimae M ‖ 8 sequitur]sequuntur M ‖

Therefore, the five rules of the older generation of composers can be gathered:
1. To the accented penultimate or antepenultimate syllable of any word many semiminimae can be adjoined[141]
2. A syllable is frequently added to a semiminima put down alone, and if to the semiminima, a syllable must also be adjoined to the first note that follows[142]
3. If two notes follow the punctus of a minima or semibrevis[143] and together they are equivalent to the value of the punctus, no syllable is given to them separately nor frequently to the note that immediately follows them

---

[141]In the manuscript, the statement of this rule reverses the positions of *semiminimae* and *syllabae*. This, too, is a slip of the pen and is noted by Lowinsky in "Treatise on Text Underlay," p. 238 and n. 18.

[142]I have translated this rule according to the context of its general statement above (196.16–20 *supra*): if a syllable is set to an isolated semiminima, a syllable must also be given to a larger note that follows the semiminima. This, too, is the context in which the rule is explained in regard to its rationale (see the second section [*confirmatio*] of chapter 21 *infra*). I have accordingly emended *prima* to *primae*, which then modifies *notae* (understood) *sequenti*. This is not entirely satisfactory, because *sequenti primae*, in addition to being somewhat awkward, does not indicate the value of the note; however, this solution does convey somewhat better the sense of this rule, which is the only rule of the five that addresses the situation of notes *not* in implied ligature.

[143]The manuscript reads *semiminimae*. This is a slip of the pen and should be emended to *semibrevis* as confirmed by (1) Stoquerus's reference to the semibrevis in his presentation of the origin of this rule (see 196.22–23 *supra* and the following discussion) and (2) his fuller explanation of the reason for this rule in the first section of chapter 22 *infra*, where the semibrevis is, indeed, specifically mentioned. There (in chapter 22), as Stoquerus explains, the two notes that follow a punctus attached to a semibrevis and equal in value to the punctus do, in fact, complete the measuring of the tempus (the division of the brevis into two semibreves):

4. Solet nonnunquam duabus minimis vel semiminimis, tanquam plurimis ultimae, una tribui syllaba, quae priori addita in sequentem extenditur.
5. Semiminimis vel minoris valoris pluribus concurrentibus non nisi una syllaba, quae primae debetur, adiici solet.
Sed nunc has ordine explicabimus, ut supra in necessariis factum.

DE ACCENTU

CAP. XX

Ad perfectam regulae de accentibus cognitionem, quatuor scitu necessaria videntur.
1. Cur accentui plures possint tribui ⟨notae⟩.
2. Quotuplex sit accentus.
3. Plenior regulae declaratio, et ad caeteras syllabas extensio.
4. Convenientia et differentia huius regulae cum caeteris quatuor.

Quod ad primam attinet, magna videtur musicae cum oratoris actione esse cognatio, quod utraque affectus in hominibus excitat, et circa vocis sonum versatur. Quare sicut in locutione longior mora illi syllabae debetur, quae accentui subiacet, ita et canendo pluribus attributa notis nonnulla cum mora proferri potest. Accedit huc quod verborum causa harmonia effingitur, quae verborum naturam et proprietatem optime exprimit. Cum igitur omnibus ver-

---

5 explicabimus]explicavimus M ‖ 10 notae]syllabae M ‖ 18 Accedit]Accidit M ‖

4. One syllable is sometimes granted to two minimae or semiminimae (in the same manner that final syllables are given to more notes),[144] in which instance, the syllable adjoined to the first note is extended to the note following
5. Only one syllable is customarily added to a succession of several semiminimae or notes of lesser value, and this syllable ought to be given to the first note.

We will now explain these rules in order, as was done above with the necessary rules.

CHAPTER 20

ON ACCENT[145]

For a perfect knowledge of the rule concerning accents, four things seem necessary to know:
1. Why several notes[146] can be granted to the accent
2. How manifold the accent is
3. A fuller clarification of the rule and its extension to the other syllables
4. Agreement and difference of this rule with the other four.

In regard to the first: there seems to be a close relationship between music and the activity of an orator in that both arouse emotions in men and both concern the sound of the voice.[147] Therefore, just as in speaking, the syllable that is subjected to an accent ought to be given more length, so too in singing, it can be delivered with some length by being attributed to several notes. In addition, harmony is fashioned for the sake of the words, since it best expresses the nature and property of the words. Since, therefore, it is proper to all words that the syllable that possesses the accent be delivered with some

---

[144]This is perhaps a reference to the exception to necessary rule 5, in which the last syllable of a textual unit would be set to a ligature occurring as the last note of a melodic unit or phrase. If this is the case, Stoquerus uses the plural forms (*plurimis ultimae*) because he is speaking in general terms.

[145]For the commentary on this chapter, see Introduction, pp. 66–70.

[146]The manuscript reads *syllabae*. This is obviously a slip of the pen and should be emended to *notae* (cf. 196.14–15 *supra*).

[147]The context of this sentence clearly suggests that *vocis* must be translated as "of the voice."

bis proprium hoc sit, ut eorum illa syllaba, quae accentum possidet, aliqua cum mora proferatur, non immerito illi plures posse notas addi putandum est.

2. Verum hic illud quoque notandum est accentum esse duplicem: alterum uniuscuiusque vocis, alterum vero integrae sententiae. Vocis cuiusque accentus satis ex grammatica notus est, cuius praecepta in musica transferri non decet; sententiae autem accentus idem fere est, qui et ultimae vocis. Iam sicut in contextu orationis singularum vocum accentus plerumque negligitur, et ideo Graeci ultimarum syllabarum accentum acutum in contextu orationis in gravem vertunt, et lectores in ecclesia ultimum sententiae cuiusque accentum expressius et tardius pronuntiant; ita et in cantionibus non tam vocum singularum quam integrae sententiae accentus considerandus est.

Quanquam interim de eo quaeri potest quam hic sententiam vocemus. Quod quamvis ex grammatica satis constat, multi tamen musici adeo aut rerum grammaticarum rudes, aut negligentes, saepe quotlibet voces connectentes, imo nec raro una voce pro integra sententia utuntur. Itaque non hic tam ex verbis sententiam intelligendam puto, quam ex cantu. Sicut enim oratio in plura membra seu sententias dividitur, ita et cantus suas quasdam partes habet, quae aut pausis aut clausulis formalibus inter se distinguuntur. Quare doctis quidem et diligentioribus musicis, sententia eadem est cum grammaticis; rudibus vero et inertioribus, eam esse puto, quae aut pausa, aut clausula aliqua formali ter-

length, one must think—not unjustly—that several notes can be adjoined to that syllable.

2. It must be noted here, however, that accent is twofold: that of each and every word[148] and that of the entire phrase.[149] The accent of any word is sufficiently known from grammar, but the precepts for it are not fittingly carried over to music. The accent of a phrase, however, is almost the same as that of the last word. For example, in the course of speech, the accent of individual words is frequently neglected, and so the Greeks, in the course of speech, turn the acute accent of final syllables into a grave accent, and lectors in church pronounce the last accent of a phrase more expressly and slowly.[150] Similarly in songs, the accent to be considered is not so much that of individual words as that of the entire phrase.

In regard to this point, however, one may ask what we are here terming a "phrase." Although this is sufficiently clear from grammar, many musicians are nevertheless unformed or negligent in grammatical matters, often connect any number of words, and not rarely use even one word as if it were an entire phrase. In consequence, I think a phrase should not be understood here so much in terms of words as in terms of song. Just as a speech is divided into several members or phrases, so too a song has its own parts, which are distinguished among themselves by pauses or formal clausulae.[151] Therefore, for the learned and more careful musicians, a phrase is the same as for the grammarians; but for the unformed and more unskilled musicians, I think a phrase is that which ends with a pause or some formal clausula, whether it consists

---

[148]In the context of this section (2), *vox* (in all of its inflections) seems best translated as "word" and as such is synonymous with *verbum* as used in this chapter. Stoquerus may have in mind a distinction between *verbum* as "word" considered abstractly and *vox* as a "word" that is pronounced (the basic meaning of *vox* is "utterance"). In turn, *syllaba* as "syllable" in this chapter is synonymous with *vox* as used in chapters 6–9 *supra*. In this instance, the distinction is between "syllable" as a component of a word (syllaba) and "syllable" as a solmization syllable (*vox*).

[149]*Sententia* connotes any self-contained group of words, such as a phrase, clause, or sentence. I have translated *sententia* as "phrase" since Stoquerus seems to be discussing word-tone coordination at the level of the phrase unit in both text and music.

[150]On these two examples, see Introduction, p. 68.

[151]I.e., rests or cadences. On the cadence as the emphatic close of a phrase, see Introduction, n. 116.

minatur, sive illa una, sive duabus vocibus aut etiam pluribus constet. Sententiae vero syllabae dividi possunt in primam, ultimam, penultimam, antepenultimam, et medias.

3. Ex praedictis igitur et ultima necessariarum regula colligitur, hunc canendi modum naturae maxime conformem esse, si primae notae prima sententiae syllaba, ultimae ultima attribuatur; mediae vero omnes, quamprimum commode fieri possit, primam sequantur, donec perveniatur ad antepenultimam vel penultimam, si illa accentum possideat, cui caeterae notae usque ad ultimam tribuantur. Ultima vero nota, ut dictum est, ultimae syllabae debetur, sicut et penultima penultimae, si accentus fuerit in antepenultima, alioqui antepenultima mediis annumerabitur.

4. Regulae igitur huic cum caeteris id commune est, quod inquirit, quae notae figura separatae, re ipsa colligatae intelligendae sint. Si enim, notis ordine in syllabas distributis, illi, quae accentum custodit, plures notae reservatae videbuntur, illae ligaturarum naturam sequentur. Differt autem haec regula a caeteris, quod illae notas colligandas ex sonorum figuris colligunt, haec autem ex natura vocum, quibus proprie accentus seu pronuntiationis mora in certis syllabis accidit.

of one word or two or even more.[152] In any event, the syllables of a phrase can be divided into first, last, penultimate, antepenultimate, and middle ones.

3.[153] It is therefore gathered from the aforesaid and from the last of the necessary rules that this way of singing most conforms to nature if the first syllable of a phrase is attributed to the first note and the last syllable to the last note. As soon as can be conveniently done, all the middle syllables should follow the first syllable, until the antepenultimate or penultimate syllable—if it possesses the accent—is reached and all the remaining notes up to the last one are granted to it. The last note, as was said, ought to be given to the last syllable, just as it was also said that the penultimate note ought to be given to the penultimate syllable if the accent was on the antepenultimate syllable; otherwise, the antepenultimate syllable is put among the middle syllables.

4. This rule is common with the other rules in that it investigates which notes, although separate in figure, are to be understood as in fact ligated together. If, after the notes are distributed in order over the syllables, several notes are seen to be left for the syllable that heeds the accent, they will follow the nature of ligatures. This rule differs from the others, however, in that the others gather the notes to be ligated on the basis of the figures of the sounds, whereas this rule gathers the notes on the basis of the nature of the words, in which the accent or length of pronunciation properly occurs on certain syllables.[154]

---

[152] I.e., the learned musician is careful to properly coordinate musical and textual phrase; the unformed musicians think primarily in terms of the musical phrase and text it with any number of words, regardless of whether or not they properly form a phrase in the grammatical sense. See Introduction, n. 117.

[153] The purpose of this section is to clarify what was said in section 2 by applying this rule within the context of necessary rule 5. According to rule 5, the first syllable of the first word of the textual unit is set to the first note of the musical unit and the last syllable of the last word is set to the last note. All the middle syllables are then set to the middle notes. The present rule indicates how best to distribute these middle syllables, that is, by placing special emphasis on the accented syllable (antepenult or penult) of the last word of the phrase. This emphasis is observed by assigning more notes to this accented syllable.

[154] The distinction of this rule from the others as stated here echoes the dichotomization in chapter 19 that traces the origin of this set of discretionary rules (see 196.14–15 *supra*).

DE SEMIMINIMA MAIORIS VALORIS NOTULAE PRAEPOSITA

CAP. XXI

1. Differentia. 2. Confirmatio. 3. Extensio. 4. Limitatio.

1. Haec regula circa ligaturas quidem, ut caeterae, versatur, sed diverso modo; in illis enim inquiritur quae notae facile colligari possint, in hac, contra, quae ligaturis ineptae sint.

2. Nam cum semiminimae syllaba debetur, maiori, si qua eam sequitur, quoque syllaba dari convenit, seu quod hae duae notae ob inaequalitatem coniungi non posse videntur, mensuramque tactus aut non implent aut superant, seu quod notarum velocitas syllabas respuit, contraque tarditas requirit. Ideoque propemodum necessario sequitur ut cum notae velociori syllaba attribuitur, tardiori eam sequenti minime negetur.

---

4 caeterae]caetera M ‖ 5 possint]possunt M ‖

CHAPTER 21

ON A SEMIMINIMA PLACED BEFORE A NOTE OF LARGER VALUE[155]

1. Difference. 2. Verification. 3. Extension. 4. Limitation.[156]

1. This rule concerns ligatures, as do the others, but in a diverse way. In those rules, it is investigated which notes can easily be ligated; in this rule, on the contrary, it is investigated which notes are unsuitable for ligatures.

2.[157] When a syllable ought to be given to a semiminima, it is agreeable that a syllable also be given to any larger note that may follow the semiminima, either because these two notes seem unable to be joined together due to their inequality, and either do not complete the measure of the tactus[158] or surpass[159] it, or because the swiftness of the notes refuses syllables, whereas the slowness of the notes requires them. And so, it follows nearly of necessity that when a syllable is attributed to a swifter note, one should by no means be denied to a slower note following it.[160]

---

[155] For the commentary on this chapter, see Introduction, pp. 70–73. *Notula* in the title (and elsewhere) is a synonym for *nota* and has no argumentational significance.

[156] The single terms that Stoquerus uses here and elsewhere to divide his discussion are probably all "topics," or *loci*, ways of discussing a subject in oratory (and transferred to expository prose) in order to establish its truth. See Introduction, n. 50. For *differentia*, for example, see Aristotle *Topica* 108a38–b6, and for *confirmatio*, see Cicero *De inventione* 1.24.34. For the proliferation of topics in the Renaissance, see Walter J. Ong, S.J., *Ramus, Method, and the Decay of Dialogue* (Cambridge: Harvard University Press, 1958), pp. 121–23.

[157] This section (and the title of this chapter) reflects this rule as presented prior to its formal statement at the end of chapter 19 (see 196.16–20 *supra*). The formal statement of the rule at the end of this same chapter does not assign any particular value to the note following the semiminima (see 200.4–5 *supra*). The next two sections discuss the text setting to notes of the same or smaller value that follow a semiminima.

[158] I.e., a semiminima followed by a minima.

[159] I.e., a semiminima followed by a brevis.

[160] Stoquerus is employing a kind of "argument from justice": if a syllable is given to a quickly moving note, one should also be given to a more slowly moving one.

3. Procedit idem etiam in aequalibus, ut si sequenti aequali primae semiminimae tribuitur syllaba, tertiae quoque semiminimae, et caeterae quotcumque sequuntur, eodem esse iure censeantur. Ineptae vero ligaturis etiam omnes minimae et caeterae maioris valoris notulae, quae forma ligaturarum carent, videri possent, nisi nimia antiquorum licentia eas contra huius artis inventorum instituta admisisset. Sed de his suo loco plura dicemus.

4. Sed etiam idem observatur, si semiminimam inaequales minoris valoris notae sequuntur. Tunc enim secundum datam regulam illi quidem, quae semiminimam immediate sequitur, sua debetur syllaba; caeterae autem illi alligatae censentur, et non semiminimae. At contra, ipsi semiminimae aequales alligari possunt; illi autem, quae eam prima sequitur, connecti non possunt. Ideoque diximus, pluribus positis semiminimis, si secundis tribuitur syllaba, primis quoque tribui suas proprias. Nam aut omnes primae connexae censentur, aut singulae separatae, ut paulo mox dicemus.

3. The same takes place also in regard to equal notes: if a syllable is granted to a semiminima that follows equal to the first, the third semiminima[161] also—and as many others that follow—should be reckoned as having the same right. Indeed, all minimae and other notes of larger value that lack a form for ligatures would seem to be unsuitable for ligatures, were it not that the excessive license of the older composers had admitted them contrary to what was established by the inventors of this art.[162] But we will say more about these matters in their proper place.[163]

4. But the same is also observed if unequal notes of smaller value follow a semiminima. In this instance, according to the rule as given,[164] the note that immediately follows a semiminima ought to be given its own syllable; however, the rest of the notes are reckoned as bound to it and not to the semiminima. Equal notes, on the other hand, can be bound to the semiminima itself, but they cannot be connected to the first semiminima that follows it.[165] And so, we said that when several semiminimae are put down, if a syllable is granted to the second ones, their own syllables are also granted to the first ones.[166] For either all are reckoned as connected to the first or each is judged to be separate, as we will say shortly.[167]

---

[161]As noted before (n. 144 *supra*), here again Stoquerus uses the plural form in the Latin when speaking in general terms (see 202.1–2 *supra* and lines 11–13 *infra* in the present chapter).

[162]Stoquerus includes these larger note values in this section to indicate the indiscriminate freedom of the older composers to make implied ligatures out of any series of equal notes regardless of their value. Stoquerus seems to be arguing here for consistency in approach. Hence, all equal notes in a series should either be treated as a ligature and given only one syllable or they should be treated as separate notes and given separate syllables.

[163]This is the substance of the second discretionary rule of the newer composers as discussed in chapter 27 *infra*.

[164]I.e., the rule formulated as discretionary rule 2 in chapter 19 (see 200.4–5 *supra*).

[165]This sentence restates the substance of what is discussed in n. 162 *supra*.

[166]I.e., a syllable cannot be assigned to the second semiminima of a series unless one is assigned to the first.

[167]I.e., in the fourth section of chapter 24 *infra*, in which Stoquerus compares discretionary rule 5 with the present rule.

DE PUNCTO MINORIS VALORIS NOTULIS PRAEPOSITO

CAP. XXII

1. Ratio. 2. Collatio cum regula superiori de puncto. 3. Collatio cum regula proxima. 4. Collatio cum regula ultima.

1. Notae duae punctum semibrevis vel ⟨minimae⟩ sequentes, et ipsi puncto aequivalentes, syllabam non admittunt, sed puncto colligatae censentur, vel quod eius sunt compartes cum eo temporis seu tactus mensuram implentes, vel quod ob magnam velocitatem syllabarum prolationi ineptae videntur, vel quod ex illius notae resolutione prodeunt, quae puncto aequipol-

---

5 minimae]semiminimae M ‖ 9 prodeunt]prodierint M ‖

CHAPTER 22

ON THE PUNCTUS PLACED BEFORE NOTES OF SMALLER VALUE[168]

1. Reason.[169] 2. Comparison with the above rule regarding the punctus. 3. Comparison with the next rule. 4. Comparison with the last rule.

1. Two notes following the punctus of a semibrevis or minima[170] and equal in value to the punctus itself do not admit a syllable, but are reckoned as ligated with the punctus either because they are its co-parts, completing with it as they do the measure of the tempus[171] or the tactus;[172] or because, owing to their great swiftness, they seem to be unsuitable for the delivery of syllables;[173] or because they issue forth from the resolution of that note, equipol-

---

[168]For the commentary on this rule, see Introduction, pp. 73–75. The emphasis on the *punctus* in the title echoes the origin (by dichotomization) of the rule as given in chapter 19 (see 196.22–198.5 *supra*).

[169]This "topic" always supplies the rationale governing the rule under discussion. It appears here in its most succinct expression (cf. 170.13, 180.6, and 202.10 *supra*).

[170]The manuscript reads *semiminimae*. This is a slip of the pen and should be emended to *minimae* in order to conform to Stoquerus's reference to the minima in his presentation of the origin of this rule and its formulation in chapter 19 (see respectively 196.22–23 and 200.6 *supra*). This is confirmed by Stoquerus's explanation, immediately following, of the first reason for this rule in the present section. Here, the completion of the measuring of the tactus (i.e., the arsis, with the semibrevis comprising the unit of the tactus) by the punctus and the two notes following can be explained only if a minima is understood as occurring on the thesis:

[171]I.e., in regard to the punctus and the two notes following a semibrevis. See n. 143 *supra*.

[172]I.e., in regard to the punctus and the two notes following a minima. See n. 170 *supra*.

[173]I.e., presumably for the delivery of a syllable on each of the two notes. Cf. Stoquerus's presentation of the origin of this rule in chapter 19 (see 198.2–5) and section 4 *infra* of the present chapter.

lens nec ipsa facile syllabae aptari posse videtur, vel denique, quod ut punctus pars notae syllabam respuit, ita et hae reliquae ad tactus vel temporis constitutionem partes, syllabae non facile fiunt participes.

2. Quare haec regula convenit partim cum regula superiori de puncto, partim cum regula proxime sequenti de duabus minimis vel semiminimis, partim cum ultima de pluribus semiminimis. Cum regula de puncto convenit, quod ut ille, quod notae pars est, syllabam non admittit, ita et hae, quod temporis seu tactus eiusdem cum nota et puncto pars sunt, syllabam respuunt.

3. Consentit et sequenti regulae; nam sicut illic notae ⟨semiminimam⟩ immediate sequenti syllaba addi prohibetur, ita et hic de duabus notis punctum sequentibus, et uni illi notae, de qua in proxima regula fit mentio, aequivalentibus dicimus.

---

9 semiminimam]syllabam M ‖

215

lent to the punctus, which itself seems unable to be easily equipped with a syllable;[174] or finally, because just as the punctus, as part of a note, refuses a syllable, so too these parts that remain for the constitution of a tactus or tempus are not easily made sharers of a syllable.[175]

2. Therefore, this rule agrees partly with the above rule concerning the punctus,[176] partly with the next following rule concerning two minimae or semiminimae, and partly with the last rule concerning several semiminimae. This rule agrees with the rule concerning the punctus because just as the punctus, as part of the note, does not admit a syllable, so these notes too, because they are a part of the same tempus or tactus with the note and its punctus, refuse a syllable.[177]

3. This rule also concurs with the following rule, for just as a syllable is prohibited there from being adjoined to a note immediately following a semiminima,[178] so here too we are talking about two notes following a punctus and equal in value to that one note, mention of which is made in the next rule.[179]

---

[174]*Nec ipsa . . . posse videtur* suggests the possibility (*pace* the measuring of the tempus or tactus) of assigning a syllable to all these notes in the figures:

as indeed often occurs in the literature; when, however, the note following the punctus is divided or resolved into two smaller notes, a syllable is given only to the first note of the pair, according to Stoquerus's argument from swiftness as given in the second reason.

[175]This fourth reason is essentially the same as the first reason. The difference is small. The first reason considers the two notes as parts of the punctus only; the fourth reason considers the two notes as parts of the entire tactus or tempus. Both reasons enter into the discussion of section 2 of this chapter.

[176]I.e., necessary rule 2 as listed at the end of chapter 11 (see 158.7 *supra*).

[177]The comparison here is based on Stoquerus's method of part-whole argumentation: that syllables are given to wholes and not to parts. Cf. Stoquerus's use of this argument in his commentary on the necessary rule concerning the punctus in the third section of chapter 14 *supra*.

[178]The manuscript reads *syllabam*. This is obviously a slip of the pen and should be emended to *semiminimam* (*minimam* is also implied since the next rule discusses both note values).

[179]That is, the two notes following the punctus are parts of the note of the next larger value or equivalent to it. This note of the next larger value is that of

4. Denique et ultimae regulae concordat, quod ut illic pluribus notis ob velocitatem syllaba adiici non permittitur, ita et hic iisdem idem fieri prohibetur.

DE DUABUS MINIMIS VEL SEMIMINIMIS

CAP. XXIII

1. Declaratio. 2. Ratio. 3. Extensio. 4. Limitatio.

1. Cum duae occurrunt minimae vel semiminimae, principalis censeri solet illa minima, quae tactum inchoat, et in semiminimis, illa, quae prior in tactus sive depressione sive elevatione sese offert; altera autem illi alligata iudicatur.

2. Cuius rei ratio haec esse videtur, quod in prima et quarta regula necessariarum diximus non partibus sed integris deberi syllabas. Quare si hic

4. Finally, this rule is also in accord with the last rule, because just as a syllable is not permitted there to be added to several notes owing to their swiftness, so here too the same is prohibited for these notes.[180]

CHAPTER 23

ON TWO MINIMAE OR SEMIMINIMAE[181]

1. Clarification. 2. Reason. 3. Extension. 4. Limitation.

1. When two minimae or semiminimae occur, the minima that begins the tactus is usually reckoned as the principal one, and in the case of semiminimae, the one that presents itself on either the thesis or arsis of the tactus; the other note, however, is judged to be bound to it.[182]

2. The reason for this seems to be what we said in the first and fourth necessary rules: syllables ought to be given not to parts but to entireties.[183]

---

which "mention is made" in the first part of the second section of the following rule (the fourth discretionary rule discussed in the next chapter). Thus, just as a single note following a punctus does not (ideally) receive a syllable, neither should the two notes as divisions of the single note receive a syllable. Here too, however, Stoquerus seems to allow for the possibility of assigning a syllable to the first note of the pair, since this is the point of the next rule.

[180]This argument from swiftness is employed at the end of the second section (*ratio*) of Stoquerus's discussion of the fifth discretionary rule in chapter 24 *infra*. Thus, although a syllable may sometimes be given to the first note of the pair of notes following a punctus, one may not be given to the second note, just as in the first rule a syllable may be given only to the first note of a series of smaller note values.

[181]For the commentary on this chapter, see Introduction, pp. 75–79.

[182]This *declaratio* is a restatement of the background of this rule as given in chapter 19 (see 198.7–10 *supra*). On Stoquerus's emphasis on the tactus as a decisive factor in text setting, see Lowinsky, "Treatise on Text Underlay," pp. 239–41. As Stoquerus will confirm in the last section (4) of the next chapter (24), the situation discussed in this rule concerns not simply a group of two minimae or semiminimae, but a series of these notes that must be ligated in groups of two to accommodate the number of available syllables.

[183]The part-whole argument is not directly referred to but implied in Stoquerus's discussion of the first necessary rule (cf. chapter 12, 162.2–5

utrisque sua adiiceretur syllaba, tanquam integrae censerentur singulae per se; at cum possit semibrevis resolvi in duas minimas, minima quoque in duas partes, scilicet semiminimas, fit ut iisdem duabus tanquam alterius partibus una sola syllaba recte possit applicari. Applicanda autem haec priori videtur,
5 vel quia illa prius occurrit, vel quia illius imprimis ratio in contrapuncto habetur. Solent enim symphonistae imprimis curare ne qua discordia occurrat cum minimis quae primum tactus locum occupant, hoc est, quae in tactus depressione canuntur; cum semiminimis vero illis, quae primae in tactus sive depressione sive elevatione sese offerunt. In sentencia principem locum obtinent illae
10 notae, quae in mensura loco impari consistunt; caeterae saepe non computantur, et quomodolibet cum quibusvis copulantur; ideoque illis, quae fere pro nullis habentur, nulla syllaba tribuenda videtur.

3. Idem quoque censendum est cum prior illa nota, cui syllaba datur, non sola separatim posita reperitur, sed simili conglutinata, ⟨quae⟩ alteram notae
15 suscipit formam, quae utramque valore adaequat, ut in clausulis formalibus,

---

14 *scripsi* ǁ

Therefore, if here to each of the two notes were added its own syllable, each note would be reckoned as an entirety in itself. But since the semibrevis can be resolved into two minimae and the minima also into two parts (namely, semiminimae), it happens that only one syllable can rightly be given to these two notes as parts of each other. This syllable, it seems, must be applied to the first note, either because it occurs first, or because special account of it is taken in the counterpoint. *Symphonistae* are customarily especially careful that a dissonance not occur with minimae that occupy the first place of the tactus, that is, that are sung on the thesis of the tactus, and with semiminimae that present themselves first on either the thesis or arsis of the tactus.[184] In a phrase, those notes obtain the foremost place that are situated on the odd place in the measure. The other notes are often not taken into account and are linked with any of them in any way.[185] And so, no syllable, it seems, should be granted to these notes, which are of practically no importance.

3.[186] This same principle must be reckoned when that first note to which a syllable is given is found not put down separately and alone but attached to one like it, which[187] takes on the other form of note that equals them both in

---

supra). He does, however, associate this argument with both the first and fourth necessary rules in his discussion of the fourth rule in chapter 15 regarding the setting of syllables to notes of the same pitch and of different pitch (see 174.12–176.5 *supra*).

[184]Stoquerus's argumentation here is derived principally from Zarlino. See Marco-Palisca, *The Art of Counterpoint*, p. 93.

[185]E.g., as passing notes.

[186]For his discussion in this section, Stoquerus presumably has in mind the cadential figure

but to make his point (that a syllable is not given to the semibrevis) he considers the figure as equivalent to

The translation, admittedly an interpretation, is based on this premise. See also Introduction, nn. 129–131.

[187]I have inserted *quae* into the text in order to associate syntactically the subject of *suscipit* with *simili*, which according to the sense of the passage seems to be that verb's referent.

maximeque in voce superiori, frequentissime contingit. Qua ratione fit ut prior illa duplicis valoris nota pari loco mensuranda aeque ac secunda occurrat. Soletque hoc casu altera illius accessoria et supplementum censeri, quod tactum suppleat, ideoque eandem cum priori syllabam occupat.

4. Videtur autem haec regula sola antiquorum propria esse, et a recentioribus prorsus neglecta. Nam recentiores minimis omnibus suas attribuunt syllabas, easque ut integras computant, semiminimis autem nullas prorsus; quod an recte necne fiat, suo loco declarabimus.

DE PLURIMIS SEMIMINIMIS

CAP. XXIIII

1. Declaratio. 2. Ratio. 3. Extensio. 4. Limitatio.

1. Pluribus semiminimis continuatis soli primae fere syllaba tribuitur, reliquis connexarum loco reputatis. Primam vero accipe non solum, quae tactum inchoat, sed quaecumque in tactu sive depressione sive elevatione prima sese offert. Nec solum primam notae figura depingendam putandum est; nam et

value, as very frequently happens in formal clausulae—particularly in the upper voice. On which account, that first note of double value[188] occurs equally as a second note measured on the even place.[189] And in this case, this other note[190] is customarily reckoned to be that note's[191] accessory and supplement—because it supplements the tactus—and therefore occupies the same syllable as the first note.

4. This rule, however, seems proper solely to the older composers and is entirely neglected by the newer ones. The newer composers attribute to all minimae their own syllables and account them as entireties; however, they give no syllables at all to semiminimae. We will clarify in its own place whether or not it is right to do this.[192]

CHAPTER 24

ON SEVERAL SEMIMINIMAE[193]

1. Clarification. 2. Reason. 3. Extension. 4. Limitation.

1. When several semiminimae[194] are placed together, a syllable is usually granted to the first semiminima only; the remaining ones are regarded as connected with it. Take as the first semiminima not only the one that begins the tactus but whatever one that presents itself first on the thesis or arsis of the tactus.[195] Nor must it only be thought that the first semiminima is depicted by

---

[188]I.e., the semibrevis, and in particular the first minima of the semibrevis conceived as two minimae.

[189]I.e., a second minima following the first minima of the cadential figure and therefore falling on the second (or even) portion (or place) of the measure (i.e., of the tactus).

[190]I.e., the second minima (i.e., the first half of the semibrevis).

[191]I.e., the first minima of the cadential figure.

[192]The assigning of separate syllables to all minimae and none at all (i.e., separately) to a series of semiminimae will be discussed, respectively, in chapters 27 and 28 *infra*.

[193]For the commentary on this chapter, see Introduction, pp. 79–82.

[194]I.e., more than two, as discussed in chapter 23 *supra*.

[195]I.e., the series can begin on the tactus or on either of its subdivisions (thesis or arsis). See the figures illustrating this in the Introduction, p. 80 *supra*.

punctus minimae pro prima habetur, quanquam tunc non puncto tanquam primae, sed ipsi notae, cui punctus accedit, communis syllaba additur.

2. Ratio autem huius rei est, quod sicut semibrevi, brevi, et aliis huiusmodi non nisi una syllaba adiicitur, ita iisdem in plurimas semiminimas resolutis non nisi una deberi videtur. Primae autem syllaba tribui solet, quod illius tum a symphonistis in contrapuncto, tum a cantoribus in ⟨coloratione⟩ et diminutione, quod vulgo glossare vocant, ratio imprimis haberi solet, caeteris fere neglectis. Denique et velocitas illarum in causa est cur singulis separatim attribui sua syllaba non potest. Sicut enim in loquendo magnam verborum obscuritatem gignit pronuntiationis velocitas, quod syllabae raptim cumulatae nec distincte prolatae auribus recte percipi non possunt, multoque minus recte intelligi, ita et in cantu ne idem accidat cavendum est.

3. Ex quo sequitur multominus aliis quam semiminimis velocioribus syllabas addi debere, ut sunt fusae et semifusae. Eadem ratione et illa, quae has

---

6 coloratione]*spatium in* M ‖ 11 distincte]distinctae M ‖

the figure of a note; even the punctus of a minima acts as the first semiminima, although in this instance the common syllable is adjoined not to the punctus as the first semiminima but to the note itself to which the punctus is added.[196]

2. The reason for this is: just as only one syllable is added to the semibrevis, brevis, and other such notes, so too only one syllable ought to be given, it seems, to these notes when they are resolved into several semiminimae.[197] A syllable is usually granted to the first semiminima, however, because special account of it is taken by *symphonistae* in their counterpoint[198] and by singers as well in coloration[199] and diminution, which they commonly term *glossare*.[200] The other semiminimae are almost neglected. Finally, their swiftness, too, is a reason why each of them cannot be attributed its own separate syllable. Just as in speaking, swiftness of pronunciation causes a great blurring of words because the syllables, rapidly accumulated and indistinctly delivered, cannot be correctly heard and much less correctly understood, so too in song, care must be taken that the same thing not happen.[201]

3. From this,[202] it follows that much less should syllables be adjoined to other notes swifter than semiminimae, as are fusae and semifusae. For that

---

[196]In this instance, necessary rule 2 takes precedence, in which the punctus is considered a part of the note to which it is attached and therefore does not receive a syllable by reason of Stoquerus's part-whole argument. See the figure illustrating this in the Introduction, p. 80 *supra*.

[197]Presumably because the semiminimae are parts of these larger note-values. See 216.10–218.4 *supra*.

[198]Stoquerus is employing here the same argument used in the *ratio* of his discretionary rule 4 discussed in the previous chapter. See 218.4–12 *supra*.

[199]The missing word in the manuscript is surely a synonym corresponding to *diminutione*. I have supplied *coloratione* (cf. 164.13–18 *supra*).

[200]I.e., the singers begin the ornamentation on the same note as appears in the unadorned version. See example 10 in Horseley, "Improvised Embellishment," p. 15.

[201]This "argument from swiftness" adds the further consideration of the intelligibility of the text being declaimed, the ultimate goal of proper text setting. Stoquerus thus argues from both a theoretical and practical viewpoint.

[202]I.e., from Stoquerus's "argument from swiftness," thus answering for the notes smaller than a semiminima as stated in the rule (see 202.3–4).

etiam semiminima maior sequitur, a syllabis libera deberet censeri, quod tamen saepius ab antiquis neglectum videtur; ideoque plura de hoc in recentiorum regulis dicentur.

4. Nec huic regulae contraria censenda est regula secunda huius ordinis, ubi diximus singulis semiminimis suam attribui syllabam, hic contra nulli praeterquam primae. Non enim illud ibi simpliciter affirmavimus, sed diximus semiminimas plures continuatas omnes ligatas censendas esse, aut singulas integras et separatim positas, de quarum his illic diximus, de illis vero haec regula intelligenda est. Si enim syllabae his subiectae abundant, singulis addendae sunt; sin minus, non nisi una omnibus adiicietur. Si denique plures quam una sint, nec tamen omnibus notis sufficere videantur, regula quarta sequenda erit. Sed huic distinctioni contraria videtur regula quarta, ubi nec omnibus notis syllabam unam, nec singulis addi oportere, sed binis potius.

---

11 videantur]videatur M ||

same reason, even the note following these—though larger than a semiminima—ought to be reckoned as free from syllables. This nevertheless seems to be frequently neglected by the older composers, and so more will said about this in the rules of the newer composers.[203]

4.[204] The second rule of this order (where we said that each syllable should be attributed to individual semiminimae)[205] should not be reckoned as contrary to this rule, where we say, oppositely, that a syllable should be attributed to no semiminima except the first. We did not make that assertion there without qualification, but we said that several semiminimae placed together are all to be reckoned as ligated or each is to be reckoned as an entirety and put down separately.[206] We talked there about the latter instance; this rule must be understood in regard to the former instance. If the syllables put under these semiminimae are abundant, they must be adjoined to them individually; but if this is not the case, then only one syllable will be added to all of them. If, finally, there are more syllables than one, and yet they do not seem to suffice for all the notes, the fourth rule will have to be followed. But the fourth rule seems contrary to this distinction; there we said that one syllable should be adjoined neither to all the notes nor to each one of them, but rather to a group of two notes.[207] Therefore, what you are to follow amidst

---

[203]The reason for not giving a syllable to the longer note following a series of these smaller notes (semiminimae included) is discussed in the first section (*ratio*) of chapter 29 *infra*. For the present, Stoquerus's reason seems to be that the temporal span between the faster note and the slower note is the same as that between the faster notes: so the slower note, too, should go without a syllable.

[204]The purpose of this section, argued scholastically by distinction, is to isolate the limitation of this rule to a series of semiminimae (or smaller notes) for which only one syllable is available (or intended) from the limitations of rules 2 and 4 of this set, in which more than one syllable is available or intended—either an equal number of notes and syllables (rule 2) or a proportion of two notes to one syllable (rule 4). This section sheds further light on the background of the rules presented in chapter 19, which discusses these rules only from the standpoint of the notes (see 196.16–198.19). The closing observation in this section further limits this rule to semiminimae and smaller notes in a ₵ mensuration.

[205]This statement of the rule refers to the rule as applying to the texting of two or more successive semiminimae as discussed in the third section of chapter 21 (see 210.1–3 *supra*).

[206]See 210.13–14 *supra*.

[207]See the statement of the rule in chapter 19 (202.1–2) *supra*.

Quare in hac opinionum varietate quid sequaris ex syllabarum cum notis collatarum defectu et copia colligendum est.

⟨Hic⟩ enim sciendum et illud est, quod recentiores in signo C utuntur seminimimis pro minimis, itaque in eiusmodi cantionibus regula haec et caeterae, quae de seminimimis loquuntur, de fusis, quae illis seminimimis aequipollent, intelligendae sunt; et similiter de aliis accipiendum est, unamquamque naturam eius sequi, cui aequipolleat.

DE REGULARUM ANTIQUORUM INTER SE CONCORDIA ATQUE ORDINE

CAP. XXV

Cum regulae hae arbitrariae sint, et antiqui ab illis facilius recesserint quam recentiores, ideoque nulla earum fere limitationibus careat, in tanta opinionum varietate quid sentiendum sit, quoque ordine canendum, summatim dicendum opinor.

Imprimis igitur primae sententiae cuiusvis notae prima syllaba tribuenda est, secundum ultimam necessariarum; deinde mediae, quae primam sequuntur, secundum primam et quintam necessariarum, et primam arbitrariarum; ita

---

3 Hic]Si M ||

this variety of opinions must be gathered from the deficiency or abundance of syllables in relation to the notes.

Here[208] it must also be known that the newer composers use semiminimae as minimae in the sign C. In consequence, in such songs, this rule and the rest that speak of semiminimae must be understood as speaking of fusae, which are equal in value to those semiminimae. And this must likewise be taken for the other notes: that each one follows the nature of that note to which it is equal in value.

CHAPTER 25

ON THE MUTUAL AGREEMENT AND ORDER OF THE RULES OF THE OLDER COMPOSERS[209]

Since these rules are discretionary and the older composers diverged from them more easily than the newer ones (and so almost none of them is lacking in limitations), I think I should say summarily what must be thought amidst such a variety of opinions and in what order these rules are to be applied in singing.

First of all, therefore, the first syllable must be granted to the first note of any phrase, according to the last necessary rule.[210] Then, the middle syllables that follow the first must be placed, according to the first and fifth necessary rule and the first discretionary rule,[211] in such a way that a syllable is never-

---

[208]The manuscript reads *Si*, presumably introducing a conditional statement; however, in the absence of an apodosis, a *si*-clause has no meaning in this particular case. Assuming a scribal reading of *si* for perhaps *hic*, I have made the emendation as indicated, with *quod . . . minimis* functioning as a noun clause in apposition to *illud*. Accordingly, this section shows that, while this rule and rules 2 and 4 are limited to compositions in a ₵ mensuration, they are also serviceable, at the level of fusae and smaller notes, in compositions of the newer generation in a C mensuration.

[209]For the commentary on this chapter, see Introduction, pp. 82–84.

[210]This rule (necessary rule 5) and the other four necessary rules observed in this chapter are listed at the end of chapter 11 (see 158.6–12 *supra*).

[211]Stoquerus's reference to necessary rule 1 is clarified by his discussion of this rule in chapter 12, section 3 *supra*, where he points to the singers' error of assigning too few syllables (i.e., not enough middle syllables) at the beginning of a phrase, resulting in their being forced to divide notes at the end in order to accommodate the remaining syllables (see 162.1–5 *supra*). For a

tamen ut a punctis et ligaturis expressis abstineatur, secundum secundam et tertiam necessariarum. Pluribus autem eodem in loco positis omnino cuilibet sua debetur per quartam necessariarum.

    Mox quod ad arbitrarias attinet, observet si semiminimis occurrentibus aliae interpositae sint, ut non continuentur; tunc enim nisi in clausulis formalibus hoc accidat, tam ipsis semiminimis, quam minimis interpositis, singulis sua addetur syllaba, secundum ⟨secundam⟩ arbitrariarum. Sin plures semiminimae continuae positae occurrunt, animadvertendum utrum abundent syllabae, ut necessario cuique semiminimae sua tribuatur syllaba, per secundam arbitrariarum. Sin notae potius abundant, omnibus una sola addatur, per quintam arbitrariarum. Quod si hac ratione aliquot abundaturae eiusdem semiminimae syllabae videantur, binis una tribuatur syllaba, per quartam. Quae omnia

---

7 secundam]tertiam M ‖

theless withheld from puncti and expressed ligatures, according to the second and third necessary rules.[212] When, however, several notes are put down in the same place,[213] each and every note ought to be given its own syllable, according to the fourth necessary rule.

Next, in what pertains to the discretionary rules, one should observe if other notes are placed between semiminimae that may occur so that the semiminimae are not placed together; for in this instance, unless this occurs in formal clausulae, a separate syllable is adjoined to the semiminimae themselves as well as to the minimae placed between them, according to the second[214] discretionary rule. But if several semiminimae occur placed together, one must notice whether there is an abundance of syllables so that each semiminima is necessarily granted its own syllable by the second discretionary rule.[215] But if, on the other hand, there is an over-abundance of notes, only one syllable is adjoined to all of them, by the fifth discretionary rule.[216] But if, by this reasoning, only a few syllables would seem to be in excess for the same semiminima, let one syllable be granted to the semiminimae in groups of two,

---

fuller statement of necessary rule 5 that includes the middle syllables, see 182.3–4 *supra*. The discretionary rules are listed at the end of chapter 19 (see 200.2–204.4 *supra*). The reference to discretionary rule 1 indicates that the accented syllable of the last word of the phrase is included among the middle notes.

[212]"Second and third," that is, in the order listed at the end of chapter 11 (see 158.7–9 *supra*). Stoquerus has also referred to these rules as numbered by the order of their discussion, respectively, in chapter 13 (the ligature rule, or the "second rule") and in chapter 14 (the rule concerning the punctus, or the "third rule" [see 176.1–5 *supra*]).

[213]"In the same place," that is, on the staff, meaning of course successive notes of the same pitch.

[214]The manuscript reads *tertiam*. I have emended this to *secundam*, since the matter discussed here is contained in section 2 of Stoquerus's discussion (chapter 21) of discretionary rule 2 (see 208.7–12 *supra*). Moreover, rule 2 is the only one of the five discretionary rules that pertains to notes *not* in ligature, notated or implied (see 208.4–6). The exception regarding formal clausulae is found in section 3 of Stoquerus's discussion (chapter 23) of discretionary rule 4 (see 218.13–220.4 *supra*).

[215]This is treated in section 3 of Stoquerus's discussion (chapter 21) of discretionary rule 2 (see 210.1–3 *supra*).

[216]As stated in the list of these rules at the end of chapter 19 (see 202.3–4 *supra*).

observanda sunt donec perveniatur ad illam syllabam, quae accentui subiecta est; illi, si plures notae, quantaecumque supersint, omnes tribuantur, donec perveniatur ad ultimam vel penultimam, si illa accentu careat, per primam arbitrariarum; vel si tot notae superesse videantur, ut sententia repeti queat, absolvatur sententia statim, nec super accentu mora fiat, ne repetitionis commoditas amittatur.

Verum id interim circa repetitiones notandum eas, si frequentes sint, fastidium et nauseam audientibus parere perinde ac si inter loquendum eiusdem vocis crebrior fiat repetitio; itaque cavendum ne nimium repetitionibus studeamus. Hae enim ut in cantu plano prorsus nullae, quod sciam, reperiuntur, ita in mensurali aut necessitatis causa in una aliqua vocum fit, donec eam caeterae voces omnes assequantur, aut perraro consulto ob sententiarum aliquarum gravitatem exprimendam, et animis hominum imprimendam contingit, sicut et ab oratoribus et poetis figurate nonnunquam vel verba tantum, vel integrae sententiae ac versus repeti solent.

by the fourth discretionary rule.[217] All these factors must be observed until one reaches the syllable that is put to the accent. That syllable is granted whatever notes are left until one reaches the last syllable or the penultimate syllable (if unaccented), by the first discretionary rule.[218] But if so many notes would seem to be left over, so that the phrase can be repeated, let the phrase be completed at once, and let there be no length on the accented syllable, lest the suitableness of the repetition be lost.[219]

In regard to repetitions, however, it must meanwhile be noted that if they are frequent, they subject listeners to the same aversion and disgust as constant repetition of the same word does in speaking. In consequence, we must be careful not to be over-eager for repetitions. As no repetitions at all—as far as I know—are found in plainsong, so in mensural music, repetition either happens out of necessity in one or other of the voices until all the other voices catch up with it, or it takes place by design, though rarely, in order to express the importance of some phrases and impress it on men's minds, just as either words alone or entire phrases and verses are sometimes wont to be repeated by orators and poets as figures of speech.[220]

---

[217]202.1–2 *supra*. The situation described here is unclear in its wording. The thought, in relation to the previous sentence, seems to be this: here, too, there are more syllables in proportion to the number of notes, so the same semiminima (in the previous sentence) to which one syllable is given and extended to the entire series must now (in this sentence) be given one syllable but extended only to the next note, with the remaining syllables assigned similarly to the remaining semiminimae in groups of two.

[218]200.2–3 *supra*. See also Stoquerus's discussion of this rule in chapter 20, where, in section 3 (206.4–11 *supra*) he includes, in reference to necessary rule 5, the accented syllable (of the last word of a phrase) among the middle notes.

[219]The repetition of the phrase is suitable because one (a composer or singer) thereby avoids an excessively long melisma on the accented syllable. Cf. Lowinsky, "Treatise on Text Underlay," p. 241, where, in addition, he points to an echo of this in Zarlino's rule 8 (in his *Istitutioni harmoniche*).

[220]On repetition as a figure of speech, see Quintilian *Institutio oratoriae* 9.1.33 (and also 2.4 and 3.28–31). For a sensible use of textual repetition, see the opening section of Willaert's "Christi virgo dilectissima," soprano, mm. 1–11, and tenor, mm. 1–9, in Edward E. Lowinsky, ed., *The Medici Codex of 1518*, Monuments of Renaissance Music, vols. 3–5 (Chicago: University of Chicago Press, 1968), 4:150.

Quam vero sententiam in musica intelligamus in prima arbitrariarum declaratum est; ibidem et in quinta necessariarum explicatum satis est quae sit ultima et penultima nota, quibus ultima syllaba et penultima accentu carens tribuenda est. Potest enim ultima non finalis tantum atque simplex intelligi, sed et composita seu ligata, sive expresse id fiat atque ipso actu, sive vi ac potestate, ut saepe iam dictum est. Omnibus enim his regulis arbitrariis nil aliud inquisitum est, quam quae notae, etiamsi formam ligaturarum non admitterent, possent tamen aliis commode connecti; sed nunc ad reliquas recentiorum observationes properemus.

DE ARBITRARIIS RECENTIORUM REGULIS

CAP. XXVI

1. Tertius quinarius. 2. Ratio sufficientiae. 3. Differentia ab arbitrariis antiquorum. 4. Ipsarum regularum enarratio.

---

4 potest]potens M ||

What we understand as a phrase in music was made clear in the first discretionary rule.[221] There and in the fifth necessary rule, it was sufficiently explained what is the last and penultimate note to be granted the last and penultimate syllable (if it lacks the accent).[222] The last note can be understood as not only a final and simple note but also a compounded and ligated note, whether this is done distinctly and actually or virtually and potentially, as has often already been said.[223] In all these discretionary rules, nothing was investigated other than which notes—even if they did not admit of the form of ligatures—could nevertheless be suitably connected to other notes.[224] But let us now hurry on to the remaining observances of the newer composers.

CHAPTER 26

ON THE DISCRETIONARY RULES OF THE NEWER COMPOSERS[225]

1. The third group of five rules. 2. The reason for the sufficiency. 3. Their difference from the discretionary rules of the older composers. 4. The listing of the rules themselves.

---

[221]See the discussion of this rule in chapter 20, section 2 (204.12–206.3 *supra*).

[222]See chapter 20, section 3 (206.4–11 *supra*) and the discussion of necessary rule 5 in chapter 16, section 4 (182.8–15 *supra*). The latter explains what is meant by the last note (either a single note or a ligature [real or implied]). The following sentence in the present chapter merely reiterates this.

[223]See, for examples, chapter 13, section 3 (168.1–6); chapter 16, section 4 (182.8–15); chapter 18 (190.27–192.3). Stoquerus here couches the same idea in scholastic terms of act and potency. Hence, the fact that a series of notes cannot be expressed in a "distinctly and actually" notated ligature and yet must be given one syllable (due to the exigencies of the notes, say, in a series of semiminimae followed by a longer note) makes the series "virtually and potentially" a ligature.

[224]Cf. 190.27–29 *supra*.

[225]For the commentary on this chapter, see Introduction, pp. 84–86.

1. Sequitur nunc tertius harum regularum quinarius; in tres enim eas ordine divisimus, et ⟨cuique⟩ ordini quinque regulas assignavimus. Nec id tam consulto effinximus, quam ipsa natura ita constitutas investigando invenimus. Ut enim superioribus nihil facile vel addi ⟨vel demi⟩ posse visum est, ita et in his rem sese habere non difficulter demonstrabimus. Nam aut notas aut verba aut utrumque considerari cantando oportet. Circa notas considerabimus utrum minimae sint, an maiores vel minores minima. Minimis enim et maioribus minima singulis sua debetur syllaba, minoribus vero non; quod adeo verum est, ut nec illi, quae has proxime et immediate sequitur, quantovis maior sit, syllaba ulla tribuatur. In verbis vero consideratur ne facile repetitio fiat, minime autem verborum, sed nonnunquam sententiarum. Denique in utrisque, hoc est, et verbis et notis simul observatur ne syllabae brevi notula longa tribuatur, vel e converso, longae brevis.

⟨2.⟩ His ego quid amplius addi possit, quod in priores non incidat, me non invenire fateor; nec praeterea, quod demi possit, reperio, cum nihil contineatur quod in superioribus traditum occurrat, nisi quis forte ultimam antiqu-

---

2 cuique]cuius M ‖ 4 *scripsi* ‖ 5 demonstrabimus]demonstravimus M ‖ 8 minima]minimum M ‖ 14 *scripsi* ‖ 15–16 contineatur]contineat M ‖

1. Of these rules, there now follows the third group of five. We have divided these rules by order into three and assigned five rules to each order. Nor did we fashion this by design as much as we found them upon investigation to be so formed by nature itself.[226] Just as it was seen that nothing could easily be added to the above rules or taken away,[227] so will we also demonstrate without difficulty that it is the same matter in regard to these rules. In singing, either the notes or the words or both together ought to be considered. In regard to the notes, we will consider whether they are minimae or whether they are larger or smaller than a minima. Individual minimae and notes larger than a minima ought each be given their own syllable; individual notes smaller than a minima, however, do not each receive their own syllable. This latter situation is so true that neither is any syllable granted to the note that immediately follows these notes, however much larger it might be. In regard to the words, it is considered that repetition not readily take place, not only of words, to be sure, but also sometimes of phrases. And finally, in respect to both, that is, words and notes together, it is observed that a long note not be granted to a short syllable nor, conversely, a short note to a long syllable.

2. I acknowledge I do not discover anything further that can be added to these rules that does not come under the previous ones. Nor, moreover, do I find anything that can be taken away, since nothing is contained here that occurs handed down in the above rules, unless perhaps someone might say that the last rule of the older composers has been carried over into this set.

---

[226]By "nature," Stoquerus means the determining properties or characteristics of the notes (their values, for example, or their juxtaposition as separate entities or as notated or implied ligatures) or of the words (their syllabic correspondence with the numbers of available notes, for example, or their accent, particularly that of the last word of a phrase). In turn, these characteristics of the notes and words are investigated through Stoquerus's scholastic looking glass and by dichotomization come into view as determinants governing the number and formulation of the rules in each set. In this respect, as the next sentence of this chapter explains, "it was seen" that nothing can be added to or taken away from the rules already presented. See 188.15–190.26 in chapter 18 *supra* and 196.11–198.19 in chapter 19 *supra*.

[227]I have inserted *vel demi* in order to complete the sense and implied contrast with *vel addi* as given in the text. Moreover, Stoquerus discusses both alternatives in section 2 of the present chapter.

orum regulam huc translatam dicat; at illa ibi conditionaliter posita est. Saepeque aliter contingit ut ibidem in penultima et antepenultima regulis habetur, hic vero minoribus minima notulis simpliciter syllabas tribui negamus.

⟨3.⟩ Differunt et hoc a superioribus, quod illae plane et mere arbitrariae
5 sint, hae autem tam necessariarum quam arbitrariarum naturam sapere videntur. Arbitrariarum, quod non necessaria ipsis causa insit, propter quam, ut necessariae, nullo modo mutari possint. Necessariarum vero vim habent, quod rationi maxime consentientes fere aeque ut necessariae semper a recentioribus observatae videntur, nec nisi perraro, necessaria aliqua urgente causa,
10 neglectae inveniuntur. Ideo longe facilior cantandi ratio, quod ad verba attinet, in recentiorum cantilenis est, quam in antiquis. Quanto enim quisque regulis maxime sese astringit, tanto minus lectorem seu cantorem ambigere sinit. Sicut enim viator minus errare potest, si una sit ei in itinere via, cuius vestigia sequatur, posita, at ubi plures quam una se viae offerunt, non potest viator

---

4 *scripsi* ‖ 10 Ideo *corr. in marg.* Imo M ‖

There, however, that rule was put down conditionally,[228] and it often happens otherwise, as is the case in the second- and third-to-last[229] rules. Here, however, we simply deny that syllables are granted to notes smaller than a minima.

3. These rules differ from the above rules in this respect as well: the above rules are distinctly and purely discretionary, whereas these rules seem to betray the nature of both the necessary and discretionary rules. They are discretionary because there is no necessary cause inherent in them on which account, like the necessary rules, they can in no way be changed; they have the force of the necessary rules, however, because in their close concurrence with reason, they seem to be always observed by the newer composers almost equal to the necessary rules, nor are they discovered to be neglected, except rarely, and then at the behest of some necessary cause.[230] Thus,[231] as far as the words are concerned, the method of singing is far easier in the cantilenas of the newer composers than in those of the older composers, for the more closely a composer restricts himself to the rules, the less does he leave the reader or singer room for uncertainty. Just as a traveller is less likely to go astray if one road for his journey is put down for him whose tracks he may follow (but when more roads than one present themselves, a traveller only can

---

[228]I.e., on the condition that only one syllable is available or intended for a series of semiminimae. If more syllables are available or intended, then other rules of the older composers become operative, as Stoquerus goes on to explain.

[229]I.e., rules 4 and 3 respectively. Rule 4 addresses the setting of syllables to semiminimae as grouped in pairs. Stoquerus's citation of rule 3, however, is misplaced and should refer instead to rule 2 or, more precisely, to that part of his discussion of this rule that allows for separate syllables to be given to *all* semiminimae in a series. See 210.1–3 in chapter 21 *supra*. Cf. 228.7–12 in chapter 25 *supra*.

[230]I.e., some overriding reason or exception.

[231]In the body of the text, *imo* is given and underlined by the scribe, which draws attention to the reading, *ideo*, placed at the right margin and preceded by the abbreviation for *aliter*. I have substituted this alternate reading in the text since the context appears to support it.

non errare, nisi quid eum vel casus, vel rationis iudicium adiuvet. Plures itaque viae cantoribus positae sunt in antiquorum cantilenis, in quibus, qui regulas ignorant, fallaci casui sese committunt; qui vero regulas supra de illis a nobis traditas percipiunt, facile rationis iudicio illis instructo errores cavent.

5   At in recentiorum cantionibus cum regulae certae sint, quasi una in illis via tantum inserta, cantorem errare fere impossibile est. Quod tamen non ita accipiendum est, quasi eas et harum regularum rudis absque errore cantare possit. Sicut enim viator errare potest, certa etiam via ei posita, si eam ipsam ignoret, urbemque aggressurus nesciat quo sese vertat, an ad Orientem, vel Occiden-
10 tem, vel Meridiem, an ad Septentrionem; ita et cantor has quantumvis certas regulas, si ignoret, non necessario observabit; nec enim adeo naturales et necessariae sunt, ut, natura duce, ab iis aberrare non possit.

⟨4.⟩ Regulae igitur ipsae hae sunt.

1. Minimae et maioribus minima singulis singulae addendae sunt syllabae.
15 2. Semiminimis iisque minoribus, quotquot sint, non nisi una tribuenda est syllaba.
3. Notulae quoque, quae semiminimas vel fusas immediate sequitur, quanticumque sit valoris, eadem cum ipsis semiminimis syllaba communis est.
20 4. Repetitio textus fugienda est, magis autem verborum quam sententiarum.
5. Syllabis brevibus notae breves, longis longae tribuendae sunt.

---

13 *scripsi* ||

go astray unless something—either chance or a judgment of reason—helps him), so too, many roads are put down for the singers in the cantilenas of the older composers, in which those who are ignorant of the rules commit themselves to chance, which is misleading, while those who grasp the rules we handed down above regarding those cantilenas easily avoid errors through the judgment of reason provided in these rules.[232] Since, however, the rules pertaining to the songs of the newer composers are certain, with only one road, as it were, set into them, it is practically impossible for the singer to go astray. But nevertheless, this should not be taken to mean that even one unformed by these rules can sing those songs without error. Just as a traveller can go astray when even a certain road is put down before him if he is ignorant of the road itself and, as he is about to proceed toward a city, does not know which way to turn—east, west, south, or north—, so too a singer will not observe these rules necessarily, no matter how certain they are, if he is ignorant of them; for they are not so natural and necessary that, with nature as a guide, it is impossible for him to depart from them.

4. These, then, are the rules themselves:
1. Individual syllables must be adjoined to a minima and individual notes larger than a minima
2. Only one syllable must be granted to semiminimae and notes smaller than semiminimae, regardless of their number
3. The note, too, that immediately follows the semiminimae or fusae, regardless of its value, shares the same syllable with the semiminimae themselves
4. Repetition of text must be avoided—more, however, of words than phrases
5. Short notes must be granted to short syllables, long notes to long syllables.

---

[232]Stoquerus reminds his readers that the discretionary rules of the older composers are grounded in reason and that a knowledge of these rules and their application in practice is far superior to random choices that may, more often than not, be erroneous, as his extended simile implies.

DE MINIMA EAQUE MAIORIBUS NOTULIS

CAP. XXVII

1. Ratio. 2. Cur proprium. 3. Extensio. 4. Limitatio.

1. Minimae eaque maioribus notulis, ob tarditatem ac pronuntiationis moram, commode syllabae applicari possunt; ideoque illis regulariter singulis singulae debentur syllabae, ideoque primi musicae autores certas ligaturarum figuras instituerunt, qua re significarunt notis illis regulariter singulis suas deberi syllabas, nec nisi in expressis ligaturarum figuris contrarium fieri licere. Minimam vero ius maiorum notarum sequi vel ex ipso nomine patet. Nec enim minorum sed maiorum respectu minima; quare maioribus annumeranda est, dictaque minima videtur, eo quod minima sit, hoc est, infimum locum obtineat, minorique cum mora pronuntietur inter eas notas, quae syllabis proprie serviunt.

2. Propria autem haec regula recentiorum ideo videtur, quod ab antiquis omnino neglecta videtur; illi enim indifferenter quotlibet et quaslibet notas uni syllabae perinde ac ligatas tribuebant.

CHAPTER 27

ON THE MINIMA AND NOTES LARGER THAN A MINIMA[233]

1. Reason. 2. Why this rule is proper. 3. Extension. 4. Limitation.

1. Syllables can suitably be applied to the minima and notes larger than it because of their slowness and length of delivery.[234] And so, as a rule, individual syllables ought to be given to these individual notes. And so, the first authors of music established certain figures of ligatures by which they signified that as a rule, individual notes ought to be given their own syllables and that the contrary was not allowed unless in expressed figures of ligatures.[235] That the minima follows the law of larger notes, however, is evident even from its very name. The minima is such, not in respect to smaller notes but to larger ones; therefore, it should be put among the larger notes and seems to be called a minima because it is the smallest of these. That is, of those notes that are properly at the service of syllables, it obtains the lowest place and is delivered with a shorter length.

2. This rule, however, seems proper to the newer composers because it seems to be entirely neglected by the older ones. The latter indiscriminately granted notes of any number and kind to one syllable, just as if these notes were ligated.[236]

---

[233]For the commentary on this chapter, see Introduction, pp. 86–88.

[234]This argument from slowness or prolonged delivery in regard to the minima and larger note-values may be considered a companion or complementary argument to Stoquerus's argument from swiftness in regard to semiminimae and smaller note-values, to which he appeals in his discussion of rule 5 of the older composers in chapter 24, section 2 *supra*. Stoquerus's appeal, in the second half of the present section, to the root meaning of *minima* and its consequent grouping with note values larger than it further confirms his argumentation in this section.

[235]Cf. 210.3–5 *supra*.

[236]The placement of this rule among those of the newer generation of composers also reflects a stylistic difference between the two generations, with the newer generation preferring a more syllabic style in which melismas occur chiefly on series of semiminimae and smaller note-values (see Introduction, n. 139).

3. Idem quoque nonnunquam observatur in semiminimis, cum in minimarum locum succedunt, quod semper fieri solet in signo C, nonnunquam etiam in ₵, quo casu vel omnes voces semiminimas sonant, vel quodammodo intervallis maioribus distantes ponuntur, et quod certius signum est, plures
5 illis quam una syllaba ascribuntur. Quod cum fit non binis, ut supra in regula quarta attribuenda erit una syllaba, sed singulae minimae iure censendae erunt, singulisque singulae addendae erunt syllabae.

4. Limitanda tamen haec regula in clausulis formalibus videtur, in quibus minima saepe syllaba destituitur.

DE SEMIMINIMIS EISQUE MINORIBUS NOTIS

CAP. XXVIII

1. Ratio. 2. Proprium. 5. Extensio. 4. Limitatio.

1. Quod nulla semiminimis attribuitur syllaba, id fieri videtur quod illae antiquis in usu non fuerint, longeque postquam musica inventa est introductae

3. This same principle is also sometimes observed in regard to semiminimae when they take the place of minimae, as always happens in the sign C, and sometimes even in ₵, in which case either all the voices articulate semiminimae or the semiminimae[237] are put down at somewhat larger intervals apart[238] and—what is a more certain sign—more syllables than one are allotted to them.[239] When this takes place, a syllable must not be attributed to groups of two, as in the fourth rule above;[240] rather, they must be reckoned by law as individual minimae and individual syllables are to be adjoined to them individually.

4. This rule, it seems, should nevertheless be limited in regard to formal clausulae, in which the minima is often left without a syllable.[241]

CHAPTER 28

ON SEMIMINIMAE AND NOTES SMALLER THAN SEMIMINIMAE[242]

1. Reason. 2. Why this rule is proper. 3. Extension. 4. Limitation.

1. The reason for the fact that no syllable is attributed to semiminimae[243] seems to be that they were not in practice among the ancients and were introduced long after music was invented.[244] This is clear even from the term

---

[237]The context of Stoquerus's argumentation here seems to require *semiminimae* as the subject of *ponuntur*.

[238]See Introduction, n. 140.

[239]I.e., Stoquerus seems to be saying that in addition to the qualifications just mentioned, the text underlay itself shows a plurality of syllables placed under the series of semiminimae.

[240]See 202.1–2 *supra*.

[241]See the explanation of this exception in chapter 23, section 3, 218.13–220.4 *supra*.

[242]For the commentary on this chapter, see Introduction, pp. 88–90.

[243]In this section, Stoquerus argues that semiminimae cannot of themselves receive individual syllables. That a syllable is in fact given to the first semiminima of a series of semiminimae will be discussed in the first section of the next chapter.

[244]See Introduction, n. 145.

sunt; quod vel ex minimae appellatione constat. Ex qua manifeste deprehenditur nullam ea notula minorem in usu primis huius scientiae autoribus fuisse. Quare cum minima sit secundum nomen suum minima ex iis, quae syllabis applicari consueverunt, merito hac minoribus notulis syllabae denegantur.
5 Nec parum ad rem facit, quod illarum notarum velocitas syllabas non admittit, oritur enim magna syllabarum confusio; distincta enim syllabarum prolatio tempore ac mora indiget.

2. Regulam vero hanc propriam esse huius loci superius capite 26 et capite proximo probatum est. Antiqui enim non semper unam syllabam omnibus
10 semiminimis continue positis attribuebant, sed vel duas vel tres vel plures, ita ut nunc duabus, nunc quatuor, nunc pluribus syllaba una, aut etiam singulis singulae tribuerentur.

3. Quod vero de semiminimis hic dicitur, idem et de minima, cum semiminimae comparatur, ut in proportione tripla, dici potest.

"minima." From this term, it is clearly detected that no note smaller than it had been in practice among the first authors of this science. Therefore, since the minima is, according to its very name, the smallest of those notes that are customarily applied to syllables,[245] syllables are justly denied to notes smaller than it. It is of no little import here that the swiftness of those notes does not admit syllables, for a great slurring of syllables results. A distinct delivery of syllables needs time and length.[246]

2. That this rule is proper to this place was proved above in chapter 26[247] and the next chapter.[248] The older composers did not always attribute one syllable to all semiminimae placed together, but even two, three, or more syllables; thus one syllable was granted now to two, now to four, now to several, or even individually to individual semiminimae.

3. What is said here concerning semiminimae can also be said concerning the minima when it is equal to the semiminima, as in *proportio tripla*.[249]

---

[245]Stoquerus now uses his argument from the meaning of *minima* (cf. 240.9–13 *supra*) to conclude that notes smaller than it should not receive syllables.

[246]Stoquerus repeats here the same argument from swiftness that he employs in his discussion of rule 5 of the older composers. See chapter 24, section 2 (in particular, 222.8–12) *supra*.

[247]See in particular section 2 (234.14–236.3) *supra*.

[248]See chapter 27, section 2 (240.14–16) *supra*.

[249]Stoquerus is perhaps referring to the common occurrence in triple time where a series of minimae ordinarily receive one syllable, as in this figure:

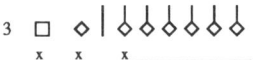

I am grateful to Don Harrán for his clarification of this as presented in the galley proofs of his *Word-Tone Relations in Musical Thought from Antiquity to the Seventeenth Century*, Musicological Studies and Documents, no. 40 (Neuhausen-Stuttgart: American Institute of Musicology and Hänssler-Verlag, 1986).

4. Quod vero haec regula non observatur, quando semiminima minimae naturam sequitur; de hoc satis supra in proxima regula diximus.

DE MINIMA AUT QUALIBET MAIORI NOTULA SEMIMINIMAS IMMEDIATE SEQUENTE

CAP. XXIX

1. Ratio. 2. Proprium. 3. Extensio ad mediatam. 4. Illatio seu corollarium de ultima.

    1. Quae semiminimas immediate maior sequitur syllabam eandem cum ipsis semiminimis communem habet. Cum enim syllaba semiminimis regulariter non attribuatur, ut supra in proxima regula diximus, primae tamen contra

---

1 quando [minima *delevi*] semiminima minimae M ||

4. This rule is not observed when the semiminima[250] follows the nature of the minima. We spoke sufficiently of this above in the previous rule.[251]

CHAPTER 29

ON THE MINIMA OR ANY LARGER NOTE IMMEDIATELY FOLLOWING THE SEMIMINIMAE[252]

1. Reason. 2. Why this rule is proper. 3. Extension to the mediated note.[253] 4. Inference or corollary concerning the last note.

1. The larger note that immediately follows the semiminimae has the same syllable in common with the semiminimae themselves. Since as a rule a syllable is not attributed to semiminimae (as we said above in the previous

---

[250]The manuscript shows *minima semiminima minimae*. *Minima* appears to be a scribal slip that was not deleted according to the scribe's customary manner of drawing a line through the word. That *minima* is not intended as an adjective modifying *semiminima* is clear from the fact that in the manuscript *minima* is capitalized (*Minima*) according to the scribe's custom of capitalizing the note names throughout the treatise. These factors seem to warrant the exclusion of *minima* in the edited text.

[251]See chapter 27, section 3 (242.1–7 *supra*).

[252]For the commentary on this chapter, see Introduction, pp. 90–93.

[253]It will become clear in Stoquerus's discussion of this topic (see section 3 *infra*) that "the mediated note" refers to the next longer note (also a minima) after the longer note that immediately (*immediate*) follows a series of semiminimae. This next longer note, then, is "mediated" (*mediata*) by the minima between it and the last semiminima of a series. "Extension" in the statement of this topic refers to the extension of the rule to include the second longer note after the semiminimae, whereas in the discussion of this topic below, "extension" refers to the extension of the same syllable to the next longer note after the semiminimae.

illarum naturam semper addatur, consequens est eam posteriori, cui convenire poterat, adimi, ut, quod uni superflue attributum videbatur, alterius privatione compensaretur. Nec vero iniuste primae semiminimarum syllaba adiicitur, nec contra posteriori, quamvis maiori, debetur, si recte rem perpendas. Quod
5 enim semiminimis syllabae non adduntur ob velocitatem, qua proferuntur, introductum est. Velocitas autem et mora non ex principio, sed fine prolationis dignoscuntur. Si enim cito deficiat prolatio, velociter pronuntiatio facta dicetur. Quare quod ad velocitatem attinet, non qua in nota incipit pronuntiatio curandum est, sed in qua desinit, quam idcirco maiorem esse oportet, ut velox
10 pronuntiatio vitetur. Ideo recte diximus ultimam maiorem cum praecedentibus eam semiminimis syllabam eandem habere communem.

---

1 naturam]natura M ||

rule[254]) and yet, contrary to their nature,[255] one is always adjoined to the first of a series, it is consistent for a syllable to be withheld from the note after the series—on which there could have agreeably been one—so that what seemed needlessly attributed to one note might be offset by a denial to the other. It is not unreasonable however, if you weigh the matter rightly, for a syllable to be added to the first of the semiminimae, but on the other hand, it ought not to be given to the note after them, although it is larger, for it has been proposed that syllables are not adjoined to semiminimae because of the swiftness with which the notes are delivered.[256] But swiftness and length are discerned not from the beginning but from the end of the delivery, for if the delivery comes to an end quickly, the pronunciation will be said to have been swiftly done. Therefore, as far as swiftness is concerned, care must be taken not on the note on which the pronunciation starts, but on the one on which it ends. For this reason, this note should be a larger one in order to avoid a swift pronunciation. Thus, we rightly said[257] that the last longer note has the same syllable in common with the semiminimae preceding it.[258]

---

[254]I.e., the second discretionary rule of this set of five rules as discussed in the previous chapter, particularly in section 1 (*ratio*) *supra*, where Stoquerus explains why semiminimae in series do not each receive separate syllables.

[255]I.e., as having too short a duration to accommodate the distinct delivery of a syllable. In the continuation of his argumentation in this section, Stoquerus completes his explanation of both why a syllable may in fact be given to the first semiminima of a series (the essential thrust of discretionary rule 2) and why one is withheld from the first longer note after a series (the thrust of discretionary rule 3 as discussed in this chapter). I have emended *natura* in the manuscript to *naturam* because it is governed by *contra*.

[256]See 244.5–7 *supra*. Also, cf. n. 246 *supra*.

[257]I.e., in the topic sentence that begins this section.

[258]Stoquerus's argumentation in this section is phenomenological, drawing from the simple fact that words or the syllables of a word require for their delivery a sufficiently measured pace in order to be understood by the listener. Hence, when words and syllables are set to notes, the notes themselves must be of such duration as to enable the listener to understand the sung text. Stoquerus's argument, based as it is on the natural judgment of the ear, expresses one facet of the humanist ideal of the proper coordination of text and music.

2. Hanc vero regulam ab antiquis non minus neglectam quam observatam videas; ideo non immerito recentioribus propria ascribitur, quando ab illis non minus quam necessariae custoditur.

3. Nonnunquam eadem syllaba etiam in alteram, quae hanc sequitur, extenditur, vel ut mora in semiminimis impedita plenius reddatur, vel ut, si semiminimas sequatur ⟨minima⟩ in tactus depressione, altera eam sequens mensuram impleat, per quartam arbitrariarum.

4. Ex his notandum est ultimam notam, cui ultima debetur syllaba, non posse semper esse eam, quae ultimo loco ponitur; quid enim si illam plurimae semiminimae praecedant, tunc enim illa semiminimis annumeratur, syllabamque propriam non admittit, ultimaque, quae syllabae capax sit, prima semiminima censenda est.

---

6 minima]semiminima M | altera]alteram M ||

2. You might see that this rule was no less neglected than observed by the older composers. Thus, it is not unjustly allotted here as proper to the newer composers, since it is heeded by them no less than the necessary rules.

3. Sometimes the same syllable is extended even to the next note that follows this longer note, either in order that the length impeded in the semiminimae might be rendered more fully, or in order that, if a minima[259] on the thesis of the tactus follows the semiminimae, the next note[260] following the minima might complete the measure, according to the fourth discretionary rule.[261]

4. From these considerations, it must be noted that the last note to which the last syllable ought to be given cannot always be the note that is put down in the last place. If several semiminimae precede it, then it is put with the semiminimae and does not admit a syllable proper to it, and the last note that is capable of a syllable must be reckoned to be the first semiminima.[262]

---

[259]*Semiminima* in the manuscript is obviously a slip of the pen and should be changed to *minima* as demanded by the context.

[260]I have emended *alteram* in the manuscript to *altera*, since the context indicates that it modifies *sequens* as the subject of *impleat*.

[261]Of the two reasons given in this section, the first is an aesthetic one (the composer might simply prefer a longer declamation of a word or syllable), the second is mensural (the composer might judge it better to assign a new syllable on the beginning of the next tactus). The second reason might indeed be preferable in the instance Stoquerus himself cites (i.e., a pair of minimae following the series of semiminimae), and hence the reference to discretionary rule 4 of the older composers, which addresses how properly to assign syllables to pairs of minimae when one syllable is not available or intended for each note of the pair. For examples illustrating these two reasons, see the commentary on this section in the Introduction.

[262]This section fulfills the promise Stoquerus made in section 4 of his discussion of necessary rule 5 in chapter 16 (see 182.8–15 *supra*) to explain more fully in the discretionary rules how best to set a syllable to the last note of a phrase that is in fact part of an implied ligature.

DE REPETITIONE VERBORUM FUGIENDA

CAP. XXX

1. Ratio. 2. Proprium. 3. Limitatio.

1. Verbum idem saepius absque nausea repeti non potest. Sicut enim in loquendo balbutientibus vitio datur, quod syllabas et voces prolaturi duplicant, imo saepius multiplicant, contraque loquacibus unam atque eandem rem saepius auribus obtundentibus offendimur, ita et in canendo eadem verba molesta sunt. Quid quod in cantu plano, qui maxime naturam ac veritatem exprimit, repetitio fieri omnino non solet.

2. Ideo non immerito reprehensione digni sunt, qui quamlibet non modo sententiam, sed et vocem quoties libet repetunt, ii qui mihi balbutire magis quam loqui, vel canere videntur. Quod cum a recentioribus non perinde atque a veteribus commissum videatur, proprie illis attributum negari non potest.

3. Interdum tamen sententiae graviores, ut animis magis imprimantur, repeti solent, sicut et figurate ab oratoribus repetitiones fieri solent; sed hoc, ut si raro fiat, virtuti ascribi potest, ita si frequenter et sine delectu fiat, in vitium incidit.

CHAPTER 30

ON AVOIDING REPETITION OF WORDS[263]

1. Reason. 2. Why this rule is proper. 3. Limitation.

1. The same word cannot be often repeated without becoming disgusting.[264] Just as in speech, it is given as a fault in stutterers that in their delivery of syllables and words, they repeat them once and often more than once, and on the other hand, we find it offensive when garrulous people often din one and the same idea into our ears, so too in singing, the same words are bothersome. And what of the fact that in plainsong, which best expresses nature and truth,[265] repetition is not wont to occur at all?

2. Hence, they are not unjustly deserving reproach who repeat not only any phrase but also any word whenever it pleases them. They seem to me more to stutter than to speak or sing. Since this does not seem to have been committed by the newer composers in the same way as by the past composers, it cannot be denied that this rule is properly attributed to the newer ones.

3. Nevertheless, sometimes weightier phrases are wont to be repeated so that they might be more firmly impressed on the minds, just as repetitions are wont to be made by orators as figures of speech.[266] But if it is done rarely, this can be allotted to virtue; so if it is done frequently and without discrimination, it is counted a fault.

---

[263]For the commentary on this chapter, see Introduction, pp. 93–94.

[264]Stoquerus's argumentation in this section and in section 3 below is essentially the same as was already given in chapter 25 (see, in particular, 230.7–15 *supra*).

[265]I.e., both the natural and reasonable manner of coordinating words and notes. The use of *natura* and *veritas* here recalls the synonyms Stoquerus uses at the beginning of chapter 19 to describe the necessary rules (*naturales*) and the discretionary ones (*verisimiles*), for which see 192.16–19 *supra*.

[266]See n. 220 *supra*.

DE SYLLABARUM QUANTITATE OBSERVANDA

CAP. XXXI

1. Declaratio. ⟨2.⟩ Ratio. 3. Proprium. 4. Limitatio.
   1. Quantitas syllabarum aliter in prosa quam in cantione observatur. In prosa enim

Caetera desiderantur.

---

3 *scripsi* ‖

CHAPTER 31

ON THE OBSERVANCE OF THE QUANTITY OF SYLLABLES[267]

1. Clarification. 2. Reason. 3. Why this rule is proper. 4. Limitation.

1. The quantity of syllables is observed differently in prose than in song.[268] For in prose . . .

The rest is missing.[269]

---

[267]For the commentary on this chapter, see Introduction, pp. 94–95.

[268]Keeping in mind the rule itself which this chapter is intended to elucidate—that short syllables be set to short notes, long syllables to long notes (see 238.21 *supra*)—one can presume from the topic sentence given here that Stoquerus intends this section to be a preliminary distinction, for purposes of clarification (*declaratio*), between how syllabic quantity is observed in a non-musical context, especially prose (*prosa*), and in a musical one (*cantio*). The following sections would then discuss the reason for the rule (*ratio*); why the newer composers observe it more closely than do the older composers (*proprium*); and its limitation (*limitatio*) to instances that are not overidden by other reasons (e.g., a contrapuntal line that may force the texting of a long syllable to a short note).

[269]For what might comprise the remainder of the treatise, see Introduction, pp. 14–16 and 95.

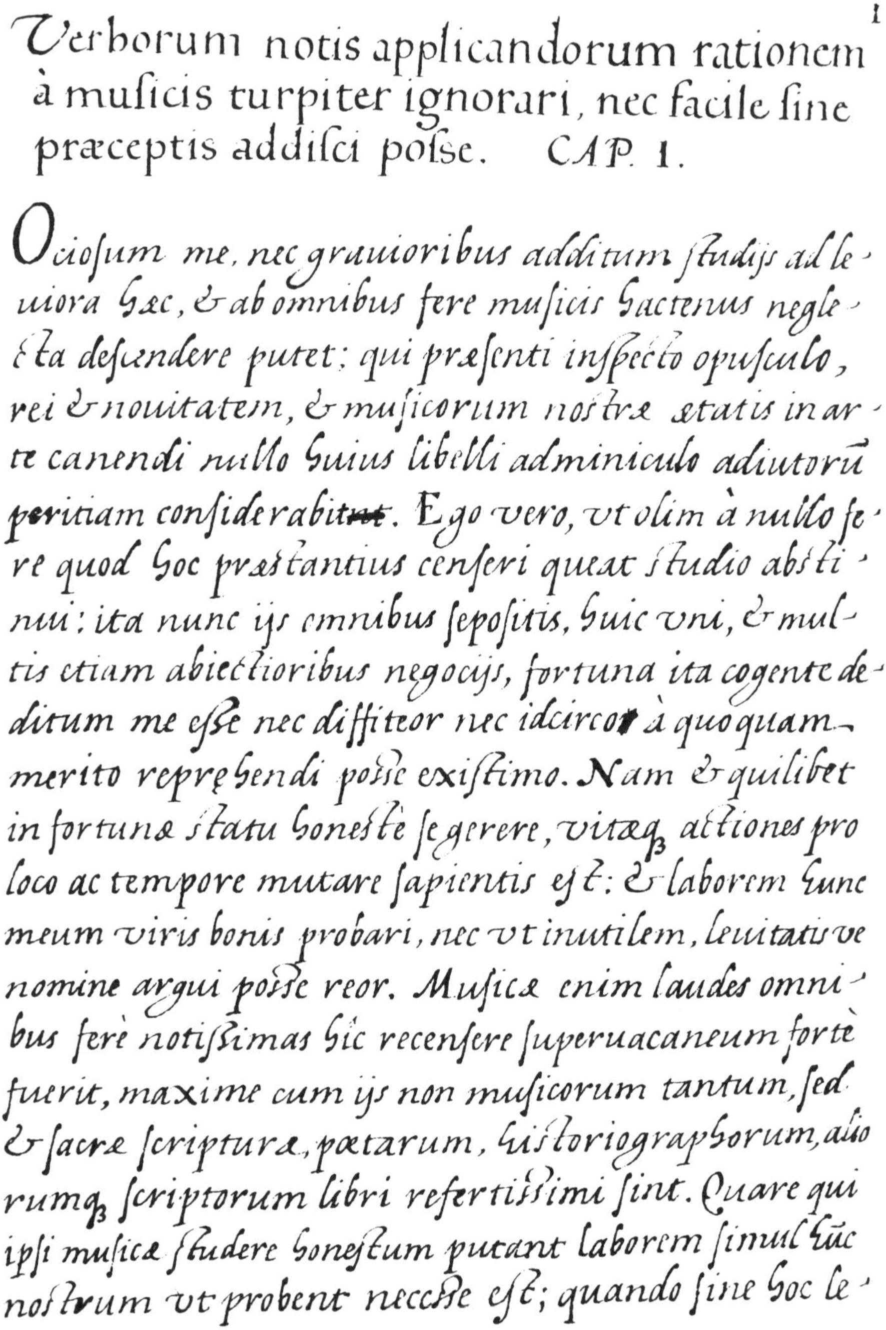

Verborum notis applicandorum rationem à musicis turpiter ignorari, nec facile sine præceptis addisci posse.   CAP. 1.

Ociosum me, nec grauioribus additum studijs ad leuiora hæc, & ab omnibus fere musicis hactenus neglecta descendere putet: qui præsenti inspecto opusculo, rei & nouitatem, & musicorum nostræ ætatis in arte canendi nullo huius libelli adminiculo adiutorū peritiam considerabit~~ur~~. Ego vero, vt olim à nullo fere quod hoc præstantius censeri queat studio abstinui: ita nunc ijs omnibus sepositis, huic vni, & multis etiam abiectioribus negocijs, fortuna ita cogente deditum me esse nec diffiteor nec idcirco à quoquam merito reprehendi posse existimo. Nam & quilibet in fortunæ statu honestè se gerere, vitæq; actiones pro loco ac tempore mutare sapientis est: & laborem hunc meum viris bonis probari, nec vt inutilem, leuitatisue nomine argui posse reor. Musicæ enim laudes omnibus fere notissimas hic recensere superuacaneum fortè fuerit, maxime cum ijs non musicorum tantum, sed & sacræ scripturæ, pœtarum, historiographorum, aliorumq; scriptorum libri refertissimi sint. Quare qui ipsi musicæ studere honestum putant laborem simul hũc nostrum vt probent necesse est; quando sine hoc le-

Plate 1. Madrid, Biblioteca Nacional, MS. 6486, f. 1r.

loqui, vel canere, videntur. Quod cum à recentioribus non perinde atq̧ à veteribus commiſſum videatur, propriè illis attributum negari non poteſt.
3. Interdum tamen sententiæ grauiores vt animis magis imprimantur, repeti solent, ſicut & figuratè ab oratoribus repetitiones fieri solent: ſed hoc, vt ſi raro fiat, virtuti aſcribi poteſt: ita ſi frequenter & ſine delectu fiat, in vitium incidit.

De ſyllabarum quantitate obſeruanda. CAP. XXXI.

1. Declaratio. Ratio. 3. Proprium. 4. Limitatio.
1. Quantitas ſyllabarum aliter in proſa, quàm in cantione obſeruatur. In proſa enim.

Cætera deſiderantur.

Plate 2. Madrid, Biblioteca Nacional, MS. 6486, f. 40v.

INDEX VERBORUM

aberrare, 154.1; 184.6; 238.12
abesse, 134.2, 6; 186.6
abiectior, 100.10
abnegare, 154.15
absolvi, 230.4–5
abstinere, 100.9; 162.10; abstineri, 228.1
abstractus, 112.13; 118.20
abundare, 224.9; 228.8, 10, 11
accedere, 112.5, 11; 116.4; 130.4, 12; 134.5; 150.16–17; 152.11; 182.10; 192.17; 202.18; 222.2
accentus, 112.18; 196.14; 200.2; 202.6, 8, 10, 11, 17; 204.1, 3, 4–5, 6, 7, 8, 9, 10; 206.8, 10; 230.1, 3, 5; 232.3
accessoria, 220.3
accidere, 152.29; 154.5; 162.1; 164.1; 166.20; 168.11; 184.13; 206.18; 222.12; 226.6
accidentaria, 134.1, 3
accipere, 118.4; 220.13; accipi, 178.7; 180.9; 196.1; 226.6; 238.6–7
acquirere, 102.18
actio, 100.13; 116.18; 156.4; 186.14; 202.14
actor, 148.22, 23; 154.16, 17
acumen, 142.5
actus, 130.8; 204.8
acutus, 122.4; 124.17; 132.6, 11; acutior, 130.2; 132.9; 134.5; 142.6
adaequare, 218.15
addere, 104.18; 138.21; addi, 100.5; 114.9; 162.11; 190.24; 200.3, 5; 202.2; 204.2; 222.2, 14; 224.10, 13; 228.7; 234.4, 14; 238.14; 242.7; 248.1, 5
addici, 190.16; 202.4; 228.10
addiscere, 114.19; addisci, 100.3; 116.10, 14; 118.9
adducere, 110.22; 192.7; adduci, 118.15; 164.3
adesse, 162.12
adiicere, 102.11; 162.5; 174.13; adiici, 164.12; 166.14; 172.11; 198.16; 200.4; 216.2; 218.1; 222.4; 224.10; 248.3
adimi, 248.2

259

adiungere, 164.7
adiuvare, 238.1; adiuvari, 100.8; 102.19
adminiculum, 100.8
admiscere, 140.8
admittere, 118.6; 188.11; 198.19; 210.6; 212.6; 214.7; 232.7; 244.5; 250.11; admitti, 150.7; 168.9
Adrianus Vuillartius, 162.9; 194.4, 9
adultus, 102.7
adversari, 128.7
adverti, 118.18
aeditus, 194.11
aequipollens, 198.3
aequipollere, 226.5–6, 7
aequivalens, 200.7; 212.6, 212.8–214.1, 11–12
aemulari, 110.7
aequalis, 190.16; 210.1 (bis), 10
aequus, 102.10; 134.11, 12
aestimari, 116.8
aetas, 100.7; 106.11
aeternus, 152.2
affectus, 202.15
afferre, 120.6; 186.7; allatus, 120.15
affirmare, 224.6; affirmari, 146.6
affirmatio, 146.8–9
agere, 104.4–5; 144.14; 154.19; 156.13 (bis); 184.1; 190.14; 192.2; agi, 104.3; 120.3; 150.20; 178.1, 4; 190.1; 192.2
aggredi, 108.9–10; 238.9
agilitas, 108.16
aio, 104.16; 108.12; 110.15; 114.3, 14; 118.16; 124.7
alacriter, 102.25
Alexander, 112.22; 156.19 (bis)
alienus, 120.6
alius, 100.17; 108.15; 110.15; 112.16, 21; 114.6, 23, 24; 118.19 (bis), 21; 122.3, 16; 144.5 (bis); 150.16 (bis); 152.4, 9, 10, 13; 154.24 (bis), 27 (bis); 156.3 (bis), 17; 170.3; 172.5, 6 (ter), 12; 180 (ter); 186.12, 13; 190.30 (bis); 222.13; 226.6; 228.5; 232.8
allegatus, 114.5
alligari, 210.9, 10; 216.9
alter, 104.6 (bis); 116.10; 126.5; 130.1, 2, 8; 134.2 (bis),6 (bis); 12; 144.9, 13; 164.6; 178.7, 8, 11; 204.3, 4; 216.9; 218.3, 14; 248.2; 250.4, 6
alteratio, *v.* punctus alterationis
altus, 124.17

261

ambae, 198.11, 14
ambigere, 190.2; 236.12; ambigi, 190.5
ambiguitas, 196.11
ambo, 106.9, 16; 118.15, 18
ambulare, 156.11–12
ambulatio, 110.10
amitti, 188.2; 230.6
amor, 106.5
amplecti, 184.18
amplexari, 102.25–26
amusus, 192.19
animadverti, 228.8
animus, 106.5; 156.6; 164.8; 230.13; 252.14
annotari, 154.10
annumerare, 162.6; annumerari, 158.6; 206.11; 240.10–11; 250.10
annus, 110.11
antecedere, 104.8, 13–14; 148.11, 18; 152.1; 178.12; 180.1
antepenultimus, 180.10–11; 200.2; 206.3, 7–8, 10, 10–11; 236.2
anterior, 148.13
antiquitas, 106.18
antiquus, 106.11; 148.19; 170.1; 192.14; 194.5; 196.1–2, 8; 200.1; 210.5; 220.5; 224.2; 226.8, 11; 232.12–13; 234.16–236.1; 236.11; 238.2; 240.14; 242.14; 244.9; 250.1; antiquior, 150.15–16; 162.9; 194.8; antiquissimus, 106.23; 110.2
aperire, 114..13; 118.10; 158.3; 182.15, 20–21; 188.11–12; 192.11; aperiri, 190.25
apparere, 124.8; 136.4; 138.7; 154.26; 168.6; 174.16
appellare, 102.2; 116.22; 142.4; 186.5
appellatio, 118.1; 244.1
applausus, 114.25; 150.13
applicare, 106.2; 108.20, 23; applicari, 100.1; 144.14; 190.4; 218.4 (bis); 240.5; 244.4
applicatio, 114.16
apponi, 172.8; 190.19; 196.23; 198.18
apprehendere, 114.15, 17; apprehendi, 184.9
approbari, 150.7
aptari, 214.1
aptus, 160.9, 14; aptior, 144.6
arbitrari, 124.11
arbitrarius, 114.24; 154.29; 156.1, 5; 158.14; 182.6,14; 186.1, 4, 5, 9; 188.3; 190.14–15, 27; 192.16; 226.11, 17; 228.4, 7, 10, 11; 230.3–4; 232.1, 6, 10, 12; 236.4, 5, 6; 250.7

arbitrium, 108.6, 20; 146.14; 156.6, 11; 186.6, 7, 8, 10
argui, 100.14; 184.1; 188.8
argumentum, 108.10–11; 110.8, 9, 10–11, 12; 112.5; 114.1 (bis)
Aristotiles, 154.2; 184.17
ars, 100.7; 102.9, 14, 17, 108.2, 7, 13; 110.4, 5, 12; 112.7, 10; 114.14, 27; 116.4, 5, 6, 11, 13, 14; 118.2, 3, 9; 146.15; 120.2; 148.30, 31; 150.2, 3, 4; 152,13; 184.6; 188.15; 192.21; 196.6; 210.5; ars oratoria, 102.15–16
artifex, 146.15; 152.10; 184.6; 194.1, 3
artificialis, 110.6; 116.1; 192.17–18; 194.1
ascendere, 122.5, 17; 128.11; 130.12, 14; 134.9–10, 13; 136.3, 5, 8, 11, 12, 18; 138.1, 8; 142.5, 7, 10, 12, 16, 16–17, 17, 18, 21, 22, 24, 26; 144.2, 3, 5, 8; ascendi, 136.14
ascribere, 192.9; ascribi, 164.1–2; 172.9; 242.5; 250.2; 252.16
assentiri, 140.21
assequi, 100.19; 114.16; 164.6; 196.7; 230.12
asserere, 142.11; 146.16
assignare, 192.4; 234.2; assignari, 126.5; 158.11–12; 166.12; 174.17
assuefieri, 184.19
astringere, 154.12–13; 194.6; 196.5; astringi, 108.19; 148.17; 154.11–12; 236.12
attinere, 120.7; 152.7; 180.10; 194.7; 198.6; 202.14; 228.4; 236.10; 248.8
attingere, 130.10, 20
attribuere, 166.14; 168.12; 174.14–15; 220.6; attribui, 116.18; 118.6; 158.8; 166.10; 168.1; 170.6–7; 182.3; 190.29; 198.13; 202.17; 206.6; 208.11–12; 222.9; 224.5; 244.10; 246.10; 248.2; 252.13
audire, 156.10; 164.12; 230.8; 242.6, 13
auditor, 118.7
auferri, 162.11
augere, 120.8; 172.10; augeri, 160.10; 164.9
augmentatio, *v.* punctus augmentationis
auris, 114.26; 118.5; 164.15; 174.3; 222.11; 252.7; *v.* commune aurium judicium, naturale aurium iudicium
autor, 108.19; 138.11; 144.18; 146.7, 15; 148.2; 154.17; 192.7; 194.10; 240.6; 244.2
autoritas, 112.2, 4; 144.17; 146.9, 15–16; 148.12, 28; 152.8, 10, 11, 14; 154.3; 192.3, 6
avaritia, 184.19
avis, 106.1, 19; 116.1
B–fa, *v.* hexachordum B–fa
B–mi, *v.* hexachordum B–mi
♮ durum, *v.* cantus ♮ durus

b molle, *v.* cantus b mollis
baculum, 102.6
balbutire. 252.5, 11
barbarismum, 118.7
beneficium, 102.14
benignior, 114.18
bibit, 156.10
biformis, 104.6
binae, 198.6, 7; 224.13; 228.12; 242.5
bonus, 100.14; 152.18; 154.1; 186.11; optimus, 154.14; *v.* bonus vir
brevis (*adj.*), 234.12, 13; 238.21 (bis)
brevis (*n.*), 222.3
Bucolici, 106.16
C, *v.* signum C
₵, *v.* signum ₵
caecus, 102.5; 142.8 (bis)
caeterus, 104.13; 106.9; 114.9–10, 15; 118.19; 120.1; 122.8, 11; 130.5, 18; 148.20; 154.6; 160.12–13; 168.9; 196.1; 198.17, 19; 202.12, 13; 206.8, 12, 16; 208.4; 210.2, 4, 9; 218.10; 222.7; 226.4–5; 230.11; 254.6
canere, 100.7; 112.13; 116.20, 21; 148.7, 20, 30; 150.11; 156.12, 16 (bis), 17; 158.2; 182.18, 21; 184.1, 3, 13, 20; 196.15; 202.17; 206.5; 252.7, 12; cani, 102.1; 108.18; 112.9; 116.3; 118.10; 134.8; 136.12; 138.4 (bis); 140.3, 4, 5; 146.19; 152.7, 24; 182.19, 22; 194.7; 218.8; 226.13
cantare, 102.3, 9–10, 18, 24; 108.21, 110.2; 148.10, 15; 154.19; 158.1; 160.16; 234.6; 236.10; 238.7; cantari, 108.12, 15–16; 112.11; 114.3; 122.2; 124.9, 14; 130.12; 136.10, 11, 11–12; 138.20–21, 22; 146.13; 148.9; 192.13
cantilena, 124.7, 13, 15; 130.17; 144.18; 146.13, 15, 19; 148.4, 18, 27; 150, 4; 152.21, 25; 162.7; 168.10; 192.11; 194.11; 236.11; 238.2
cantio, 102.8; 148.2; 152.17; 160.15, 16; 164.2, 5; 172.17; 190.9; 194.6, 13; 204.10; 226.4; 238.5; 254.4
cantor, 108.6; 118.10; 124.6; 146.18, 19; 148.3, 7, 20, 22, 25, 29; 152.17, 20, 23, 26; 154.18–19; 162.1; 164.4, 13; 170.1; 190.2; 222.6; 236.12; 238.2, 6, 10
cantus (mensuralis), 146.18; 172.3–4; 186.3; 196.16; 204.16, 17; 222.12; 230.11
cantus (re solfizatione), 106.20; 116.1; 122.5, 12; 124.5, 6, 7, 8; 140.15; 142.4; 144.4; cantus naturalis, 122.7, 14–15; 124.2 (bis), 3; 130.16; 136.7; cantus b mollis, 122.7; 122.3, 15; 124.3, 7, 9, 15–16, 17; 130.9, 16; cantus ♮ durus, 122.7, 15; 124.3–4, 7, 9–10, 12, 17; 130.9, 16;
cantus planus, 172.3; 230.10; 252.8
capax, 250.11

carere, 116.5; 140.18; 170.8; 178.2; 188.4; 210.5; 226.12; 230.3; 232.3
casus, 238.1, 3; 242.3
causa, 156.7; 164.1; 172.17; 178.9; 182.20; 188.15; 222.8; 236.6, 9
caveri, 160.3; 174.2; 190.13; 222.12; 230.9; 238.4
censere, 158.14; censeri, 100.9, 20; 118.2; 156.12; 188.10; 198.1, 10; 210.3, 10, 13; 212.6–7; 216.7; 218.1, 13; 220.3; 224.1, 4, 7; 242.6; 250.12
certitudo, 104.7; 128.5
certus, 104.4; 106.2, 4; 108.21, 22; 112.8; 130.11; 134.7; 136.15; 140.13; 150.11; 166.11; 182.8; 188.11; 190.18; 194.5; 206.18; 238.5, 8, 10; 240.6; 242.4
choraedus, 148.21
circumstantia, 188.9, 11
cithara, 156.19
cito, 102.24; citius, 102.19
civilis, 152.4
clarus, 192.7
clausula formalis, 204.18, 20; 218.15; 228.5–6; 242.8
clavis, 122.1, 3, 4, 10, 12, 13, 14; 124.12, 14, 15, 16, 18; 126.1, 4; 128.8; 130.7, 14–15; 134.7, 8; 138.17, 18, 19 (bis); 140.1 (bis), 2, 5, 7, 11, 16, 20, 24
clericus, 104.20
coepisse, 106.20; 110.3; 148.28
cogere, 100.11; 156.13; 164.2; 166.20; cogi, 120.3, 144.19; 162.4
cognatio, 202.15
cognatus, 126.1
cognitio, 106.25; 122.3; 190.27; 202.8
cognoscere, 120.11; cognosci, 144.14; 188.12
cohaerere, 196.16
collatio, 212.3 (bis), 4
colligare, 184.21; colligari, 112.19; 166.11; 170.6; 176.10; 178.8; 190.23; 192.5; 196.17, 21; 206.13, 16; 208.5; 212.6
colligere, 110.16; 206.16; colligi, 146.8, 11; 180.6; 192.12; 200.1; 206.4; 226.2
collocari, 126.11; 130.5
colorare, 164.17
coloratio, 222.6
combinatio, 168.5; 170.3–4
comedere, 156.9
comicus, 146.5
comitari, 102.26; 144.17, 19
committere, 118.7; 238.3; committi, 126.11; 166.18; 184.3, 9, 15; 252.13

commixtio, 124.1
commoditas, 230.5
commovere, 106.6
communis, 106.9; 120.4; 150.5, 9; 152.5; 154.9; 206.12; 222.2; 238.18; 246.9; 248.11; commune aurium iudicium, 150.16
comoedia, 148.23; 154.16
comparari, 244.14
compars, 212.7
compensari, 248.3
compleri, 134.13
complures, 104.10; 140.11
componere, 108.17; 144.19; 148.5, 14, 18; 152.24, 28; 184.2 (bis), 3, 5–6; componi, 110.11; 112.2; 138.1–2; 146.4, 6; 148.16; 152.25; 232.5
compositio, 102.27; 114.26; 146.12; 148.1, 8, 11
compositor, 108.21, 22; 114.20; 148.1; 150.4
comprehendere, 180.11; comprehendi, 192.20–21
computare, 220.7; computari, 160.11; 218.10–11
conari, 108.23
concedere, 146.3; concedi, 116.2; 118.3; 128.6; 146.3; 164.14
concordare, 216.1
concretus, 112.13; 120.1
concurrere, 190.3, 9, 11; 202.3
conferre, 168.3; 180.3; conferri, 226.1–2
confirmare, 110.1
confirmatio, 174.8; 208.3
conformis, 206.5
confusio, 244.6
confusus, 174.18
confutare, 110.8, 12
conglutinari, 218.14
congruere, 188.1; 192.17
coniectura, 196.13
coniungere, 106.16; coniungi, 166.9; 208.9
connectere, 184.11; 204.14; connecti, 112.19; 184.11, 21, 22; 196.19; 210.11, 13; 220.13; 232.8
connectio, 184.20
consecqui, 248.1
consentaneus, 148.10–11; 176.2
consensus, 150.9
consentire, 152.6; 188.4; 194.1; 214.9; 236.8
consequentia, 166.21
consequi, 102.17, 20, 25; consecutus, 102.13

considerare, 100.8; 234.6–7; considerari, 112.18; 116.1; 120.1; 140.17; 142.5; 160.4; 174.18; 176.5; 188.14; 204.11; 234.6, 10
consistere, 126.10; 164.3; 170.4; 182.13; 218.10
consonare, 150.9, 12
constare, 102.13; 104.11, 21; 108.21–22; 110.4, 12; 112.5; 116.9; 118.4; 140.3; 142.22; 172.8, 16; 190.27; 204.13; 206.1; 244.1
constituere, 120.2; 130.2; 146.2; constitui, 130.7, 14; 198.11; 234.3
constitutio, 214.2–3
consuescere, 194.15; 244.4
consuetudo, 152.3
consulere, 102.16
contemni, 102.21
contemplatio, 128.6
contendere, 110.9–10; 148.10
contextus, 204.8
continere, 106.25–26; 114.4; 122.5; 138.12; contineri, 102.1; 108.5–6; 122.14; 148.30–31; 184.2; 234.15–16
contingere, 106.3; 108.6; 114.19; 136.1, 10; 150.6; 156.5–6, 14; 164.8; 168.5; 192.12; 220.1; 230.13; 236.2
continuari, 166.8; 220.12; 224.7; 228.5
continuus, 228.8
contrahere, 164.14; 174.15; 176.7; contrahi, 166.9; 174.13
contrapunctus, 174.1; 218.5; 222.6
contrarium (*n.*), 136.4; 148.26; 160.8; 162.7; 240.8
contrarius (*adj.*), 138.15; 150.18; 184.17 (bis), 19; 188.6; 224.4, 12
controversia, 118.12
convenientia, 174.8; 202.13
convenire, 106.21; 142.15; 148.3 (bis), 4, 5, 19; 152.17, 21 (bis), 23. 27, 29, 29–30, 30, (bis), 31 (bis); 154.1; 174.10; 182.6, 15; 208.8; 214.4, 6; 248.1
copia, 226.2
copulari, 218.11
cornicen, 106.3
corollarium, 138.6; 246.6
correlativus, 146.18; 152.16
corrigere, 154.17; 166.18; corrigi, 152.18; 184.15–16
correspondere, 132.7–8
corruptio, 162.11
creatio, 106.20; 110.2–3
creber, 230.9
crescere, 192.9
cumulari, 222.10

cupiditas, 196.9
curare, 218.6; 248.9
currus deambulatoriis, 102.6
cursum, 198.19
custodire, 196.10; 206.14; custodiri, 196.3–4; 250.3
Cyprianus, 194.13
Daemonicus, 102.21
dare, 110.14; 120.10; 144.15; dari, 110.5; 152.26; 196.18; 200.7; 208.8; 210.8; 218.13; 252.5
deambulatorium, v. currus deambulatoriis
debere, 136.3; 176.9; 196.17; 222.14; deberi, 136.17; 148.28; 152.13, 23; 158.10; 166.6; 172.12–13; 182.1; 190.20; 196.15; 198.12; 202.4, 16; 206.9; 208.7; 210.9; 216.11; 222.5; 224.1; 228.3; 234.8; 240.6, 8; 248.4; 250.8
Decalogus, 150.20, 21; 152.1
decantari, 106.4
decere, 102.4; 114.13; 118.10; 152.30; 204.6
decima, 134.2–3; 178.10
declaratio, 192.10; 202.12; 216.6; 220.11; 254.3
declarare, 220.8; declarari, 166.3; 170.2; 190.7; 232.1–2
dedecere, 118.11
dedere, 124.18; dedi, 100.11; 124.12
deduci, 104.20; 128.6
deesse, 104.8; 128.14; 130.5, 7; 134.4
deficere, 128.12–13
defectus, 102.17; 152.25; 190.11, 13; 226.2
defendi, 150.10; 152.8–9
deficere, 162.2–3; 248.7
definitio, 108.9; 116.16; 118.9
delectari, 126.1
delectus, 252.16
delinquere, 184.4; 188.7
demens, 114.8
demi, 234.4, 15
demirari, 102.5; 104.11
demonstrare, 192.4; 234.5; demonstrari, 108.10; 110.11; 186.13; 190.25
demonstratio, 138.12
denegare, 244.4
denominari, 116.19
dependere, 152.15; 156.7, 17; 186.6
depingi, 220.15
deponere, 102.5

deprehendi, 122.10; 196.22; 244.1–2
depressio, 198.9–10; 216.9; 218.7–8, 8–9; 220.14; 250.6
depromi, 186.4
derogare, 154.3
descendere, 100.6; 122.5, 122.17–124.1; 128.11; 130.13, 14; 132.1; 134.10; 136.2, 7–8, 10, 12, 18; 138.1, 8; 142.4, 7, 10, 11, 15–16, 17 (bis), 19, 20, 22, 24; 144.1 (bis), 3, 6, 8
desiderare, 154.2; desiderari, 104.14; 254.6
desiderium, 146.1
designare, 170.2
desinere, 248.9
destitui, 178.9; 242.9
destruere, 166.15
detegere, 114.2
Deus, 150.21, 156.8
deviare, 150.14
dexteritas, 108.16
diapason, 128.12, 14; 130.5, 10, 12; 136.13, 16
diapente, 132.3; 136.14, 17, 19; 138.2, 3
diatessaron, 132.2–3, 5; 136.14, 16, 17; 138.2 (bis)
dicere, 110.2; 114.15; 116.19; 118.8, 9, 19; 120.4; 140.21; 142.8; 146.10, 11; 150.2; 154.27; 156.14, 20, 21; 160.14; 166.13; 176.11; 178.10; 184.4; 190.10, 29; 192.17; 196.11; 210.6, 12, 14; 214.12; 216.11; 224.5, 6, 8; 236.1; 246.2, 10; 248.10; dici, 102.10; 112.12; 114.20; 116.14; 128.10–11; 130.21; 148.12, 31; 150.3; 154.16; 162.7; 166.19; 186.4; 192.16; 194.2; 196.13; 198.14; 206.9; 224.3; 226.14; 232.6; 240.11; 244.13, 14; 248.7–8
dictio, 106.4
differre, 174.9, 12; 196.4; 206.15; 236.4
differentia, 144.6–7; 174.8; 202.13; 208.3; 232.12
difficilis, 116.7; difficilior, 116.7, 8; difficillimus, 116.8
difficultas, 194.7
diffiteri, 100.11
digere, 156.10
dignus, 252.10; dignissimus, 106.24
dignitas, 104.7
dignoscere, 150.18; dignosci, 190.23; 248.7
diiudicare, 170.1
diligens, 148.24; 182.21; diligentior, 204.19
dilui, 156.19
dimidius, 172.8
diminuere, 164.16

diminutio, 222.7
Diogenes, 110.8
discantus, 124.18
discedere, 188.1
discindere, 164.16
discipulus, 162.9
discordia, 218.6
discretus, 182.13
disdiapason, 136.13, 14
dissimilitudo, 196.16
dissolvi, 190.10
dissolutus, 182.13
dissonantia, 174.3
distare, 112.17; 132.2, 6, 7, 8, 11; 166.11; 176.1–2, 8; 190.16–17; 242.4
distinctio, 224.12
distinguere, 112.18; 154.29; distingui, 188.14; 204.18; distinctus, 118.18; 174.19; 244.6
distractio, 184.20–21, 22
distrahi, 184.12
distribui, 206.14
diversitas, 114.12; 170.1–2
diversus, 110.14; 114.8; 122.13; 126.8; 130.15; 136.18; 138.11; 150.6; 176.5, 6, 10; 208.4
dividere, 134.11; 142.3; 152.3; 164.14; 174.14; 234.2; dividi, 136.13, 14; 166.20; 174.12; 194.2 (bis); 204.17; 206.2
divisio, 104.1, 5; 118.12; 142.1, 15, 23; 156.2; 162.4; 180.6; *v.* punctus divisionis
docere, 118.5; 122.6; 140.6; 152.4; 182.7, 11; 194.12; doceri, 104.3; 112.3; 138.22; 152.19; 160.11
doctrina, 120.8
doctus, 150.15; 204.18; doctior, 154.18
dominus, 104.9; 112.1
domire, 156.10
dubitari, 144.16; 152.18–19; 190.4
dubium, 106.19; 114.24; 172.16; 174.4, 8; 188.15; 190.10, 11
ducere, 182.20; duci, 184.18
dulcior, 164.2
duo, 106.14, 16; 118.14, 19; 130.1, 23; 134.4, 10, 11; 136.13; 142.14, 22; 160.11, 15; 178.2; 184.10; 194.2; 198.12, 14; 202.1; 206.1; 208.8; 212.5; 214.5, 10; 216.4, 7; 218.2 (bis), 3; 244.10, 11
duplex, 124.6, 8; 164.1; 172.17; 188.15; 194.3; 198.3; 204.3; 220.2
duplicare, 252.5–6

dux, 146.6; 238.12
ecclesia, 204.9
edere, 156.11
edisci, 122.1–2
efferri, 164.10
efficere, 164.4; effici, 116.13; 174.16; effectus, 104.17
effingere, 146.15; 154.12; 234.3; effingi, 102.3; 202.18
effrenatus, 146.1
elegantior, 196.5
elevatio, 216.9; 218.9; 220.14
eligere, 122.5; 124.13
enarratio, 232.13
enormius, 154.19
enuntiare, 106.13
enuntiatio, 104.21
errare, 236.13; 238.1, 6, 8; errari, 154.17
error, 114.2; 128.4; 138.11; 150.18; 166.18; 172.16; 184.1, 2, 15; 238.4, 7
essentia, 166.15
Ethicus, 154.2; 184.17
evadere, 102.15; 116.3
evertere, 166.18
evitare, 154.19
exactius, 194.11
examinare, 114.2; 120.20; 192.12
excellentissimus, 110.13
exceptio, 178.2
excessum, 190.12, 15
excitare, 202.15
excludere, 144.3–4
excogitare, 196.3
excolari, 154.25–26
executio, 156.8
exemplum, 162.5; 178.5, 6; 192.6, 7, 8–9, 9, 10, 12
exercere, 124.12; exerceri, 104.18; 112.3; 120.10; 124.18; 154.26
exercitari, 104.19; 124.13
exercitatio, 140.16
exercitium, 102.14, 26
exhibere, 178.10
existere, 168.6; 194.10
existimare, 100.12; 102, 19
exordiri, 194.4
exordium, 130.15

271

expectare, 104.4
experiri, 124.16
expers, 112.7; 150.2
explicare, 128.4–5; 202.5; explicari, 190.7; 232.2
explicatio, 158.13–14; 160.1; 182.20
expoliri, 114.28
exponere, 106.11; exponi, 158.14
expositio, 182.21
expressio, 106.1; 116.2
exprimere, 112.15; 174.5; 194.14; 202.19; 252.9; exprimi, 102.3; 114.22; 148.8; 168.3, 7; 170.4; 172.15; 174.3; 182.10, 13; 190.17, 22; 228.1; 230.13; 240.8
exquiri, 148.24
extare, 104.10; 106.19; 108.19; 112.9; 146.10, 13 (bis); 148.7, 27; 150.21; 152.11; 168.10; 190.23; 192.8; 194.14
extendere, 198.5; extendi, 202.2; 250.5
extensio, 202.12; 208.3; 216.6; 220.11; 240.3; 242.12; 246.6
facere, 104.15; 152.28; 154.18, 21, 21; 162.4; 244.5; fieri, 102.26; 152.26, 27; 156.5; 162.5; 164.5, 18; 172.3; 174.18; 176.3 (bis), 9 (bis); 178.2, 7; 182.15; 184.5, 8; 188.3, 5 (bis); 192.7; 202.5; 206.7; 214.3, 11; 216.2; 218.3; 220.1, 8; 230.5, 9, 11; 232.5; 234.11; 240.8; 242.2, 5, 13; 248.7; 252.9, 15, 16 (bis)
facilior, 112.11; 120.16; 134.8; 136.1
facultas, 102.18; 114.27
fallax, 238.3
falsitas, 108.10
falsus, 110.11 (bis); 142.8; falsissimus, 142.23
fastidium, 230.7–8
fateri, 114.7; 176.8; 234.15
ferri, 110.10; 156.20
fidere, 140.18
fidicen, 148.20
figura, 102.2; 106.13; 112.19; 118.5; 138.9; 166.8, 11, 15; 168.2, 6, 7, 10; 170.4, 6; 172.1, 2; 174.15; 176.10; 182.10, 11, 12, 13; 190.20, 23, 30; 206.13, 16; 220.15; 240.7, 8
figurate (*adv.*), 230.14; 252.15
finalis, 232.4
finis, 100.19; 102.10, 11, 24; 104.11, 12, 20; 106.7, 25; 116.8, 13; 192.10; 194.9; 248.6
foelicitas, 114.15
fons, 188.12
forma, 190.21, 28; 196.13; 210.4; 218.15; 232.7

formalis, *v.* clausula formalis
fortuna, 100.10, 12
Franchinus (Gaffurius), 104.15, 18, 20
Franciscus Salinas, 104.9; 112.1
frequens, 230.7
fuga, 164.5
fugire, 164.13; fugiri, 238.20; 252.1
fundamentum, 140.18
fungi, 148.22, 23
fusa, 138.21; 222.14; 226.5; 238.17
futurus, 148.17; 154.11; 156.21 (bis); 158.3
generalis, 116.22; generalior, 118.1
gens, 152.4; 154.8
genus, 124.13; 170.5–6, 12; 184.10; 194.3
gerere, 100.12; 170.2
Germanus, 106.2; 116.20; 164.17
gignere, 222.10
glossare, 164.16; 222.7
Gordianus, 112.22
Graecus, 204.8
grammatica (*n.*) 146.7; 148.11, 29; 190.1; 204.5, 13
grammaticus (*n.*), 118.2; 148.12; 154.5, 10; 204.19
grammaticus (*adj.*), 204.14
gratus, 150.14; gratior, 164.12
gravis, 132.3, 11; 204.8–9; gravior, 100.5; 124.17; 130.1; 134.5; 164.8; 252.14
gravitas, 142.5; 230.13
Guido, 106.11
habere, 108.12; 112.21; 128.4; 154.7; 156.16; 172.4; 204.17; 234.5; 236.7; 246.9; 248.11; haberi, 144.20; 146.16; 148.2, 9; 152.10; 170.8; 192.8; 222.1, 7; 236.2
harmonia, 164.2, 7, 15; 202.18; 218.5–6, 12
harmonicus, *v.* Institutiones harmonicae
hexachordum, 122.12–13, 16; 124.1; 128.14; 130.4, 11–12, 14, 20, 21, 22; 132.1, 7 (bis), 9; 134.10, 12; hexachordum maius, 130.3; hexachordum naturale, 130.9, 15; 132.2, 4 (bis); 134.1; hexachordum B–mi, 132.3, 5 (bis), 10; hexachordum B–fa, 132.2, 4, 5, 11
Hispanus, 116.19; 126.3; 164.16
historiographus, 100.17
homo, 106.5, 20, 21; 110.5; 116.2; 146.4, 17; 156.4 (bis); 156.9 (bis), 12, 14; 158.2 (bis); 186.14; 192.21; 202.15
honestus, 100.18; 150.8, 20

hortari, 112.3
humana vox, 104.10
humanitas, 158.1
humanus, 106.21
hypothesis, 128.5; 130.20, 21–22
ignarus, 104.3; 152.13, 19
ignorantia, 152.28–29
ignorare, 118.11; 120.21; 154.23, 28; 182.19; 184.6; 238.3, 8, 11; ignorari, 100.2,
illatio, 246.6
illigari, 194.15
imitari, 102.7; 106.1–2; 110.5; 148.6; 154.14; 168.12–170.1; 194.10
immediate, 136.8 (bis)
immorari, 106.22
immutare, 148.23
impar, 218.10
impediri, 154.21; 250.5
imperitia, 184.8
imperitior, 118.7
imperium, 156.8
implere, 198.1; 208.9; 212.8; 250.7; impleri, 128.14; 134.15; 164.5
impossibilis, 238.6
imprimi, 164.8; 230.13; 252.14
improbare, 102.25; 108.4; 120.15
improbatio, 138.10
inaequalis, 190.5, 11; 210.7
inaequalitas, 208.8
inanis, 108.8
incertus, 136.16; 182.18
inchoare, 122.17; 136.10; 182.12; 216.8; 220.14; inchoari, 136.5, 17
incidere, 140.19; 234.14; 252.17
incipere, 182.12; 248.8
includi, 184.10
inconveniens, 160.7
incumbere, 120.9
incuria, 184.8
incurrere, 188.2
indigere, 108.7; 158.14; 244.7
indignus, 106.21
indi, 154.25
indicari, 166.13
indoctus, 192.19

inducere, 140.11
ineptus, 136.9; 208.6; 210.3; 212.8
inesse, 236.6
infans, 102.6
inferior, 132.10; 134.3, 10; 142.3, 4
infimus, 132.1; 136.15; 240.11
infinitus, 138.8; 154.8; 192.8
infirmus, 102.6
ingeniosus, 192.21
ingenium, 102.16; 108.14
ingredi, 140.9
initiari, 104.18
initium, 124.7; 198.9
inniti, 164.11
innumerus, 154.3
inquam, 106.16; 108.18; 122.2
inquirere; 146.5; 206.12; inquiri, 120.19; 122.10; 126.4, 9; 192.1; 208.5; 232.7
inquisitio, 140.21
insanire, 138.16
insculptus, 150.12
inserere, 168.10; inseri, 150.8; 154.13; 238.6
inspectio, 102.13
inspici, 100.6, 122.16; 134.8; 140.19
instituere, 240.7; institui, 106.25; 140.3; 210.6
Institutiones de jure naturali et gentium et civili, 152.3–5
Institutiones harmonicae, 110.17
instrui, 238.4
instrumentalis, 104.7
instrumentum, 102.5
integer, 104.4; 106.4; 196.17; 198.11; 204.11, 15; 216.11; 218.1; 220.7; 224.8; 230.14
intelligere, 140.1; 232.1; intelligi, 138.14; 160.5, 13; 172.5; 178.11; 196.17, 18; 204.16; 206.13; 222.12; 224.9; 226.6; 232.4
intentio, 108.18, 22; 144.10, 16; 146.14; 152.22, 27, 28
intentus, 124.5
interesse, 158.1; 164.18
internoscere, 138.18
interponi, 228.5, 6
intervallum, 104.8; 136.1; 176.1; 190.16, 21; 242.4
intolerabilis, 184.15
introduci, 242.14; 248.6

introductorium, 122.1
inutilis, 100.14; 182.19
invenire, 124.6; 126.7; 140.22; 196.3; 234.3–4, 15; inveniri, 106.12, 19, 23; 110.3; 112.8, 10; 140.8; 172.2; 188.6; 210.6; 236.10; 242.14
investigare, 234.3; investigari, 122.2; 128.1
invitus (*adj.*), 164.2
invitare, 164.4
ira, 106.5
Isocrates, 102.20
Italia, 126.7
Italicus, 194.13–14
Italus, 106.3; 164.16; 194.14
iter, 236.13
iubere, 122.2; 126.4; 138.17; 140.1, 7, 11, 12, 19; 146.2; iuberi, 156.19
iucundus, 164.7
iudicare, 194.12; iudicari, 120.21; 154.6; 160.8; 162.11; 216.9
iudicium, 122.3–4; 148.24, 25; 154.22 (bis), 186.8; 238.1, 4; *v.* commune aurium iudicium, naturale aurium iudicium
iuncus, 102.4 (bis); 108.13 (bis); 114.5
iureconsultus, 146.16; 152.2; 186.7
ius, 152.2; 176.1; 210.3; 240.9
Iusquinus, 194.8
iuvari, 124.11
labor, 100.13, 18; 102.19–20; 114.18
largitio, 150.10
latere, 104.5; 174.2
Latinus, 116.20; 194.13
laudabilis, 186.14
laus, 100.15; 188.10; 196.7
lectio, 102.25–26
lector, 104.3; 120.7, 20; 128.5; 190.1; 204.9; 236.12
legere, 120.21
legitimus, 100.19; 102.24
Le pecorine, 194.14
levis, 102.10; levior, 100.5
levitas, 100.14
lex, 146.2, 16 (bis); 150.1, 7, 19; 152.10, 12, 13
libellus, 100.8
liber (*n.*), 100.17; 102.16; 104.10; 126.3; 156.15
liberalitas, 184.18
liberior, 112.11
libertas, 108.17; 114.20; 194.5; 196.9

liberus, 158.4; 186.11; 224.1
libere (v.), 186.6; 252.11
librarius, 184.8
licentia, 196.4; 210.5
licere, 116.22; 142.18; 154.17, 18, 19, 21; 158.13; 174.1; 240.9
ligari, 224.7; 232.5; 240.16
ligatura, 158.8; 160.9; 166.1, 4, 6, 7, 11, 12, 16, 19; 168.1, 2, 7, 8, 11; 170.3; 176.5, 7, 11; 182.10, 12 (bis); 190.21, 22, 28, 29, 29–30; 196.12; 206.15; 208.4, 6; 210.3,4; 228.1; 232.7; 240.6, 8
limitari, 242.8
limitatio, 174.9; 180.7; 208.3; 216.6; 220.11; 226.12; 240.3; 242.12; 252.3; 254.3
linea, 106.13; 124.12, 14, 15, 16; 126.10 (bis)
lingua, 116.20; 154.6, 7
litera, 106.13, 15, 19; 128.8, 10, 12; 130.13, 19, 20, 21, 22; 132.8; 134.1, 4, 9. 10, 13
localis, 124.11
locari, 126.10
locus, 100.13; 106.8; 108.19; 110.14; 112.14, 21; 114.4, 6; 118.8; 120.16; 130.2, 5; 140.17; 150.6, 17, 152.8; 154.7, 8; 156.15; 158.10; 160.14; 172.4; 174.6, 9; 176.5, 6, 7; 188.8, 11; 210.6; 218.7, 9, 19; 220.2, 13; 228.2; 240.14; 242.2; 244.8; 250.9
locutio, 202.16
longus, 104.8; 114.18; 234.13 (bis); 238.21 (bis); longior, 196.14; 202.16
loquax, 252.6
loqui, 114.27; 144.4; 156.10, 12; 172.7; 222.9; 226.5; 230.8; 252.5, 12
magnus, 194.6; 202.14; 212.8; 222.9; 244.6; maior, 140.16; 150.12; 196.7, 18; 208.1, 7; 210.4; 224.1; 234.7, 8, 10; 238.14; 240.1, 4, 9, 10 (bis), 12; 242.4; 246.3, 8; 248.4; 248.9, 10; v. hexachordum maius
maior, v. magnus
male, 108.21
malus, 144.20–146.1
mandare, 164.3
manere, 130.22; 174.2
manifestare, 128.2; manifestari, 134.7
manifestus, 116.12
manus, 122.1
materia, 106.6
mathematicus (adj.), 154.7
maxima (n.), 168.3
maximus (adj.), 114.16
mederi, 184.17

mediare, 136.9, 11; mediari, 246.6
mediocris, 102.14, 26; 106.21
meditatio, 102.26; 154.25
medius, 106.8; 124.16; 126.10; 172.9; 180.8 (bis), 11; 182.4 (bis), 5; 206.3, 6, 11; *v.* media mutatio
melodia, 164.11
membrum, 142.23 (bis); 204.17
meminisse, 106.17; 116.21; 118.16
memoria, 124.11; 140.16, 18
mens, 150.5, 8, 11
mensura, 196.23; 198.8–9; 208.9; 212.7; 218.10; 250.7
mensuralis, *v.* cantus mensuralis
mensurari, 220.2
mentio, 214.11
Meridies, 238.10
merito (*adv.*), 100.11
meta, 148.13
metaphora, 164.17
minima (*n.*), 138.21; 196.22; 198.8, 11, 12, 14, 18; 200.5, 6; 202.1; 210.4; 212.5; 214.5; 216.4, 7, 8; 218.2 (bis), 7, 220.6; 222.1; 226.4; 228.6; 234.7 (ter), 8; 238.14 (bis); 240.1, 4, 9, 10, 11; 242.1–2, 6, 9; 244.1, 3, 13; 246.1, 3; 250.6
minimus (*adj.*), *v.* minor
minor, 160.13; 170.5; 178.3; 202.3; 210.7; 212.1; 234.7, 8; 236.3; 238.15; 242.10; 244.2, 4; minimus, 164.16; 240.11; 244.3
misericordia, 106.5
modulamen, 104.20
modulatio, 104.16–17
modus, 120.11, 14, 19; 126.2, 4, 8; 128.1, 4; 138.10; 142.25; 150.11; 152.24; 154.7; 156.12; 158.2; 160.6, 15; 182.21, 21; 190.23; 192.13; 206.5; 208.5; 236.7
molestus, 252.8
momentaneus, 148.25
momentum, 108.9; 148.16
monstrare, 112.21
mora, 196.15; 202.16, 17; 204.2; 206.18; 230.5; 240.5, 12; 244.7; 248.6; 250.5
mos, 110.8; 150.20
motus, 110.9, 11
movere, 144.3
multiplicare, 252.6
multitudo, 138.18; 140.2, 23

multus, 100.10; 102.12, 14; 110.9, 15; 114.18, 150.11; 194.11; 204.13; plus, 110.22; 112.19; 114.11; 120.5; 124.5; 126.1; 134.7; 140.11, 20; 150.7, 13; 152.13; 158.6, 10; 160.8, 14; 162.2, 4, 8; 164.1, 3, 4, 13, 14; 166.7, 8, 13–14, 14; 168.2; 172.1; 174.6, 11 (bis), 12, 13 (bis), 14 (bis), 15 (bis), 16, 17; 176.1, 6, 8 (bis), 10; 188.17 (bis), 18, (bis); 190.3, 4–5, 5, 8, 9, 15, 20, 28; 192.4; 196.11, 15; 198.7, 16, 17; 200.3; 202.3, 10, 17; 204.2; 206.1, 14; 210.6, 12; 214.6; 216.1; 220.12; 224.2, 7, 10; 228.2, 7; 230.2; 236.14; 238.1; 242.4; 244.10, 11; plurimus, 164.16; 194.13; 202.1; 220.9; 222.4; 250.9

munus, 148.23

musica (*n*.), 100.15, 18; 102.4, 9; 104.1, 4; 112.7; 116.11, 18; 150.3; 154.6; 156.15; 158.1; 194.9; 202.14; 204.5; 232.1; 240.6; 242.14; musica sonorum, 118.17; musica verbalis, 116.16, 21–22; 118.4, 12, 14, 17; 120.8–9; 144.9, 13; musica verborum, 116.21–22; musica vocalis, 106.7; 108.1; 110.4; 116.5, 22; 118.18

musicalis, *v*. voces musicales

musice (*n*.), 104.5; 108.14; 112.2; 194.4

musicus, (*adj*.), 106.1

musicus (*n*.), 100.2, 6, 7, 16, 20; 102.8; 106.11, 25; 108.15; 110.13; 114.14; 120.12–13; 142.3; 154.3, 5; 156.5, 12, 21; 158.3 (bis), 13; 186.6, 10, 11; 188.5; 204.13, 19

mutabilis, 156.11

mutare, 100.13; mutari, 186.4, 12, 14; 188.8; 236.7

mutatio, 122.17; 136.1, 5, 7, 9; 140.8 (bis), 10–11; 188.11; media mutatio, 136.15; 144.5, 6

mutilus, 120.2; 162.7

natare, 102.4 (bis); 108.13 (bis)

natura, 102.14, 17 (bis); 104.7, 12; 106.21; 110.5 (bis); 114.15, 18; 116.2; 146.19 (bis); 150.5, 12; 152.17, 18; 154.24, 25; 156.7, 10; 184.12; 186.4; 188.13; 192.2, 19; 196.21; 202.19; 206.5, 15, 17; 226.7; 234.3; 236.5; 238.12; 246.2; 248.1; 252.8

naturalis, 110.6; 114.27, 28; 124.12–13; 152.1, 14; 184.5; 192.18; 238.11; naturale aurium iudicium, 152.5; *v*. cantus naturalis, hexachordum naturale

natus, 102.18

nausea, 230.8; 252.4

necessarius, 110.15–16; 114.23; 120.13; 154.30; 156.1, 4, 15, 18; 162.6, 10; 170.7; 178.1; 182.16; 184.14; 186.3, 9–10, 12; 188.13; 190.7, 14, 22; 192.1–2; 196.10; 202.5, 8; 226.16, 17; 228.2; 232.2; 236.5, 6, 7, 8, 9; 238.12; 250.3

necesse, 100.19; 120.8; 122.13; 190.5; 192.6

necessitas, 164.2, 5, 6–7; 174.8; 180.6, 13; 182.20; 186.5, 12; 192.2, 3; 230.11
negare, 110.12; 112.6; 142.6; 150.1; 176.9; 236.3; negari, 110.4; 208.12; 252.13
neglectius, 104.10
negligere, 102.1, 112.15; 196.10; 204.14; negligi, 100.6. 114.21; 156.7; 162.7; 186.7; 188.6, 10; 204.7; 222.8; 224.2; 236.10; 240.15; 250.1
negocium, 100.10
neotericus, 194.7; 196.10
nequire, 118.3; 186.14
nescire, 238.9
neuter, 178.4
Nicolaus Vicentinus, 116.12
nimius, 196.4, 9; 198.4; 210.5
niti, 108.11; 192.3
nodus, 108.4; 112.22
nomen, 100.14; 102.2; 112.14; 116.18; 118.4; 188.2; 240.9; 244.3
nominari, 192.18
norma, 152.24
noscere, 124.14;
nota (*n.*), 100.1; 102.1; 108.23; 112.17; 114.9, 11 (bis); 118.5, 6; 158.6, 7, 8, 10, 11; 160.3, 5, 8, 9, 10, 12; 162.2, 3, 4 (bis), 6; 164.1, 3, 6, 9, 10, 12, 13, 15; 168.10, 12; 170.4, 11; 172.1, 7, 8, 11, 14; 174.2, 3, 5, 10, 12, 13, 14, 15; 176.1, 8, 10; 178.2; 180.1, 3, 8, 12, 14; 182.1 (bis), 2, 3, 9, 10, 13; 186.3–4; 188.16; 190.9, 15, 17, 18, 20, 27; 196.11–12, 14, 15, 16, 22, 23; 198.1, 2, 3, 5, 6, 116; 200.6; 202.10, 17; 204.2; 206.5, 8, 9, 13 (bis), 14, 16; 208.5, 8, 11; 212.5; 214.2, 7, 8, 9, 10, 11; 216.1; 218.10, 13, 14; 220.2, 15; 222.2; 224.11, 13; 226.1, 15; 228.10; 230.4; 232.3, 7; 234.5, 6, 12; 238.21; 240.7, 9, 12, 15; 242.10; 248.8; 250.8
notari, 122.14; 140.7, 12, 15; 190.18, 23; 204.3; 230.7; 250.8
notula, 208.1; 210.4; 212.1; 234.12; 238.17; 240.1, 4; 244.2; 246.3
notus, 106.14; 154.24, 29; 204.5; notior, 154.24, 27; notissimus, 100.15; 154.29
notitia, 150.8; 154.13; 196.11
novem, 168.5; 170.3
novitas, 100.7
novus, 114.10, 12; 120.5, 15; 154.4, 5, 12; 190.25; 194.4, 10, 12; 196.2
nullus, 100.7, 9; 108.19; 110.3, 9; 158.13; 170.13; 172.11; 184.18; 190.10; 192.10; 200.7; 218.12 (bis); 220.7; 224.5; 226.12; 230.10; 236.7; 242.13; 244.2

numerus, 106.16; 116.20; 118.14, 16; 150.10; 160.10; 164.9, 11; 190.5, 9, 11, 12
nuncupare, 152.3; nuncupari, 186.12
obiicere, 108.17; 118.16; obiici, 152.20
oblectare, 164.15
obscuritas, 222.10
observare, 112.16; 114.24; 122.9; 140.23; 156.18; 184.14; 238.11; observari, 112.15; 114.24; 138.17; 140.1, 6, 11, 14; 152.5; 156.6; 158.4, 5; 160.7, 11; 166.5; 182.14; 188.5–6; 190.26; 196.2; 198.2; 210.7; 230.1; 234.12; 236.9; 242.1; 246.1; 250.1; 254.1, 4
observatio, 124.5; 232.9
observator, 152.13
obstare, 150.19; 152.16; 154.16
obtinere, 106.8; 112.4; 138.19; 198.2; 218.9; 240.12; obtineri, 116.9 (bis); 172.7
obtundere, 252.7
obviare, 188.6
obvius, 192.9
Occidens, 238.9–10
occupare, 130.2; 218.7; 220.4
occurrere, 138.21; 154.20; 156.18; 188.9; 198.7, 8, 10; 218.5, 6; 220.2; 228.4, 8; 234.16
ociosus, 100.5
ocium, 108.8
octavus, 122.4; 126.6; 128.10; 130.3
oculatus, 102.7
odium, 106.5
offendi, 118.8; 252.7
offensio, 118.6
offerre, 192.20; 198.16; 216.9; 218.9; 220.15; 236.14
oleum, 108.8
omittere, 106.1; 162.3–4; omitti, 112.14; 124.5; 168.3
omnis, 100.5–6, 10, 15; 104.8, 12, 13; 112.14; 114, 10, 21 (ter), 24; 120.8; 122.4; 124.7; 142.3; 144.4, 6, 7; 150.5, 9; 154.1, 13, 23; 156.16; 158.5; 160.9; 184.10; 186.5; 188.2, 5, 15; 190.13, 26; 192.8, 13; 194.1, 8, 10; 196.11; 206.6; 210.4; 224.7, 10, 11; 228.10, 12; 230.2, 12; 232.6; 242.3; 244.9
opera, 102.12, 15, 25; 108.4, 7
opinari, 142.9; 226.14
opinio, 108.7, 10; 110.1, 13; 120.14; 128.7; 150.18; 152.7; 226.1, 12–13
oportere, 116.6; 130.4, 11; 142.23; 146.18; 148.21; 152.21; 154.27; 162.12; 166.10; 178.10; 184.11; 188.16; 224.13; 234.5; 248.9

opponere, 114.20
optare, 102.25; 154.1
optimus, *v.* bonus
opus, 102.13; 108.7, 9, 14; 114.10, 12; 144.6; 156.10, 14; 162.13; 190.25; 192.9; 196.6
opusculum, 100.7; 120.6
orare, 102.14, 18
oratio, 204.7, 8, 16
orator, 202.14; 230.14; 252.15
oratoria, *v.* ars oratoria
ordo, 122.9, 11; 128.5. 130.11; 134.7, 8, 9; 138.7; 140.5, 24; 142.5; 154.28; 180.3 (bis), 13; 182.2; 194.2; 196.7; 202.5; 206.14; 226.9, 13; 234.2 (bis)
Oriens, 238.9
origo, 188.12
oriri, 148.27, 188.15; 190.10, 12; 244.6
Orlandus, 194.12
ornatior, 116.3
ostendere, 126.2; 140.25; ostendi, 114.5; 140.9; 192.6
ovis, 194.15
par, 190.9; 220.2
parare, 108.16
parere, 230.8
pars, 102.11; 104.4, 12, 21; 106.24; 108.14; 112.2, 7, 15; 114.16; 116.18; 118.15; 120.1, 4, 14; 134.11; 144.9, 13; 148.30, 150.1; 172.9 (bis), 11, 12; 174.18; 176.3 (bis), 4; 190.7; 198.10, 11, 15; 204.17; 214.2, 2, 7, 8; 218.3 (bis)
particeps, 214.3
pater, 194.9
patere, 118.16; 122.11; 126.6, 9; 128.13; 130.20; 140.24; 172.12; 192.1, 19; 240.9
pati, 184.12
paucus, 110.16; 164.15; 192.11; paucior, 158.6; 160.3; 162.2, 3, 8; 164.4, 9, 14 (bis); 180.14
Paulus, 152.2
pausa, 204.18, 20
peccari, 160.6, 15; 184.21
peculiaris, 178.8; 196.19
pellis, 194.15
penultimus, 180.10; 200.2; 206.2, 8, 10 (bis); 230.3; 232.3 (bis); 236.2
peragi, 104.10
percipere, 108.7; 238.4; percipi, 108.15; 114.14; 116.11; 222.11

perdere, 102.15; 108.8
perdiscere, 192.13
perelegans, 196.8
perfectio, *v.* punctus perfectionis
perfectior, 122.4
perfici, 112.9; perfectus, 100.20; 106.26
peritia, 100.8
peritus, 102.4, 5, 14; 192.21
permitti, 216.2
permultus, 106.10
perpendere, 248.4
perscribi, 106.14–15
perspicere, 128.7; perspici, 118.9; 140.5
pertinere, 104.13; 182.11
pertractari, 120.5
perveniri, 206.7; 230.1, 3
peti, 134.13
pictor, 164.17
pietas, 106.5
planus, *v.* cantus planus
plenior, 164.12; 202.12
plerusque, 114.14; 146.10
plurimus, *v.* multus
plus, *v.* multus
poena, 150.10; 152.2
poenitudo, 102.27
poeta, 100.17; 148.23; 154.18 (bis); 230.14
politus, 116.1
ponere, 120.19, 20; 148.13; 196.8; poni, 112.19; 124.14, 16; 158.10; 178,3; 180.2; 184.11; 200.4; 210.12; 218.14; 228.2; 236.1, 14; 238.2, 8; 242.4; 244.10; 250.7
possidere, 124.15; 130.8, 19, 23; 198.15; 200.3; 204.1; 224.8; 206.8
posterus, 116.4; posterior, 106.14; 148.14; 178.3, 4; 190.6; 248.1, 4
postponi, 150.14
postulare, 146.18; 196.20
potentia, 130.8
potestas, 232.5–6
practicus, 104.6, 7, 9–10, 15
praecavere, 104.5
praecedere, 134.14–15; 138.2; 144.16, 17, 20; 146.8, 10, 11; 150.4; 166.13; 168.7; 178.7–8; 180.2; 196.19; 248.10; 250.10
praeceptor, 156.18, 20

praeceptum, 100.3; 102.15, 19, 21; 108.5 (bis); 110.14, 15; 112.10; 114.12, 19; 120.10; 148.31; 150.20; 152.1, 12; 154.3, 4–5; 162.1, 6; 190.1, 2; 194.10–11, 12; 196.2, 5, 6; 204.5
praecipi, 182.14
praedicere, 120.10; praedici, 114.28; 130.2, 14–15, 21; 206.4
praeditus, 114.18; 192.21
praeferri, 148.24; 150.15; 154.22–23
praemeditari, 154.22
praemittere, 128.5; praemitti, 150.18
praepari, 116.9
praeponi, 208.1; 210.1
praescribi, 148.14; 152.7
praesens, 100.6
praestantior, 100.9; praestantissimus, 102.11; 104.12; 106.22; 112.2
praevius, 104.5
praxis, 192.10
primus, *v.* prior
principalis, 216.7
princeps (*adj.*), 218.9
princeps (*n.*), 146.1; 194.8, 9
principium, 120.7; 130.16; 136.4; 162.2; 184.4, 6; 248.6
prior, 106.22, 24; 110.6; 116.10; 144.13; 168.4; 178.3, 5, 7; 198.9, 10, 13; 202.2; 216.8; 218.4, 13; 220.1, 4; 234.14; primus, 104.15–16, 18, 21; 106.7, 11, 14; 110.3; 116.7, 10, 19; 122.10, 16; 126.4; 128.10; 130.20; 136.15; 138.16; 140.10; 152.9; 154.13; 158.8, 11 (bis); 160.1; 168.1; 172.12; 176.3, 4; 180.8, 9, 12 (bis), 13, 14; 182.3 (bis), 8, 9, 11; 190.13; 198.8, 18; 200.5; 202.4, 14; 206.2, 5 (bis), 7; 210.1, 11, 12, 13; 216.10; 218.7, 8; 220.12, 13, 14, 15; 222.1, 1–2, 5; 224.6; 226.15 (bis), 16, 17 (bis); 230.3; 232.1; 240.6; 244.2; 246.10; 248.3; 250.11
privatio, 248.2
probabilis, 190.26; 192.16
probare, 100.19; 110.9, 13; 140.21; probari, 100.14; 140.10; 192.7; 244.9
procedere, 134.9; 138.9; 210.1
prodigus, 184.18
prodire, 212.9
produci, 158.9; 198.13
proferri, 144.1; 202.18; 204.2; 222.11; 248.5; 252.5
prohiberi, 174.12; 176.2, 3; 214.10; 216.3–4
progressus, 120.11, 17; 138.10, 14
prolatio, 212.8; 244.6; 248.6, 7
promittere, 144.15
pronuntiare, 106.15; 204.10; pronuntiari, 138.19–20; 240.12

pronuntiatio, 104.18; 196.14–15; 206.17; 240.4; 248.7, 8, 10
properare, 232.9
proponere, 120.2; 122.2; 124.6, 9
proportio tripla, 244.14
proprietas, 198.6; 202.19
proprius (*adj.*), 102.8; 120.1; 124.18; 170.7; 190.20; 204.2; 210.13; 220.51; 240.3, 14; 242.12; 244.8; 246.6; 250.2, 11; 252.3; 254.3
prosa, 254.4, 5
proximus, 110.1; 126.10, 11; 134.1, 12; 136.9; 140.9; 160.10; 166.10; 212.4; 214.11; 244.9; 246.2, 10
prudenter, 102.20
publicum, 194.11
puer, 104.18–19; 122.1; 124.11, 13
punctum, 170.11; 172.1, 2
punctus, 170.9; 170.12; 172.5; punctus perfectionis, 172.5–6; punctus divisionis, 172.6; punctus alterationis, 172.6; punctus augmentationis, 158.7; 160.10; 172.6, 7, 14, 17; 174, 1–2, 3, 4; 178.11, 12; 180.1; 190.17, 18, 19; 196.21, 22, 23 (bis); 198.2, 3; 200.6 (bis); 212.1, 3, 5, 6 (bis), 9; 214.1, 4, 6, 8, 10; 222.1 (bis), 2; 228.1
puniri, 150.21
putare, 100.6, 18; 104.5; 108.10; 114.5; 122.3, 10, 14, 17; 126.9; 148.26; 154.5; 158.13; 160.4; 204.20; putari, 160.10; 182.11; 188.14; 204.2; 220.15
quaerere, 108.5; quaeri, 152.9; 204.12
quaestio, 146.8
qualitas, 196.22
quantitas, 112.18; 254.1, 4
quartus, 124.12; 134.2, 6; 190.21; 216.10; 224.11, 12; 228.3, 12; 242.6; 250.7
quatuor, 134.14; 138.3; 142.11, 14; 158.5; 166.3; 202.13; 244.11
quinarius, 232.12; 234.1
quinque, 158.5; 168.5; 200.1; 234.2
quintus, 134.2, 6; 162.1; 226.17; 228.10–11; 232.2
quire, 100.9; 102.7; 108.9; 116.10; 138.9; 190.25; 230.4
raptus, 148.25
rarior, 168.3
ratio, 100.1; 102.1; 110.2; 112.4, 9, 11; 114.4, 8 (bis); 116.3; 120.15; 140.20; 144.4; 146.1, 2, 5, 6, 18; 148.7, 10; 150.1, 11; 154.9; 156.7, 17; 166.13; 168.2; 170.7, 13; 174.2; 176.2; 180.6; 182.6, 19; 184.1; 188.5, 6; 192.1, 3, 4, 21; 194.7; 212.3; 216.6, 10; 218.5; 220.1, 11; 222.3, 7, 14; 228.11; 232.12; 236.8, 10; 238.1, 4; 240.3; 242.12; 246.6;

252.3; 254.3; recta ratio, 152.12, 24; 154.15; 164.11; 186.9, 11–12, 13; 188.1, 4; 192.17
recedere, 150.13; 152.25; 154.14, 16; 226.11
recensere, 100.15
recentior, 148.19; 150.15; 196.1; 220.5–6; 224.2–3; 226.3, 12; 232.8, 10; 236.8–9, 11; 238.5; 240.14; 250.2; 252.12
recipi, 114.26; 150.13; 154.4, 10; 168.8
rectus, 188.7; recta ratio, *v.* ratio
reddere, 106.26; 120.15; 162.7; reddi, 164.12; 180.13; 250.5
refertissimus, 100.17
regi, 148.30
regula, 108.19, 21, 22; 110.11, 12; 112.2, 6, 9, 16; 114.7 (bis), 10, 21, 23; 124.1, 8; 144.15, 18 (bis), 20; 146.4, 6, 7, 9, 13, 14 (bis), 16; 148.2 (ter), 7, 8, 10, 15, 19, 26, 29; 150.4, 8, 19; 152.4, 8, 9, 13, 16, 19, 26, 29; 154.9, 14, 23, 28; 156.1, 17; 158.3; 160.1, 5; 160.11 (bis), 15; 166.10, 18; 172.3, 12, 16; 174.4, 10; 176.3, 5; 178.1, 10; 180.2, 10, 13; 182.5, 6, 8, 18, 20, 21; 184.1–2, 5, 9, 14 (bis); 186.3, 11; 188.3, 7, 8, 10, 12; 190.6, 10, 13 (bis), 22, 25, 27; 192.1, 11, 14, 16; 194.6; 196.8; 200.1; 202.8, 12; 206.4, 12, 16; 208.4; 210.8; 212.3 (bis), 4; 214.4 (bis), 5, 6, 9, 11; 216.1, 10; 224.3, 4 (bis), 9, 11, 12; 226.4, 8, 11; 232.6, 10, 13; 234.1, 2; 236.1, 2, 11; 238.3 (bis), 5, 7, 11, 13; 240.14; 242.5, 8; 244.8; 246.1, 2, 10; 250.1
reiicere, 196.2; reiici, 140.6; 144.4
relinqui, 106.22; 158.4; 162.3; 186.11
reliquus, 126.5; 168.3; 190.13; 214.2; 220.12–13; 232.8
remittere, 120.7
reperire, 234.15; reperiri, 122.13; 170.7; 218.14; 230.10
repetere, 138.8; 252.11; repeti, 164.10; 230.4, 15; 252.4, 15
repetitio, 230.5, 7, 9 (bis); 234.10; 238.20; 252.1, 9, 15
repraesentare, 148.4–5; 172.9
reprehendere, 102.12; reprehendi, 100.11–12; 140, 2; 142.1; 168.9; 188.2–3
reprehensibilis, 140.14
reprehensio, 252.10
repugnare, 150.9
reputari, 220.13
requirere, 140.16; 208.10; 166.17; requiri, 118.15; 164.1
reri, 100.15
res, 100.7; 102.10, 11; 104.12, 13; 108.5, 8; 110.12, 15; 116.12; 118.4; 140.17; 144.14; 150.2; 152.19; 156.7; 166.16; 168.2 (bis); 170.6; 174.16; 188.14; 190.30; 196.13; 204.13; 206.13; 222.3; 234.5; 240.7; 244.5; 248.4; 252.6
rescindere, 112.22

reservari, 206.14–15
resolutio, 212.9
resolvi, 198.12, 14; 218.2; 222.4–5
respectus, 240.10
respondere, 114.27; 128.8; 134.9; 138.14–15; 154.4; 156.20; respondi, 128.7; 152.9, 23
responsum, 156.19
respuere, 208.10; 214.2, 8
restare, 138.14; 196.11
restituere, 120.16
rex, 156.21
Romani, 152.2
rudis, 114.28; 192.19; 204.14, 19; 238.7; rudior, 116.3
sacra scriptura, 100.16–17
Salinas, *v.* Franciscus Salinas
Salmantica, 112.3; 126.3
sanus, 102.7
sapere, 114.4; 188.13; 236.5
sapiens, 100.13
satisfacere, 120.12
scientia, 102.13, 24; 154.7, 24; 244.2
scire, 154.28; 202.8; 230.10; sciri, 104.4; 106.24; 110.15; 122.11; 140.4; 198.7; 226.3
scirpus, 108.5
scribere, 102.16, 21; 104.8; 114.24; 184.20; scribi, 124.8 (bis); 138.4 (bis); 146.8; 148.4, 8, 9; 148.28, 30; 150.6, 15; 152.3 (bis), 8, 14; 164.3; 182.2
scriptor, 100.17; 150.6; 152.8, 14; 154.14
secundum quid, 150.3
secundus, 104.16, 19; 106.7, 8 (bis), 11, 14, 18 (bis); 110.4; 152.7; 176.3, 5; 192.1; 210.12; 220.2; 224.4; 228.1, 7, 9
seiungere, 118.17
semen, 154.25
semibrevis, 170.5; 196.22; 198.12; 200.6; 212.5; 218.2; 222.3
semiditonum, 128.14; 130.1, 4, 11
semifusa, 222.14
semiminima, 138.21; 160.12; 178.3, 9; 180.1–2; 196.18, 19; 198.8, 9, 13–14, 14, 17; 200.3, 4, 4–5; 202.1, 3; 208.1, 7; 210.1–2, 2, 7, 8–9, 10 (bis), 12; 214.5, 6, 9; 216.4, 7, 8; 218.3, 8; 220.7, 9, 12; 222.4, 13; 224.1, 5, 7; 226.4, 5 (bis); 228.4, 6, 7–8, 9, 11–12; 238.15, 17, 18; 242.1, 3, 10, 13; 244.10, 13, 13–14; 246.1, 4, 8, 9 (bis); 248.3, 5, 11; 250.5, 6, 10 (bis), 12

semitonium, 130.1
sensus, 190.30; 192.20
sententia, 118.9; 146.5; 150.5; 158.11; 164.8, 10–11; 204.4, 6, 9, 11, 12, 15, 16, 17, 19; 206.1–2, 5–6; 218.9; 226.15; 230.4, 5, 12, 15; 232.1; 234.11; 238.20; 252.11, 14
sentire, 128.4; 148.26; sentiri, 226.13
separatim, 118.20
separari, 106.10; 170.6; 174.2, 4; 188.13; 206.13; 210.14
seponi, 100.10
septem, 128.9; 130.3; 134.9 (bis), 11, 13; 138.7; 140.1
septenarius, 134.11, 15
Septentrio, 238.10
septimus, 130.4, 7, 21; 140.13
sequi, 102.25; 104.22; 108.21, 23; 112, 6, 11; 114.5, 8, 21, 22; 134.15; 138.3, 7, 9; 142.8; 144.17 (bis), 19; 146.6, 7, 8; 148.6 (bis), 7, 11, 21, 27; 150.2; 152.10, 17, 18; 154.4, 5; 160.7; 168, 5, 6; 172.16; 174.4; 182.2, 22; 184.15, 21–22; 190.14, 22, 25; 192.8; 194.8, 11; 196.7, 9, 18; 198.1, 2, 5, 10, 13; 200.5, 6, 8; 202.2; 206.7, 15; 208.7, 11, 12; 210.1, 3, 8, 9, 11; 212.5; 214.5, 9, 10, 11; 222.13; 224.1, 12; 226.1, 7, 16–17; 234.1, 9; 236.14; 238.17; 240.9; 246.2, 4, 8; 250.4, 6 (bis)
servire, 106.24; 240.13
sex, 104.21, 128.8; 130.2
signari, 124.12; 130.17; 140.17; 172.12; 190.20, 28
signatura, 138.19
significare, 118.1; 240.7
signum, 242.4; signum C, 226.3; 242.2; signum ₵, 242.3
silere, 110.8
similis, 114.10; 152.16; 154.17; 178.7, 12; 180.1; 218.14
similitudo, 114.5
simplex, 166.19; 168.10; 170.6; 172.2; 176.7; 182.8–9
simpliciter, 126.8; 150.3
sinere, 190.2; 236.12
singulus, 112.17; 114.1; 122.6; 138.16 (bis); 170.4; 182.5, 20; 184.11; 190.24 (bis); 192.3; 198.6; 204.7, 10–11; 210.14; 218.1; 222.8; 224.5, 7. 9, 13; 228.6; 234.8; 238.14 (bis); 240.5, 6, 7; 242.6, 7 (bis); 244.11, 12
situs (*adj.*), 176.7
solere, 104.19; 130.17; 140.17; 184.13; 202.1, 4; 216.7; 218.6; 220.3; 222.7; 230.15; 242.2; 252.9, 15 (bis)
solfizare, 100.20; 104.16
solfizatio, 102.3, 8–9; 108.12, 14, 15; 112.5, 8, 9, 14–15, 16–17, 17; 114.3, 6, 9, 14; 120.4; 190.1–2

solus, 102.14; 106.1, 4, 9, 12, 14, 24; 108.6 13; 112.4; 118.20; 126.4, 8; 142.16; 144.20; 168.12; 172.7; 180.1; 188.18; 196.4; 200.4; 218.4, 14; 220.5, 12; 228.10
solutio, 112.22
solvere, 114.1; solvi, 112.19
sonare, 242.3
sonus, 104.16, 17; 106.1, 2, 12, 13, 15; 108.20; 116.2; 118.14, 17; 120.3, 5, 7, 8; 136.9; 144.13, 14; 166.9, 10; 172.2; 174.5, 10; 188.17 (bis), 18; 190.1, 5, 15, 16, 17, 21; 202.15; 206.16; *v.* musica sonorum
sortiri, 148.1; 190.19
spacium, 124.14; 126.11 (bis)
species, 106.7; 108.1; 110.4; 114.28; 116.5, 10; 118.2, 18, 19; 120.1; 130.1; 166.7; 168.8; 170.3
spectare, 142.7
stare, 182.1
statuere, 182.9–10; statui, 116.5
status, 100.12; 146.16
studere, 100.18; 108.9; 184.19; 230.9–10
studiosus, 116.11
studium, 100.5, 9; 102.11
stylus, 148.4
suadere, 186.13–14
suavior, 164.15
subdere, 196.6
subiacere, 156.8; 202.17
subiicere, 118.2-3; 118.18; subiici, 106.6; 114.11; 120.2, 130.22; 144.18–19; 152.2; 196.8; 224.9; 230.1
subitus, 154.22
sublatio, 198.9
subrogari, 144.4–5; subrogatum, 114.4, 7
subsistere, 106.9; 118.19
subtrahi, 162.11
succedere, 112.14; 114.6, 12; 188.16, 18; 242.2
sudor, 120.6
sufficere, 108.13; 112.1; 122.3; 178.11; 190.1; 224.11
sufficientia, 232.12
sumere, 124.15; sumi, 136.4; 164.17; 196.14; 200.7
superare, 104.9; 208.9–10
superesse, 230.2, 4
superfluus, 162.10
superior, 134.3, 9–10; 140.19; 142.3, 4, 6; 174.10; 192.18; 212.3; 214.4; 220.1; 234.4, 16; 236.4

supervacaneus, 100.15–16
supervenire, 186.12–13
supplementum, 220.3
supplere, 102.17–18; 220.4; suppleri, 152.25
surgere, 110.10
suscipere, 106.26; 218.15
suspicari, 104.11
suus, 158.7, 10; 190.18; 196.23; 210.13; 218.1; 224.5; 228.7; 234.8; 240.7; 244.3
syllaba, 104.17, 21, 22; 106.2, 3, 12; 112.17, 18; 114.9, 11 (bis); 118.5, 6; 158.6, 7, 8, 10, 11; 160.3, 8, 9, 11, 13; 162.2, 3 (bis), 4, 8; 164.9, 11–12; 166.4, 7, 9–10, 12, 14 (bis), 16; 168.1, 12; 170.6, 13; 172.11, 12; 174.11, 13, 15, 17; 176.8–9; 178.4, 8, 9; 180.2, 3, 6, 8, 9, 12, 14; 180.14–182.1; 182.3, 8; 188.17, 17–18, 18; 190.5, 9, 12, 15, 19, 20, 24, 28; 196.12, 18, 19–20; 198.2, 4, 6, 7, 12, 13, 15, 16, 18–19, 19; 200.2, 4, 7; 202.2, 4, 12, 16; 204.1, 8; 206.2, 6, 9, 14, 18; 208.7, 8, 10, 11; 210.2, 9, 12; 212.6, 8; 214.1, 2, 3, 7, 8, 10; 216.2, 11; 218.1, 4, 12, 13; 220.4, 12; 222.2, 4, 5, 9, 10, 13–14; 224.1, 5, 9, 13; 226.1, 15; 228.7, 8–9, 9, 12 (bis); 230.1; 232.3; 234.8, 10, 12; 236.3; 238.14, 16, 18, 21; 240.5, 6, 8, 12–13, 16; 242.5, 6, 7, 9, 13; 244.3, 4, 5, 6 (bis), 9, 11; 246.8, 9; 248.3, 5, 11; 250.4, 8, 10–11, 11; 252.5; 254.1, 4
symphoneta, 108.17; 146.9; 148.4, 6, 7–8, 17, 21, 22, 24; 152.20, 23; 154.11, 18, 22, 23; 164.3; 168.12; 184.4
symphonista, 144.10, 14; 152.22, 25, 27; 164.7; 166.12; 184.8; 218.6; 222.6
tactus, 198.10, 11; 208.9; 212.7; 216.8 (bis); 218.7 (bis), 8; 220.3–4, 13, 14; 250.6
tangere, 156.19, 20
tantus, 170.1; 226.12
tardior, 112.20; 208.12
tarditas, 208.10; 240.4
temerarius, 154.22
tempus, 100.13; 114.19; 116.10; 188.8; 196.7; 212.7; 244.7
tempus (in mensuratione), 164.5; 196.23
tendere, 102.10
tenere, 106.17; 116.21, 118.16
tenor, 124.11
tentare, 102.10
terminari, 204.20–206.1
terra, 108.19
tertius, 104.17, 19; 106.3, 8, 18; 108.1; 110.5; 116.6, 8; 148.3; 152.20; 176.4; 190.19; 210.2; 228.2; 232.12; 234.1

testari, 116.12
testimonium, 110.22
textus, 108.12; 116.20; 172.17; 174.1; 238.20
theorema, 128.1; 140.9, 13, 24; 142.12, 13, 14
theoricus, 104.6, 7
tollere, 194.5; 196.5; tolli, 120.13; 144.7; 162.12; 184.3, 14, 22
tonus, 136.2
totus, 150.1 (bis); 172.12; 176.3, 4
tractare, 112.6–7; tractari, 104.11; 106.25; 108.2
tradere, 108.5; 124.1; 148.16; tradi, 104.19; 120.12; 138.11, 14; 144.7; 182.5, 21; 234.16; 238.4
trahi, 166.20
transferri, 204.5; 236.1
transgredi, 148.14, 29; 158.13
transgressor, 150.21
transilire, 148.13
transire, 120.14; 158.14; transiri, 136.7
transitus, 124.3
tres, 106.7; 122.13 (bis); 124.1; 130.15, 21; 134.15; 138.2, 3; 140.7; 142.10 (bis), 11, 12, 13; 160.3; 168.3; 190.13; 234.1; 244.10
tribuere, 112.17; 162.2; 198.18; tribui, 122.12; 130.13; 142.15; 166.4; 172.11–12; 174.11; 176.9; 190.3, 5, 6; 196.12, 15; 198.4, 6–7, 8; 202.2, 10; 206.9; 210.2, 12, 13; 218.12; 220.12; 222.5; 226.15; 228.12; 230.2; 232.3–4; 234.10, 13; 236.3; 238.15, 21; 240.16; 244.12
triplex, 104.15; 122.12 (bis); 124.5
triplicari, 130.18 (bis)
triplus, *v.* proportio tripla
turpis, 150.8
turpitudo, 102.7
typus, 168.6
tyrannus, 146.1
tyro, 102.9; 120.9; 192.11
tyrocinium, 102.5; 120.7
ullus, 168.1; 234.10
ultimus, 102.9; 106.25; 140.13; 158.11 (bis); 182.3 (bis), 8, 9, 11; 204.8, 9; 206.2, 4, 9 (bis); 212.4; 226.16; 230.3; 232.3 (bis), 4; 234.16; 246.7; 248.10; 250.8 (bis), 9, 11
undecimus, 134.4
unicus, 140.12 (bis), 20, 22 (bis); 156.18; 198.3
unisonus, 166.8; 190.16, 17, 20
unus, 100.10; 110.15; 112.1; 128.12; 130.20; 134.12; 150.7; 152.20; 158.8, 10; 166.8; 168.12; 176.4, 7; 182.1; 190.3 (ter); 192.6; 198.15,

16; 202.2, 3; 206.1; 222.4, 5; 224.10, 11, 13; 228.12; 230.11; 236.13, 14; 236.5; 238.15; 240.15; 242.5, 6; 244.9, 11; 248.2
urgere, 236.9
usus, 106.12; 108.6, 16; 114.15, 16; 118.9; 138.21; 142.6, 18; 154.4, 10, 25; 182.16, 18; 188.17 (bis); 242.14; 244.2
uter, 104.9
uti, 106.12–13, 14; 114.6; 122.6; 142.4, 7, 10, 12, 13 (bis), 16, 19, 24, 26; 144.8; 172.17; 186.7 (bis); 192.10; 204.15; 226.3
vagari, 182.18
vagus, 194.5; 196.9
valor, 160.13; 164.16; 172.8; 178.3, 7, 11, 12; 180.1; 198.3, 18; 202.3; 208.1; 210.4, 7; 212.1; 218.15; 220.2; 238.18
variatus, 136.2
varietas, 140.14–15; 142.6–7; 154.8; 156.16; 226.1, 13
varius, 108.19 (bis); 114.23; 120.11, 14; 128.4; 138.10; 140.3, 17 (bis); 146.4; 154.8
velle, 102.11
velocitas, 208.10; 212.8; 216.2; 222.8, 10; 244.5; 248.5, 6, 8
velox, 112.19; 248.9; velocior, 208.11; 222.13; velocissimus, 198.19
vendicare, 158.7; 178.8
vendicatio, 150.2
venire, 138.21; 142.18
verbalis, *v.* musica verbalis
verbum, 100.1; 102.1, 2, 8; 104.17 (bis); 106.6, 15, 16, 17; 108.15, 18, 20, 23; 110.16; 112.8–9, 11, 13, 14; 114.3, 16, 24; 116.2, 20, 21; 118.1, 2, 5, 14; 120.2; 122.6; 144.9, 14; 164.1, 6, 10, 11; 182.1, 2; 188.16, 18; 194.7; 196.13, 14; 202.18, 19, 202.19–204.1, 204.15–16; 222.9; 230.14; 234.6, 10, 11, 12; 236.10; 238.20; 252.1, 4, 7
verisimilis, 190.26; 192.16
veritas, 112.5; 128.7; 152.12; 192.17; 252.8
versari, 126.7; 130.10; 140.21–22; 184.19; 188.15; 190.15, 27; 202.16; 208.4
versiculum, 136.5
versus, 230.15
verus, 108.7; 114.7, 128.1; 152.24
vertere, 204.9; 238.9
vestigium, 236.13
vetus (*n.*), 140.2–3; 194.10; 252.13
via, 236.13, 14; 238.2, 5, 8
viator, 236.13, 14; 238.8
Vicentinus, *v.* Nicolaus Vicentinus
victoria, 112.4

videre, 102.7; 118.3; 120.20; 126.8; 132.3; 138.9; 154.27; 156.10; 176.1; 250.2; videri, 104.9; 106.22; 108.11, 13; 110.1, 5, 6; 112.5; 114.1; 116.7; 120.6–7; 120.13; 126.7; 134.2, 5; 138.16; 140.2, 14; 142.15; 144.4, 5, 20; 146.12 (bis); 148.17, 20; 150.19 (bis); 152.7, 22; 156.17; 160.9, 11, 14; 164.15; 166.3, 13, 15; 168.2, 9; 170.8; 172.3; 174.1, 18; 176.2, 6; 178.8; 184.5, 10; 186.10; 188.5, 16; 192.19; 194.1, 5, 9; 196.12, 17; 202.9, 14; 206.15; 208.9; 210.5; 212.9; 216.10; 218.4, 12; 220.5; 224.2, 11, 12; 228.12; 230.4; 234.4; 236.5–6, 9; 240.11, 14, 15; 242.8, 13; 248.2; 252.12, 13
vincere, 106.18
violator, 152.1
vir, 100.14; bonus vir, 186.8
Virgilianus, 118.15
Virgilius, 106.15–16; 116.21
virtus, 184.18; 188.2, 7, 9; 252.16
vis, 112.4, 15; 166.20; 172.7; 232.5; 236.7
vita, 100.13; 150.20
vitari, 162.9; 248.10
vitiosus, 176.6; 184.20
vitium, 114.17; 118.7; 140.19; 154.19; 160.15; 162.8; 184.9, 10, 13, 19, 20; 188.2, 3; 252.5, 16
vocabulum, 106.22
vocalis, 104.7; 116.22; *v.* musica vocalis
vocare, 102.1; 104.21; 118.20; 122.1; 164.17; 166.11; 186.9; 204.12; 222.7; vocari. 154.10; 194.14
voces musicales, 102.2; 104.21; 118.1; 120.11, 17, 19; 128.8
voluntarius, 186.14
voluntas, 144.20; 146.1, 2–3, 4, 14; 150.9; 152.8; 156.8–9, 11, 16, 17; 186.6
voluptas, 194.6
vox, 112.14, 17; 116.2, 22; 118.2; 122.2, 5, 6, 7, 9, 10, 11 (bis), 16; 124.6, 14, 17, 18; 126.1, 4, 9, 10; 128.1, 10, 12; 130.2, 3, 5, 6, 7, 11, 12, 13, 18, 19, 23; 132.2, 7, 9; 134.1, 4, 12, 13; 136.1, 10, 11, 17; 138.2, 3, 7, 10, 14, 17, 18, 19, 22; 140.1, 3, 5, 6, 8, 10, 11, 12, 22, 23, 24; 142.1, 3, 22, 24; 144.5 (bis), 6, 7; 148.4; 164.6, 8; 166.8; 186.7; 202.15; 204.4 (bis), 6, 7, 10, 14, 15; 206.1, 17; 220.1; 230.9, 11, 12; 242.3; 252.11; *v.* humana vox, voces musicales
Vuillartius, *v.* Adrianus Vuillartius
vulgatus, 184.17
vulgus, 114.26; 194.14; 222.7
Zarlinus, 110.15, 22
Zeno, 110.9

INDEX NOMINUM ET RERUM

accented syllable, setting of notes to: *see* discretionary rule 1, older composers
Aelianus, 157–59n.77
Agricola, Martin, 29n.60
Alexander (the Great), 112–15, 156–57
Aquinas, Thomas, St., 13n.31, 18n.36, 19n.38, 23n.48, 45n.74, 48n.79
analogy: *see* scholastic method
argument from authority, 21
argument from swiftness, 75, 81, 89, 92, 212–13, 222–23, 244–45; 248–49
Aristotle, 22n.46, 25n.50, 41n.69, 58, 58n.102, 154–55, 184–85
ars vs. *usus*, 20–21n.42
Aventinus, Johannes, 27–28n.57
axioms: *see* scholastic method
barbarism, 25, 118–19
Bonaventura da Brescia, 27–28n.57
Bourgeois, Loys, 37n.64
Cicero, 147n.63
common opinions: *see* scholastic method
consonance and dissonance as factor in text placement, 51–52, 78, 80, 172–75, 218–19, 222–23
Curtius, 157–59n.77
Decalogue, 43, 150–53
definition: *see* scholastic method
De modo, tempore, et prolatione: a distinct treatise in Codex 6486, 4n.6; *see also* Stoquerus
De musica verbali: division into two books, 13–16; focus of, 16, 100–103
    missing elements of, 16; *see also* Stoquerus
De vera solfizationis docendae ratione ad Magistrum Franciscum Salinam Dominum suum: *see* Stoquerus
dichotomization: *see* scholastic method
Diogenes (the Cynic), 110–11
discretionary rule 1, newer composers, 85, 86; statement of, 238–39; reason in, why minimae and larger notes receive separate syllables, 86–87, 240–41; why properly applicable to newer composers, 87, 240–41; application

of, to semiminimae in C and ₵ mensurations and when spaced apart at larger intervals, 87–88, 242–43; exception to, in syncopated cadence, 88, 242–43

discretionary rule 2, newer composers, 85; statement of, 238–39; reason in, why syllables not given individually to semiminimae and smaller notes, 89–90, 242–245; why properly applicable to newer composers, 90, 244–45; application of, to minimae in *proportio tripla*, 90, 244–45; exception to, in C mensuration, 90, 246–47

discretionary rule 3, newer composers, 85; statement of, 238–39; reason in, why longer note after a series of semiminimae should not receive a syllable, 91–92, 246–49; why properly applicable to newer composers, 92, 250–51; extension of, to note following longer note after semiminimae, 92–93, 250–51; corollary to, concerning final note at end of phrase if preceded by series of semiminimae, 93, 250–51

discretionary rule 4, newer composers, 85; statement of, 238–39; reason in, for avoiding repetition of text, 93–94, 252–53; why properly applicable to newer composers, 94, 252–53; allowance in, for occasional repetition, 94, 252–53

discretionary rule 5, newer composers, 85; statement of, 238–39; beginning of clarification of, correct observance of quantity of syllables in regard to text placement, 94, 252–255

discretionary rule 1, older composers, 65, 83, 84, 226–27, 230–31; statement of, 200–201; reason for assigning more notes to accented syllable in, 67, 202–5; particular accented syllable involved in, 67–68, 204–5; application of, in practice, 69, 206–7; relation of, to other rules of this set, 70, 206–7

discretionary rule 2, older composers, 65, 83, 228–29; statement of, 200–201; relation of, to other rules of this set, 70, 208–9; reason in, for assigning a syllable to a longer note following a single texted semiminima, 71, 208–9; situation in, of assigning a syllable to each semiminima in a series, 72, 210–11; situation in, when shorter notes follow the semiminima, 72–73, 210–11

discretionary rule 3, older composers, 66, 83; statement of, 200–201; reason in, why two notes following a punctus do not receive a syllable, 74–75, 212–15; relation of, to necessary rule 2 and rules 4 and 5 of this set, 75, 214–17

discretionary rule 4, older composers, 66, 75, 83, 228–31, 250–51; statement of, 200–201; clarification of, concerning pairs of minimae or semiminimae, 76, 216–17; reason in and manner of observance of, 76–77, 216–19; syncopated cadence in relation to, 77–78, 218–21; considered as proper to older composers, 78–79, 220–21

discretionary rule 5, older composers, 66, 75, 83, 86, 228–29; statement of, 200–201; clarification of, concerning the first semiminima of a series, 79–

80, 220–23; reasons in, for assigning one syllable to series of semiminimae, 80–81, 222–23; application of, to series smaller than semiminimae and longer note following, 81, 222–25; limitation of, to number of syllables available for series of semiminimae, 81–82, 224–27; application of rule to C mensuration, 82, 226–27

discretionary rules in general, 23, 47, 114–15, 154–55; meaning of "discretionary" in, 59, 186–87; definition of, 186–87; demonstration of need for, in addition to necessary rules, 60–62, 188–93; classification of, into those of older composers and newer composers, 62–66, 192–203; *see also* rules of verbal music

discretionary rules of newer composers: origin of, in nature, 85, 234–35; why set of five rules of, is complete, 85–86, 234–37; comparison of, with discretionary rules of older composers, 86, 236–39; list of, 238–39

discretionary rules of older composers: factors determining, 64–66; 196–99; listed, 200–203; summary of, in order used in practice, 82–84, 226–33

division: *see* scholastic method

division of music, 17–18, 105–6; *see also* verbal music; vocal music

Faber, Heinrich, 28n.59

formal clausulae: *see* syncopated cadence

Gaffurius, Franchinus, 6–9, 18–19; *Practica musicae* of, 104–5

Gerson, Guillaume, 27–28n.57

Glareanus, Henricus, 6–9

Guido of Arezzo, 106–7; hand of, 27, 122–23

Harrán, Don, *passim* in notes

Heyden, Sebald, 29n.60, 38–39n.65

humanism: humanist tradition at University of Salamanca, 9–10n.18; interaction of, and scholasticism in Renaissance, 11n.21

human nature, scholastic philosophy of, as basis for division of rules of verbal music into necessary and discretionary rules: *see* rules of verbal music

Institutes, 152–53; *see also* Justinian

Introductorium, 122–23

Isocrates, 102–3

Jones, George M.: *see* Reese, Gustave, and George M. Jones

Josquin des Prez, 9; as leader of older generation of composers, 63, 194–95; style of, compared with Willaert's, 63–64, 194–95

Justinian, 147n.65, 151n.69, 153n.73

Juvenal, 147n.62

Koswick, Michael, 27–28n.57

Kristeller, Paul Oskar, 5 and *passim* in notes

Lampadius, 28n.59

Lanfranco, Giovanni Maria, *passim* in notes

La Peccorina: *see* Willaert

ligatures: notated, 56, 61, 182–83; unnotated (*also* implied), 57, 61, 182–83; *see also* necessary rule 3

Lowinsky, Edward E., 1–7 and *passim* in notes

Madrid Codex 6486: contents of, 1; discovery and dating of, 5–6; *see also* Stoquerus

minimae, placement of syllables on: individual minimae, 86–87, 240–41; minima or larger note following a series of semiminimae, 90–93, 246–51; minimae grouped in pairs, 216–21

musica verbalis, 14–15; definition of, 24–25, 116–18; division of, 25–26, 118–21; *see also* verbal music

musical examples, missing, 15–16, 62, 192–93; *see also* staves

mutation: *see* solmization

necessary rule 1, 61, 76, 83, 172–73, 176–77, 190–91; 216–17, 226–27; statement of, 158–59; notes involved in, 46, 160–61; ways violated, 46–47, 160–63; text placement in opposite situation to, 47, 162–65

necessary rule 2, 61, 75, 83, 166–67, 176–77, 190–91, 214–15, 228–29; statement of, 158–59; *punctus augmentationis* as subject of, 51, 170–73; reason in, why no syllable assigned to punctus, 51, 172–73; exception to, 51–52, 172–75

necessary rule 3, 61, 83, 176–77, 190–91, 228–29; statement of, 158–59; reason in, for assigning one syllable to a ligature, 48–49, 166–67; observance of, in case of notational error, 49, 166–67; situation in, when syllable not given to ligature, 49–50, 168–71; notated and unnotated ligatures in, 49–50, 168–71

necessary rule 4, 61, 76, 83, 190–91; 216–17, 228–29; statement of, 158–59; reason in, why successive notes of same pitch given separate syllables, 53, 174–75; exception to, concerning two successive notes of the same pitch, 53–55, 178–81

necessary rule 5, 61, 83, 84, 162–63, 190–91, 226–27; statement of, 158–59; classification in, of syllables and notes of a phrase, 55, 180–81; establishment of necessity of, 56, 180–83; deferral of middle syllables and notes to discretionary rules, 56, 182–83; application of, to notated and unnotated ligatures at beginning and end of a phrase, 56–57, 182–83

necessary rules, 23, 44, 46, 114–15, 154–55; list of 158–59; in practice, 57–58, 182–85; *see also* rules of verbal music

Nicomachean Ethics: *see* Aristotle

notes, available, placement of syllables on: *see* necessary rule 1

Pandectae, 146–47, 150–51; *see also* Justinian

part-whole argument, 53, 76, 80, 174–77, 216–17, 222–23

phrase, placement of syllables of a phrase to notes of: *see* necessary rule 5; discretionary rule 1, older composers

plainsong, no repetition of text in, 93–94, 230–31, 252–53

Plutarch, 115n.17
punctus augmentationis: *see* necessary rule 2; discretionary rule 3, older composers
quaestio: *see* scholastic method
Quintilian, 17n.34, 25nn.49 and 51, 67n.112
reason, reasoning: *see* scholastic method
recta ratio: *see* right reason
Reese, Gustave, and George M. Jones, 4n.5 and *passim* in notes from 46n.75
repetition of text, 84, 85, 230–31, 234–35; *see also* discretionary rule 4, newer composers
right reason, 43–44, 59–60, 63, 152–55, 186–89, 192–93, 236–37
rules of verbal music: division of, into necessary and discretionary rules, 44–46; relationship of, to composition and performance, 40–44, 144–55;
Salinas, Francisco de, 1, 5–7, 112–13; *De musica libri septem* of, 1n.1, 6, 17, 104–5
scholastic method, elements of, used by Stoquerus: analogy, 13, 45, 58, 86, 236–39; axioms, 12–13, 22, 23, 41, 42, 112–15, 146–51, 184–85; common opinions, 13; definition, 12, 25, 59; division and dichotomization, 12, 61, 64–65, 85; *quaestio*, 13, 21, 40, 145n.6; reason and reasoning, 12; *see also* Stoquerus
semiminimae, placement of syllables on: single semiminima and longer note after the semiminima, 71, 208–9; one syllable to each semiminima in a series, 72, 210–11; a semiminima and a series of shorter notes following, 72–73; 210–11; semiminimae grouped in pairs, 75–77, 216–21; series of semiminimae, 79–82, 88–90, 220–27, 242–47; semiminimae in C mensuration, 88, 242–43
solmization, progression of solmization syllables along gamut in: methods of, current in Stoquerus's time, 26–30, 120–27; Stoquerus's method of, 30–36, 128–39; Stoquerus's criticism of current methods of, 36–38, 138–41; customary classification of mutation syllables in, 38, 142–43; Stoquerus's classification of syllables for, when mutation is involved, 39, 142–45; importance of Stoquerus's survey of current methods and presentation of his own, 39–40
Spangenberg, Johann, 38–39n.65
staves, blank, 160–63, 168–69, 172–73, 178–79
Stoquerus, Gaspar: life and character of, 6–7; treatises and historical significance of, 1–5; *De musica verbali libri duo* of, 1–5, 8–10, 95–96; *De vera solfizationis quam vocant docendae ratione ad Magistrum Franciscum Salinam Dominum suum* of, 1, 4–5, 8–10; *De modo, tempore, et prolatione* of, 1, 4–5, 8–11; humanist and scholastic milieu of, 9–13; tetrastich of, 1n.1; establishment of topics and sources of treatises of, 7–9

successive notes of same pitch, placement of syllables on: *see* necessary rule 4

syncopated cadence, texting of: *see* discretionary rule 4, older composers

tactus, as influence in text placement, 71, 74, 76, 79, 92, 208–9, 212–15, 216–17, 220–21, 250–51

Terence, 147n.63

text placement: *see* ligatures; minimae; notes, available; phrase; *punctus augmentationis*; semiminimae; successive notes of same pitch

Tinctoris, Johannes, 28n.58, 38–39n.65

Tzwyvel (Tzwiefel), 30n.62

usus: *see ars*

Vanneo, Stephano, 38–39n.65

Vergil, 20, 116–17, 118–19; *Eclogues* of, 106–7

verbal music: as a species of vocal music, 17–20, 24–25, 104–7; definition of, 24–25, 118–19; division of, 25–26, 118–21; established as an art, 20–24, 108–17; *see also musica verbalis*, rules of verbal music, vocal music

Vicentino, Nicola, 6–9, 116–17

vocal music, division of, 17–20, 104–7; Gaffurius's, 18, 104–5; Stoquerus's elaboration of Gaffurius's, 19–20, 104–7

voces musicales: see solmization

words, setting of, to notes: *see* accented syllable

Willaert, Adrian, 5, 7, 47, 162–63; as leader of newer generation of composers, 63, 194–95; *La Peccorina* of, 63, 194–95; *Musica nova* of, 5; style of, compared with Josquin's, 63–64, 194–95; older style of, compared with newer style, 194–95

Zarlino, Gioseffo, 6–9; *Istitutioni harmoniche* of, 21, 110–11 and *passim* in notes

Zeno, 110–11, 111n.14